# auto body
## repairing and repainting

MODERN, SIMPLIFIED METHODS

by

**BILL TOBOLDT**

Senior Associate Editor
Motor Service Magazine
Member Society of Automotive Engineers
Associate Member Automotive Engine Rebuilders Association

South Holland, Ill.
**THE GOODHEART-WILLCOX CO., Inc.**
**Publishers**

122-L

# INTRODUCTION

In the automotive field, the repairing and repainting of car bodies is growing faster than any other service branch.

Each year there are more cars on the road. As a result, there are more collisions, more wrecked bodies, more damaged fenders. This means plenty of work at top pay for those who have the know-how required to do quality work.

AUTO BODY REPAIRING AND REPAINTING covers all phases of body repairing--use of modern tools and equipment, step-by-step procedure for handling typical jobs. It includes also a chapter on customizing and building auto bodies using fiber glass.

AUTO BODY REPAIRING AND REPAINTING is an authoritative text for students and apprentices who need a substantial background in fundamentals. It is well suited for those now engaged in auto body repairing who want to increase their skills, and for owners who wish to do repair jobs that do not involve heavy structural members.

Bill Toboldt

# CONTENTS

# Contents

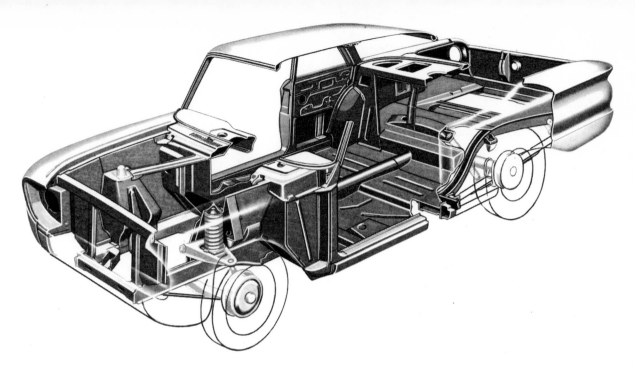

Fig. 1-1. Typical unitized body construction.

# Chapter 1

# AUTO BODY CONSTRUCTION

Today there are two principal types of auto body construction:

A. The unitized body construction.

B. The body and frame construction.

In the unitized body construction, Fig. 1-1, individual metal parts are welded together to make up the body assembly and provide overall body rigidity through an integral all steel welded construction.

The attachment provisions for the power train and suspension systems are provided by the underbody area, Fig. 1-2, which also contributes to the strength of the vehicle. The floor pan, Fig. 1-2, and related sections become an integral part of the frame thus eliminating the conventional separate body and frame. This is accomplished through the welded combination of boxed sections

Fig. 1-2. Underbody of unitized body.

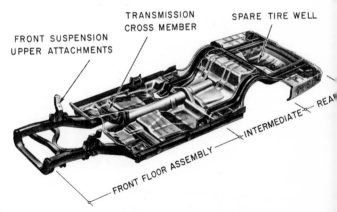

TRANSMISSION CROSS MEMBER

SPARE TIRE WELL

FRONT SUSPENSION UPPER ATTACHMENTS

INTERMEDIATE

REAR

FRONT FLOOR ASSEMBLY

(rocker panel areas and frame rails) and the floor pan.

The separate frame and body construction is a type of construction that has been in use for many years and continues to be used in the majority of cars.

Late model frames are shown in Figs. 1-3, and 1-4. A body used with a separate frame is shown in Fig. 1-5.

## BODY DESIGN DETAILS

In working in auto body repairing and repainting, it is important to learn the names of the different parts of the automobile

## SAFETY IN THE AUTO BODY SHOP

AN IMPORTANT PART OF YOUR EXPERIENCE IN THE AUTO BODY SHOP WILL BE LEARNING TO FOLLOW SAFE PRACTICES AND PROCEDURES THAT WILL PREVENT INJURIES TO YOURSELF AND TO OTHERS.

IT IS IMPORTANT AT THIS TIME, FOR YOU TO STUDY AND TO BECOME THOROUGHLY FAMILIAR WITH BASIC RULES OF SAFETY, AS DISCUSSED IN CHAPTER 33, PAGE 219.

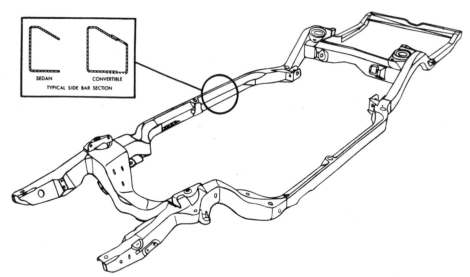

Fig. 1-3. Perimeter type chassis frame on which the body is mounted.

Fig. 1-4. Chassis frame ready for car body.

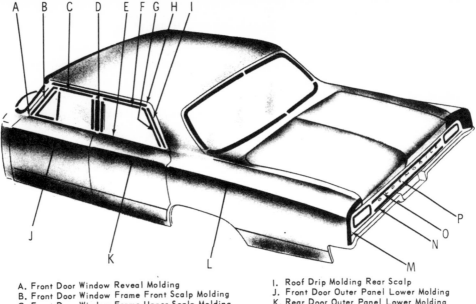

A. Front Door Window Reveal Molding
B. Front Door Window Frame Front Scalp Molding
C. Front Door Window Frame Upper Scalp Molding
D. Center Pillar Scalp Molding
E. Rear Door Window Reveal Molding
F. Rear Door Window Frame Upper Scalp Molding
G. Rear Door Window Frame Rear Scalp Molding
H. Roof Drip Molding Front Scalp
I. Roof Drip Molding Rear Scalp
J. Front Door Outer Panel Lower Molding
K. Rear Door Outer Panel Lower Molding
L. Rear Fender Lower Molding
M. Rear Fender Extension
N. Rear End Outer Panel Lower Molding
O. Rear End Outer Panel Upper Molding
P. Rear End Outer Panel Name Plate

*Fig. 1-5. Modern auto body as used with separate frame. Note locations and names of different types of decorative moldings.*

*Fig. 1-6. Sheet metal parts of modern four door sedan:*

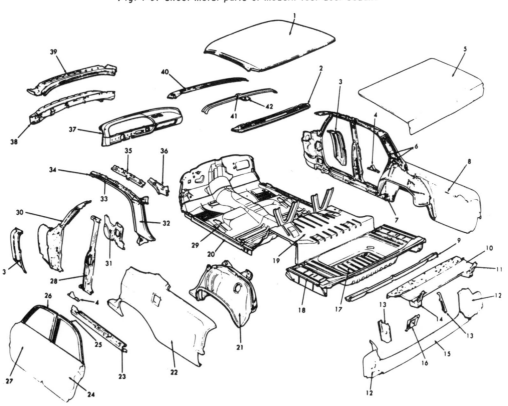

1. Panel, Roof. 2. Panel, Back Window Inner. 3. Panel, Shroud Lower Side. 4. Filler, Center Pillar Outer Panel Lower. 5. Lid, Rear Compartment. 6. Panel, Body Lock Pillar. 7. Filler, Rocker Panel Rear. 8. Gutter, Rear Compartment Lid Side. 9. Bar, Rear Cross. 10. Panel, Rear Compartment Front And Shelf. 11. Strap, Lid Hinge. 12. Hinge, Quarter Outer Extension. 13. Brace, Gutter To Pan. 14. Box, Lid Hinge. 15. Panel, Rear End. 16. Plate Lid Lock Anchor. 17. Pan, Rear Compartment Rear. 18. Filler, Pan To Quarter. 19. Pan, Rear Compartment Front. 20. Panel, Rocker Inner. 21. Panel, Wheelhouse. 22. Panel, Quarter Outer. 23. Panel, Rocker Outer. 24. Panel, Outer. 25. Door, Rear. 26. Door, Front. 27. Panel, Outer. 28. Pillar, Center. 29. Pan. 30. Panel, Front Body Hinge Pillar. 31. Reinforcement, Pillar To Rocker. 32. Panel, Roof Extension. 33. Rail, Side Roof Outer. 34. Molding, Roof Drip. 35. Rail, Inner Front. 36. Rail, Inner Rear. 37. Panel, Instrument. 38. Panel, Assembly Dash. 39. Panel, Shroud Upper. 40. Frame, Inner Upper. 41. Bow, Roof. 42. Support, Dome Light.

body, and also the methods used in assembling the various parts.

Typical bodies with various panels indentified are shown in Figs. 1-6 and 1-7. Note the names of the different panels and the location of the seams where they are joined to the other body panels or sections. Such seams vary with different makes and models of

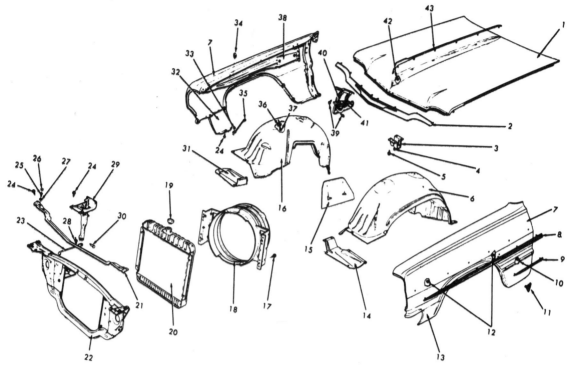

1. Panel Assembly. 2. Moulding Assembly. 3. Plate Assembly. 4. Bolt. 5. Bolt. 6. Skirt. 7. Fender. 8. Moulding Unit. 9. Moulding Unit. 10. Nut. 11. Emblem. 12. Nut. 13. Extension. 14. Extension. 15. Shield. 16. Skirt. 17. Bolt. 18. Shroud Assembly. 19. Cap Assembly. 20. Core. 21. Bar Assembly. 22. Support Assembly. 23. Extension. 24. Bolt. 25. Screw. 26. Bumper. 27. Nut. 28. Spring. 29. Catch Assembly. 30. Pin. 31. Extension. 32. Extension. 33. Nut. 34. Bumper. 35. Brace. 36. Reinforcement. 37. Bolt. 38. Reinforcement Assembly. 39. Bolt. 40. Hinge Assembly. 41. Spring. 42. Nut. 43. Moulding Unit.

*Fig. 1-7. Sheet metalwork of front end:*

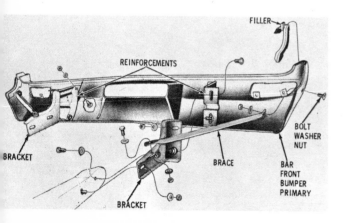

*Fig. 1-8. Details of typical front bumper construction.*

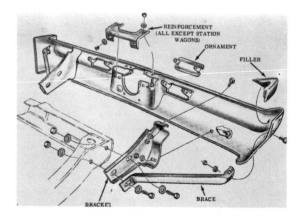

*Fig. 1-9. Exploded view of typical rear bumper assembly.*

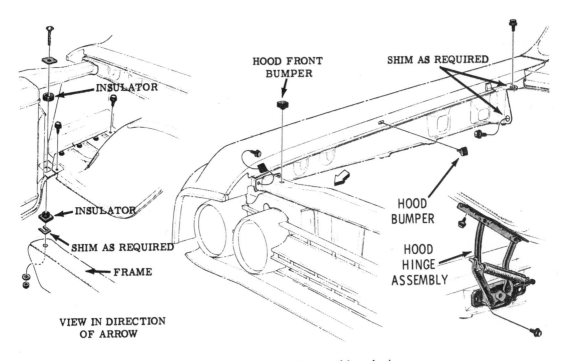

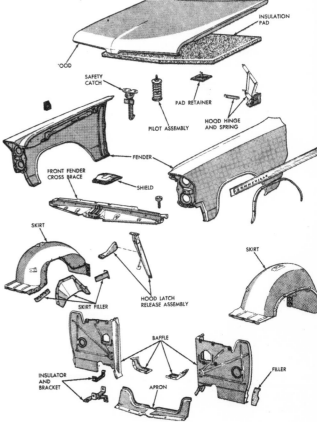

INSULATOR

INSULATOR

SHIM AS REQUIRED

FRAME

VIEW IN DIRECTION
OF ARROW

HOOD FRONT
BUMPER

SHIM AS REQUIRED

HOOD
BUMPER

HOOD
HINGE
ASSEMBLY

*Fig. 1-10. Installation drawing of front fender.*

bodies, but the illustrations are typical and can be used as a general guide when ordering replacement panels. The illustrations will be found useful when removing panels for replacement or reassembling bodies.

Details of front and rear bumper construction and method of mounting are shown in Figs. 1-8 and 1-9. A method used in attaching front fenders is shown in Figs. 1-10 and 1-11. Details of typical hood and fender construction are shown in Fig. 1-12.

*Fig. 1-11. Arrows show points of front fender attachment on Volkswagen.*

INSULATION
PAD

'OOD

SAFETY
CATCH

PAD RETAINER

PILOT ASSEMBLY

HOOD HINGE
AND SPRING

FENDER

FRONT FENDER
CROSS BRACE

SHIELD

SKIRT

SKIRT

HOOD LATCH
RELEASE ASSEMBLY

SKIRT FILLER

BAFFLE

FILLER

INSULATOR
AND
BRACKET

APRON

*Fig. 1-12. Typical installation details of front end sheet metal parts.*

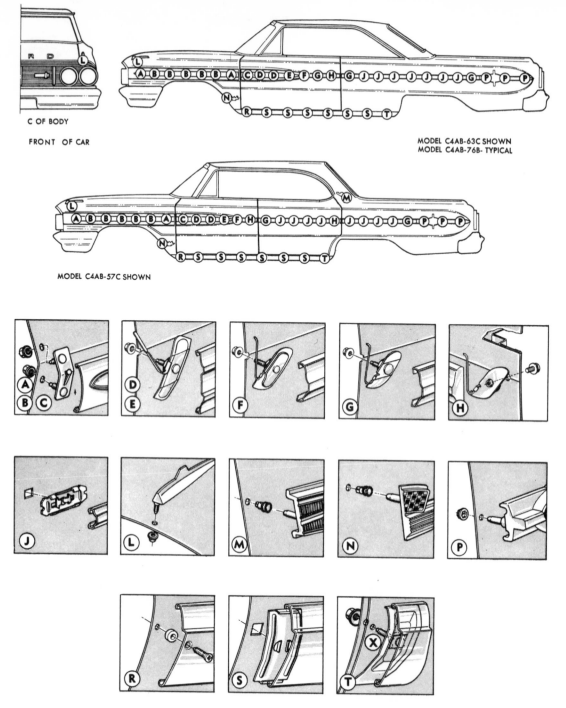

C OF BODY

FRONT OF CAR

MODEL C4AB-63C SHOWN
MODEL C4AB-76B- TYPICAL

MODEL C4AB-57C SHOWN

Fig. 1-13. Exterior mouldings and method of attachment on typical Ford body.

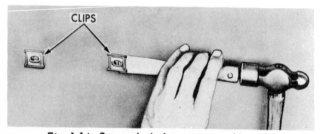

CLIPS

Fig. 1-14. One method of removing moulding clip.

There are many different methods of attaching moldings. Typical methods are illustrated in Fig. 1-13 and methods of removal and installation of the attaching clips for such molding are illustrated in Figs. 1-14 and 1-15. Further details on removal and installation of trim and hardware are given in later chapters.

Before straightening any damaged body, it

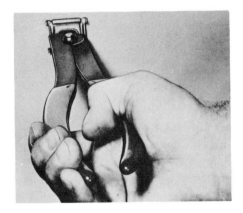

*Fig. 1-15. Removing moulding clip with plier-type tool.*

is necessary to determine the type of construction: That is, whether the body is of the unitized type, or whether the car has a conventional frame and body. This is necessary as the repair procedure will vary with the type of construction. Naturally in the case of minor damage, such as a dented panel, the procedure is the same regardless of the type

of construction. In the case of the frame-body type of design, it is necessary to first straighten the frame, if that is damaged. In the case of the unitized body, the car is treated as a single unit.

## QUIZ - Chapter 1

1. How many basic types of body construction are in common use?
   One.
   Two.
   Three.
   Four.
2. Does the unitized body construction provide overall body rigidity?
   Yes.
   No.
3. Where is the rocker panel located?
   Below the rear deck.
   Below the doors.
   Below the radiator.
   Above the rear quarter panel.

*Fig. 1-16. Underbody, cowl, body side panels, roof, front end structure and back panels of the Ford Fairlane are welded into a single unit to provide rigidity. The numbers indicate areas where special sound deadening materials are located.*

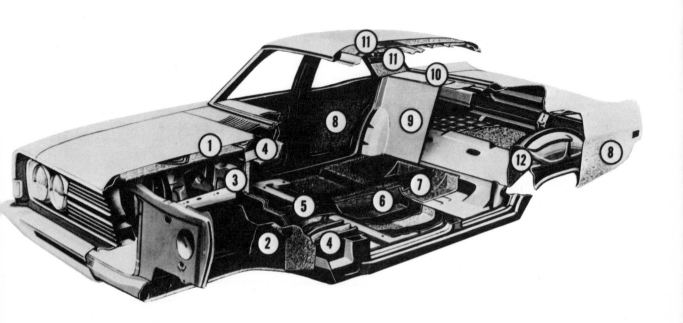

# Chapter 2

# BASIC HAND TOOLS
# FOR BODY SHOP MECHANICS

Before attempting to remove dents from a damaged panel, you should become thoroughly familiar with the different types of tools usually used, and under what conditions each should be used. The basic hand tools used in a body shop are:

1. Assorted hammers.
2. Assorted dollies.
3. Pick tools.
4. Adjustable file holder.
5. Solder paddle.
6. Vise grip pliers.
7. Fender beading tools.
8. Assorted wrenches.
9. Assorted screwdrivers.
10. Cold chisels.

## HAMMERS

Probably the most frequently used tool in the body shop is some form of dinging hammer, A, Fig. 2-1. These hammers, used together with a dolly block, B, Fig. 2-1, are used to remove dents from sheet metal. In A, Fig. 2-1, the hammer on the left is known as a combination or pick hammer. Next is a conventional dinging hammer with a long reach. Next is a dinging hammer with a shorter reach. The one on the right in Fig. 2-1, is another utility or pick hammer. While there is some difference in opinion as to names which should be used to identify different types of hammers, the ones given are accepted by most authorities.

The face of the dinging hammer may be round or square. The round-face hammer is used for general dinging, while the square-face is used for working close to a bead or other ornamentation. Also the face of the hammer may be flat or have a slight crown.

The overall length of the head of a dinging hammer may vary from 4 to 6 in. This variation in "reach" is needed because working spaces vary considerably: Some fenders are crowned more than others; also the space available for swinging the hammer varies.

The combination hammer, (any hammer with a pointed end) is used to remove small dents, which would be difficult to remove with a conventional hammer and dolly block. Such hammers are available in varying weights and point sharpness and are known as "pick" hammers.

In addition to the hammers listed, heavy roughing hammers are also available. Such hammers vary in design but are much heavier than any of those illustrated.

Hammers resembling a conventional dinging hammer, but with a corrugated face, are also used for shrinking metal. (See Chapter on Shrinking.)

Conventional ball peen or mechanic hammers are used with cold chisels and for similar work.

Under certain conditions, some mechanics prefer to use a mallet with a rubber head, for preliminary straightening and rough work. But in general such practice is discouraged in favor of other methods as explained in the chapter on the use of hand tools.

## DOLLY BLOCKS

These are basically anvils and a variety of different shapes and sizes are available. Three popular shapes are shown in B, Fig. 2-1, additional shapes are shown in Fig. 2-2. These are held on one side of the dented sheet metal, while the other side of the dent is struck with the dinging hammer. It will be

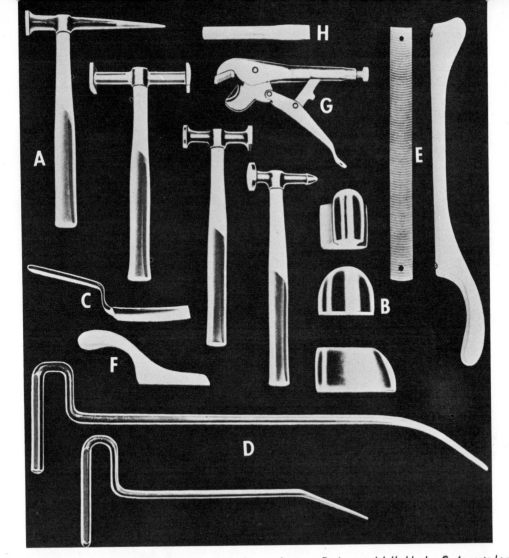

Fig. 2-1. Basic hand tools for the body mechanic. A—Dinging hammer, B—Assorted dolly blocks, C—Assorted spoons, D—Assorted pick tools, E—File and file holder, F—Solder paddle, G—Vise-grip pliers, H—Cold Chisels.

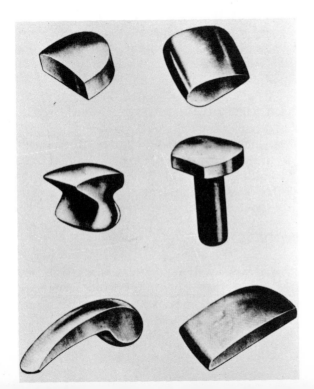

Fig. 2-2. Assortment of dolly blocks. Upper, heel and utility dollies. Center, general purpose and mushroom dollies. Lower, wedge and toe dollies.

noted in B, Fig. 2-2, that the surfaces of the dollies are finished in different radii. This is done so that the dolly will conform to the curve of the panel being straightened.

## SPOONS

These multi-purpose tools, shown in C, Fig. 2-1, are used as pry bars to pry the metal back into position, and are also used as dolly blocks when the area to be straightened cannot be reached with a conventional dolly block. Additional types are shown in Fig. 2-3. For example, dents in doors or deck lids can often be backed up with a spoon inserted through openings in the reenforcing on the back side of the door. Spoons are also used to distribute the hammer blows over wider areas. In such cases the spoon is placed on the ridge or damaged area and then struck

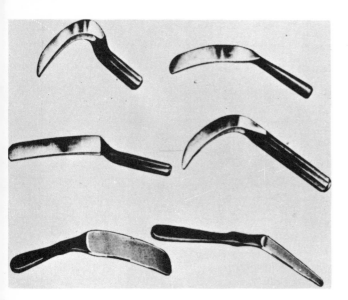

Fig. 2-3. *Various types of spoons. Upper, short elbow and curved spoons. Center, offset straight and long elbow spoons. Lower, curved flat and flat top spoons.*

with the hammer. Not only is the hammer blow distributed over a wider area in this manner, but also more important, the paint is not marred. Spoons are also used at times as "slappers," that is, the dented metal is slapped with the spoon in order to remove the dent.

## PICK TOOLS

These are specialized pry bars, shown in D, Fig. 2-1, and are designed to reach behind brackets and reenforcing bars in order to pry the metal. They are also used as spoons. The pointed end of the pick tool is so designed that it can be placed at the high point of a dent which is then forced out. Most, but not all, pick tools have pointed ends; some are flattened.

## FILE HOLDER

This important tool holds the flexible file for filing body panels. Illustrated in E, Fig.

2-1, is an unadjustable type. Adjustable types are also available as shown in Fig. 2-4. By

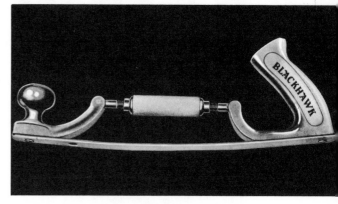

Fig. 2-4. *Body file with flexible handle.*

means of the adjustment the file is bent to conform to the curvature of the panel being repaired. The adjustment is made by turning the turnbuckle, Fig. 2-4. By filing the surface of the damaged panel, after dinging work, the high spots are quickly shown so that further work with dolly block and hammer can be performed.

## SOLDER PADDLE

This tool is made of close-grained maple, and is designed for spreading the solder over the surface of the panel. A special body worker's solder which is kept in plastic condition by means of a torch, is used to fill low spots in the panel. A typical solder paddle is shown in F, Fig. 2-1. Paddles in various shapes are available.

## VISE-GRIP PLIERS

The vise-grip plier G, Fig. 2-1, has many uses in the body shop. The most frequent use is to hold two adjoining pieces of sheet metal together so that they are in proper alignment while being welded.

## PRY BARS

There are various types and sizes of pry bars which are used for bending fender brackets, door hinges, and other parts. Some have forked ends; others are flat.

Tools described in preceding paragraphs of this chapter may be considered as basic tools, by the body repairman. In addition to these, specialized auto body mechanic's kits of tools (general purpose tools) such as shown in Fig. 2-5, are also needed to disassemble

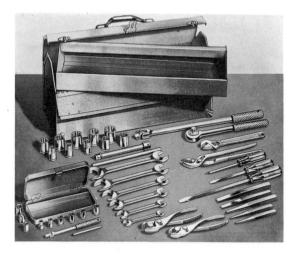

Fig. 2-5. Wrenches and other hand tools for disassembling body parts.

parts of the vehicle to permit replacement or repair of panels. Other specialized tools and equipment will be described and illustrated in appropriate sections of this text.

## QUIZ - Chapter 2

1. How many basic hand tools are used in a body shop?
    Five.
    Seven.
    Eight.
    Ten.
    Fifteen.
2. A combination or pick hammer is
    Flat on both faces.
    Pointed on both faces.
    Flat on one face and pointed on the other.
3. The overall length of the head on a dinging hammer is approximately how long?
    Ranges from 4 to 6 in.
    Ranges from 8 to 10 in.
    Ranges from 2 to 3 in.
4. The surfaces of the dolly blocks are all of the same radii.
    True.
    False.
5. Spoons are a single purpose tool.
    True.
    False.
6. How are file holders adjusted to different arcs?
    By means of a setscrew.
    By means of a turnbuckle.

# Chapter 3
# HOW TO
# USE HAND TOOLS

## USING THE HAMMER AND DOLLY

The most frequently used tools in the mechanic repairman's kit are the dinging hammer and the dolly block. As previously pointed out, the dolly is held in one hand and acts as an anvil. It is held against the damaged area while the other side of the area is struck with the dinging hammer, Fig. 3-1. Care should be taken when selecting the dolly and

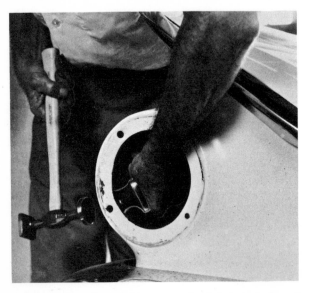

Fig. 3-1. The dolly is held on one side of the panel where it acts as an anvil, while the other side of the panel is struck with the hammer.

the hammer to be used for the job at hand. First the curve of the dolly should conform approximately to the curve or crown of the panel being straightened, Fig. 3-2. In other words, never use a flat surface of a dolly on a crowned panel. The curve of the dolly should always be the same or have a smaller radius

than the curve of the panel being straightened. Similarly, when selecting a dinging hammer for work on a specific panel, the radius of the face of the hammer should always be less than the curve of the panel. A flat face of a

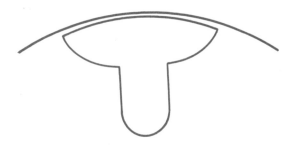

Fig. 3-2. The arc of the dolly block should coincide with the contour of the body panel.

hammer used on a concave surface would produce a lot of nicks which would have to be filled before refinishing. The curved face of the hammer, as shown in Fig. 3-3, should be used on concave surfaces, and the flat face

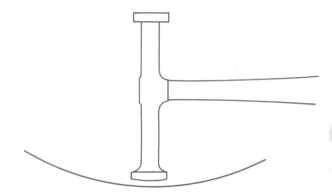

Fig. 3-3. Use the curved face of the hammer on a concave surface as shown, to avoid making small dents and nicks in the surface.

18

on convex. Fig. 3-4, shows the dinging operation in its simplest form. The dolly is held
against one side of the dent, while the ham-

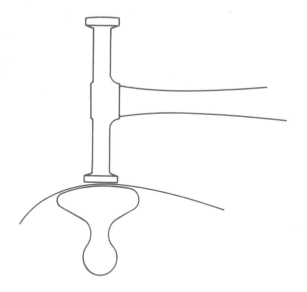

Fig. 3-4. Simplest form of ding work. Note that radius of the
dolly block face is less than the basic curve of the body.

mer blows are directed against the rim of
the dent. Note that the radius of the dolly face
is less than the basic curve of the panel. Also
note that the hammer face for this surface is
flat. If the dolly had been held on the upper
surface and the hammer blows on the lower,
a flat-faced dolly and a curved-face hammer
should have been used.

The condition illustrated in Fig. 3-5, is

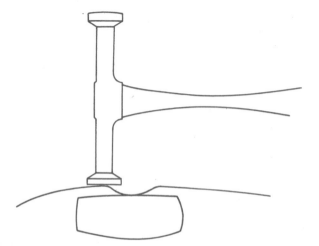

Fig. 3-5. Dinging OFF the dolly. Note that the dolly is directly
under the dent, while the hammer blows are directed against
the edge of the dent.

known as dinging OFF the dolly. In this case,
the hammer is driving one area down while
the reaction of the dolly is driving an adjacent
area upward. When the dolly is held directly
under the area being struck by the hammer,
as shown in Fig. 3-6, it is known as dinging
ON the dolly. The result is that the dented
metal is ironed smooth between the working
faces of the dolly and the hammer. Each blow
of the hammer forms a smooth spot about
1/4-in. to 3/8-in. in diameter, depending on
the amount of crown of the hammer. As the
dolly is moved along the surface of the panel,
the succeeding hammer blows will leave a
series of overlapping spots on the panel. Then
another row is dinged next to the original row
until the panel is straightened. As a result
the area will be covered with parallel rows
of spots made by the dinging hammer.

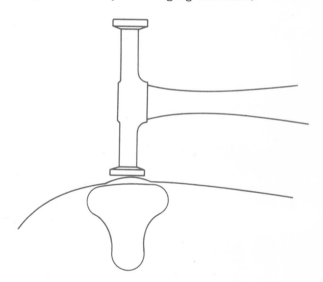

Fig. 3-6. When the dolly is held directly under the area being
struck by the hammer, it is known as dinging ON the dolly.

## USING THE DINGING HAMMER

Considerable care must be taken when using
the dinging hammer. First of all, heavy blows
will tend to make the metal of the body panel
thinner, spreading it out and stretching it.
This will cause it to have a greater area than
it had originally. The face of the hammer
must strike the panel squarely. Should the
edge of the hammer strike the panel, a nick
will be made which later will have to be filled
in order to have a smooth surface.

When driving a nail with a hammer, considerable force is used with what is known as follow-through so that the nail is driven into the wood. When using a dinging hammer, no follow-through is used. Instead, it has more of a slapping action. In that way the metal is not thinned so much and stretching is kept to a minimum.

The hammer is not gripped tightly, but rather loosely, and it is held close to the end of the handle, Fig. 3-7. It is swung with more of a wrist action, rather than the full arm swing. Usually a body repairman strikes

Fig. 3-8. One method of using a spoon is as a pry bar. It can also be used as a dolly in restricted areas where a conventional dolly cannot be used.

the curve of a dolly be less than the curve of the panel. Dollies with a straight edge are used along the edge of straight molding.

## USING THE SPOON

Heavy type spoons are often used as pry bars, Fig. 3-8. They are particularly helpful in prying out sheet metal on doors or trunk lids where the damaged metal is backed up by strengthening braces and panels. The heavier type spoons are also used as dollies when the design permits reaching into areas too small for the conventional dolly, Fig. 3-9.

Fig. 3-7. Dolly must be held firmly against the surface of the metal.

about 100 blows per minute in doing ding work. However, this varies with different men and the character of the straightening job.

## USING THE DOLLY

The dolly block is pressed firmly against the opposite side of the panel, Fig. 3-7. As a dented area is struck with a dinging hammer, the dolly block will rebound from the panel, but will return immediately, due to the pressure of the mechanic's hand. As previously pointed out, a dolly is selected so that the surface conforms to the curve of the panel being straightened. In no case should

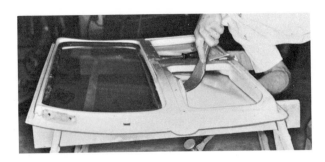

Fig. 3-9. Spoons are also used in the same manner as a dolly when space is limited.

In such cases, one end of the spoon is held by the mechanic, while the other end backs up the damaged area of the panel. The lighter type spoons are designed to hammer over a wider area. In such cases they are placed on top of the ridge of the damaged area and struck with the dinging hammer. In that way a larger area receives the hammer blow, and at the same time there is a reduced possibility of marring the painted surface.

Do not take a firm grip on the spoon, unless it is being used as a lever. Under normal conditions it should be held loosely, the hand acting as a guide and as a positioner.

exercised concerning the weight of the blow used with the hammer, otherwise too much metal will be raised.

## USING PICK TOOLS

The pick tool, Fig. 2-1, is a lever-type tool, and is used primarily to push out small

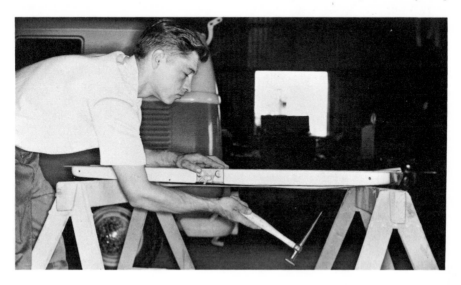

*Fig. 3-10. Using a pick hammer to remove small dents.*

## USING THE PICK HAMMER

A pick hammer is used to raise a low spot or small dent which has been disclosed after the surface has been filed, Fig. 3-10. A fine-pointed end of a pick hammer is used on small dents, and more rounded ends on larger dents. In some cases the mechanic will place the point of the hammer on the high point of the dent, and then strike the head of the pick hammer with another hammer. In other cases the mechanics will strike the dent with the point of the pick hammer, using the hammer in the conventional manner. Care must be

*Fig. 3-11. Using a pick tool.*

dents in areas where normal hammer and dolly work cannot be performed, Fig. 3-11. Doors are a good example. In such cases, by working through one of the access holes in the rear face of the door, the tool can be used to force out dents on the outside panel of the door. Another method of removing such dents is by means of pull rods, as described in another chapter.

## TIPS ON FILING

The fender file is used mostly to locate high and how spots, rather than to remove metal. It must be remembered that the sheet metal of which auto bodies are made is approximately 1/32-in. thick, and a file will quickly cut through it. There are adjustable file holders, Fig. 3-12, also nonadjustable file holders available. When using a body file it is pushed forward at an angle and not straight forward, Fig. 3-12. Pushing it straight forward will tend to cut a groove in the panel. Only light pressure should be

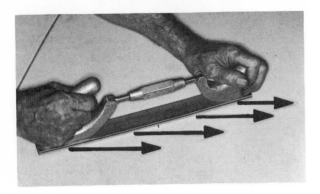

Fig. 3-12. When using a body file it should be pushed forward at an angle.

placed on the file as it is placed forward. Heavy pressure will tend to make the file teeth dig into the metal rather than cut it. However, sufficient pressure must be used to prevent chattering.

At the start of the cut, the teeth at the forward end of the file are doing the cutting. Then as the stroke progresses, the teeth which are actually doing the cutting, progress toward the heel or rear of the file. In that way, at the end of the stroke, all the file teeth from the front to the rear have been used. Strokes should be long and regular, not short and choppy.

If the file holder is of the flexible or adjustable type, it may be adjusted to conform approximately to the contour of the panel being filed. However, care must be exercised that the file is not flexed too far as there is always a possibility of breaking the file.

After the low and high spots which are located by the file have been removed by means of the dolly block and hammer, the file or disc sander is again used to remove scratches and tool marks.

## QUIZ - Chapter 3

1. Which are the most frequently used tools in the auto body repairman's kit?
    Screwdriver.
    Welding torch.
    Dinging hammer and dolly block.
    File.
2. How is the dolly used?
    As a hammer.
    As an anvil.
    In the same manner as a pry bar.
3. The flat face of the hammer is used on concave surfaces.
    True.
    False.
4. The radius of the dolly face should be greater or less than the basic curve of the dent being straightened.
    Greater.
    Less.
    The same.
5. When using a dinging hammer it should be used in the same manner as when driving a nail.
    True.
    False.
6. Describe the manner in which a dinging hammer should be used.
7. The dolly block is held loosely against the surface of the metal.
    True.
    False.
8. Is a fender file used mostly to remove metal or to locate high and low spots?
    Remove metal.
    Locate high and low spots.
9. When using a fender file it should be pushed.
    Straight forward.
    Forward at an angle.
10. After the dents have been removed by means of the dolly block and hammer, what tool is used to remove tool marks and other slight imperfections?
    Pick hammer.
    Adjustable file.
    Power sander.

# Chapter 4

# SIMPLIFIED
# METAL STRAIGHTENING

## FUNDAMENTALS

Straightening a damaged panel on an automobile is not as difficult as it would seem from the appearance of the panel. First, carefully study the damaged area to determine the best procedure to follow in removing the damage. If the wrong procedure is used first, additional work will often be required to complete the straightening operation. If the correct method is followed, much of the damaged area will automatically flex back into shape, and the total time for complete restoration is reduced.

Before starting any panel straightening operation, it is therefore important to examine the damage carefully to ascertain the best method of straightening. Basically the procedure is to remove the damage in reverse of the way it occurred.

The uninformed body mechanic will usually seize a rubber mallet or hammer and start the job by striking at the center of the damaged area. While this will force a large area of the sheet metal back into approximately its original position, actually additional damage is being created. In fact this roughing out procedure has not corrected any of the basic damage. That is still there and in most cases some marks of the roughing hammer or mallet plus some stretched metal have been added to the original damage. Extra time is, therefore, required to restore the panel.

## STARTING THE JOB RIGHT

To keep the work of straightening to a minimum, the damage must be removed in the reverse order to which it was created.

The damage caused by a collision does not occur instantaneously, but progresses from the instant of impact until the vehicle comes to rest. In other words a panel is first pushed in, and as the force continues, damage spreads further in a series of ridges. These ridges become deeper and more sharply bent, the farther they are from the point of initial contact.

Therefore, the first job of the repairman is to analyze the damage to determine where the panel was struck first and which ridges were formed last. It is these last formed ridges which must be removed first. As they are removed, the metal that is merely flexed out of position must spring back without any work being done directly on it by the mechanic.

The point of initial impact, that is the point where the damage started, can usually be

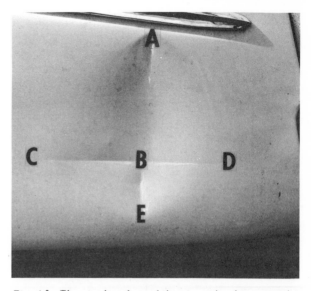

Fig. 4-1. *The simplest form of dent is made when a panel is struck a direct blow.*

recognized by the fact that the paint is deeply scratched, and in severe cases the metal may be torn.

The simplest form of damage occurs when a part is struck a direct blow by another vehicle. An example of such damage is seen in Fig. 4-1. More complicated damage occurs if the moving vehicle strikes a parked car on an angle so that the metal will be pushed into a series of ridges, Fig. 4-2.

is that the straightening process should start at the farthest edge of the damage, not at the center. The ridges are removed in reverse order to which they were formed.

The complete procedure for removing a simple dent, such as is illustrated in Fig. 4-1, is as follows: First, remove all dust and undercoating from the damaged area. Then using a dolly and dinging hammer, place the dolly under the spot A, Fig. 4-1, strike

Fig. 4-2. When the body is struck at an angle a more complicated series of dents and wrinkles is formed.

The most complicated damage results when a vehicle is struck a series of blows so that one set of wrinkles and dents is superimposed on another. Such a condition would result when a car is rolled over and over, Fig. 4-3.

Obviously, the damage illustrated in Fig. 4-1 was caused by a direct push from a bumper and bumper guard of another vehicle, with the force centering at B. The deepest ridge is at A. This is farthest from B, therefore, A should be removed first. As the ridge at A is removed, the entire area of damage will tend to spring back into place. On the other hand, if the mechanic works first on the area B, the ridge at A will still be there. C-D is not termed as a ridge but as a crease put in the metal by the bumper bar.

Actually the damaged area may be considered as a wheel, with its center at B, and the points A, C, E and D forming the rim of the wheel. Removing the ridges at A and E will permit the rest of the area to flex back into shape. The important point to remember

the outer surface of the panel with the dinging hammer. Keep working around that area until the panel tends to spring back into position. Then follow through with the dolly and hammer to point C, D and E. The panel should now be virtually smooth. Run the palm of a hand over the surface panel in an effort to locate any low spots by feel. Low spots can

Fig. 4-3. When a car is rolled, the most complicated series of dents are formed.

also be located by changing the position of trouble lights. Then when the panel appears to be perfectly smooth, use the body workers file. Draw it lightly over the surface, and any areas that are not touched by the file are obviously low, and will have to be raised by additional work with the dolly and dinging hammer. The areas that have been filed are high and will have to be hammered down. When the low and high spots are small in area, more like dimples, some mechanics will use a pick hammer to remove them. Both sharp and blunt-pointed pick hammers are available. The dent can be removed by using the pick hammer as a hammer, or the pointed end can be placed against the dent, and the other end struck with another hammer. Proceed in that manner until no further low or high spots are revealed by the use of the fender file. Following the initial filing, the surface should be smoothed by means of a power sander.

In order to understand how to remove the dents from a body panel, it is important to understand what happens to a piece of sheet metal (such as is used in an auto body) when it is damaged. A careful study of Fig. 4-1, shows that the damage consists of both ridges A and E, and the V-channels, C-D. In addition, in cases of more severe damage, the metal will be stretched and in some cases torn.

In the simplest type of damage, where the metal is pushed in without the formation of any ridges, or V-channels, a condition exists such as is shown in Fig. 4-4. By releasing the

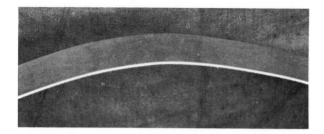

Fig. 4-4. When there is no sharp ridge, the panel will spring back into position when stress is released.

strain, the panel will automatically spring back into its original shape. The metal has not been severely stressed. If the metal does not spring back, then it has been stressed beyond its elastic limit. Every material has the property of elasticity up to a certain point,

which is called its elastic limit. When stressed beyond that point, it will not return to its original shape and form.

Fig. 4-5, shows metal that has been bent into a sharp ridge. Simply pulling each end of the metal, Fig. 4-6, will not remove the ridge as it has been stressed beyond its elastic limit. Whenever metal is bent beyond its elastic limit and takes a permanent set, the metal becomes work hardened and is actually

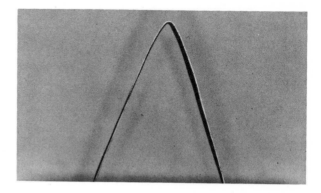

Fig. 4-5. Illustration of metal bent into a sharp edge.

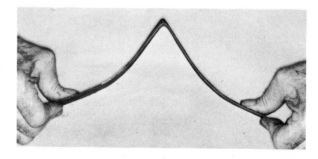

Fig. 4-6. Simply pulling on the ends of such a ridge will not remove the damage.

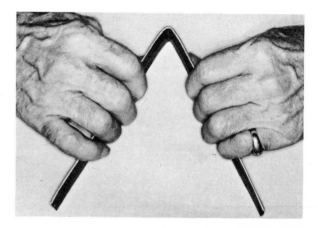

Fig. 4-7. Force must be applied at the bend area to remove the sharp ridge.

stiffer at the area of the bend than it was originally.

Restoring damaged panels to their original shape is largely a problem of removing the V-channels and ridges.

If an attempt is made to straighten the sheet metal, Fig. 4-5, by simply bending up the ends, Fig. 4-6, the ridge has not been changed, but two bends have been added. That is what happens when an attempt is made to straighten a damaged panel by working at the point of original impact.

However, if force is applied at the bent area, or ridge, Fig. 4-7, the metal will go back to its original shape without any difficulty.

## QUIZ - Chapter 4

1. When removing a dent from an auto body panel where should the work be started?

At the center of the dent.

At the area farthest from the center of the dent.

2. To keep the work of straightening at a minimum, the damage must be removed in the same order in which it was created.

True.

False.

3. It is not necessary to remove dirt and undercoating before removing any dents.

True.

False.

4. When removing dents, should the straightening process proceed directly toward the center, or should it proceed in a circular manner toward the center.

Directly.

In a circular manner.

5. When metal is stressed beyond its elastic limit, it will spring back to its original shape when the strain is released.

True.

False.

Fig. 5-1. Typical disk-type portable sander.

# Chapter 5

# HOW TO USE SANDERS

There are three main types of sanders used in the auto body repair work:

A. Rotary or Disk.

B. Oscillating.

C. Belt.

The disk-type sander is available in both the portable type, Fig. 5-1, and the flexible shaft type, Fig. 5-2.

The conventional portable disk-type sander and grinder is usually available in 7-in. and 9-in. sizes. A 7-in. tool is one that can be fitted with 7-in. diameter abrasive disks; a 9-in. grinder uses 9-in. diameter disks. The usual grinder-sander used in auto body shops operates on a 110 V, 60 cycle current. Such tools are also available to operate at higher voltages. Pneumatic (air-operated) tools are also available.

*Fig. 5-2. Flexible shaft sander.*

## SAFETY PRECAUTIONS

Before attempting to use a sander, or any other electrical tool, there are certain precautions that must be observed.

Make sure that any extension cables are of adequate size to carry the current being used. For example, if an extension cable of 50 ft. is being used, and a grinder or other electrical tool draws 5 amp., the extension cable must be of at least 18 gauge. The size cable for other currents and cable length is as given in the following table:

Based on current equivalent to 150 per cent of full load of tool and a loss in voltage of not over 5 volts. This table for 115-volt tools. For 220-volt tools use wire size corresponding to an extension length of one-half the contemplated length.

| Full-load ampere rating (on nameplate) | 0– 2.00 | 2.10– 3.4 | 3.5– 5.00 | 5.10– 7.0 | 7.10– 12 | 12.1– 16.0 |
|---|---|---|---|---|---|---|
| Ext. Cable Length | Wire size (B & S gauge) | | | | | |
| 25 ft. | 18 | 18 | 18 | 18 | 16 | 14 |
| 50 ft. | 18 | 18 | 18 | 16 | 14 | 12 |
| 75 ft. | 18 | 18 | 16 | 14 | 12 | 10 |
| 100 ft. | 18 | 16 | 14 | 12 | 10 | 8 |
| 200 ft. | 16 | 14 | 12 | 10 | 8 | 6 |
| 300 ft. | 14 | 12 | 10 | 8 | 6 | 4 |
| 400 ft. | 12 | 10 | 8 | 6 | 4 | 4 |
| 500 ft. | 12 | 10 | 8 | 6 | 4 | 2 |
| 600 ft. | 10 | 8 | 6 | 4 | 2 | 2 |
| 800 ft. | 10 | 8 | 6 | 4 | 2 | 1 |
| 1000 ft. | 8 | 6 | 4 | 2 | 1 | 0 |

Note—If voltage is already low at the source (outlet), have voltage increased to standard, or use a much larger cable than listed in order to prevent any further loss in voltage.

Make sure every electrical tool is grounded. This is an important safety precaution and is an underwriters' requirement. Electrical tools should have a three conductor cable and a three blade grounding type attachment plug cap. This is used with the proper type wall receptacle.

If the shop does not have the proper type wall receptacle or outlet, special adaptor plugs are available. Such plugs, which will fit a two-prong outlet and receive the three-prong connector on the end of the electrical grinder cable, are also provided with a short ground wire which is then connected to the cover screw on the outlet box.

Electric tools should never be used by an operator standing on a wet floor, or with wet hands.

If arcing is noted at the motor brushes, the electrical tool should be repaired, as arcing will start a fire in areas where lacquers are being sprayed.

In addition to the electrical safety precautions, operators of grinding equipment should always wear safety goggles or a face mask. A respirator is also advisable. The operator shown in Fig. 5-2 is wearing a combination face mask and a respirator.

## USING DISK SANDER

When using a disk sander, the tool should be held firmly but without undue pressure of the tool against the auto body. Heavy pressure will slow cutting action, and reduce the life of the abrasive disk.

The rotary sander should be used with a long sweeping motion, back and forth to produce smooth continuous coverage. The sander should not be operated in one spot, as this will tend to burn the metal. Neither should a circular motion be used. If the angle of the tool is too great, only a small area of the disk will contact the surface of the panel and a rough cut surface will be obtained. If the disk is placed flat against the work surface, the cutting action will be irregular and bumpy. In addition, it will be difficult to control the motion of the tool. For best results, the sander should be tipped with just enough pressure to bend the disk, as shown in Fig. 5-3.

Disk sanders are used to remove paint and

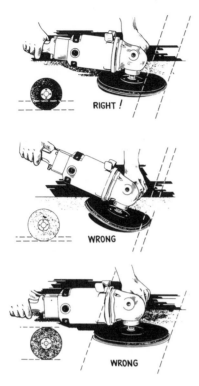

Fig. 5-3. Illustrating the correct and wrong way of using an electric sander.

to locate low spots in panels. The low spots disclosed by means of a sander are clearly shown in Fig. 5-2. When used for grinding, the disk sander is normally moved from left to right, and to remove grinding marks is moved at right angles to the grind marks.

Fig. 5-4. A cone-shaped mandrel with abrasive is used to sand sharp curved surfaces.

On most surfaces, the conventional flat disk is used with the sander-grinder. However, on curved surfaces, cone shaped mandrels and abrasives, Fig. 5-4, and curved pads with disk abrasives, Fig. 5-5, are available.

Fig. 5-5. Here a curved disk and abrasive is being used to sand a panel that is moderately curved.

## OSCILLATING AND ORBITAL SANDERS

These sanders, which are used primarily for finish sanding of the metal and paint surface, are available in electrical and pneumatic types, Fig. 5-6. Some of these sanders

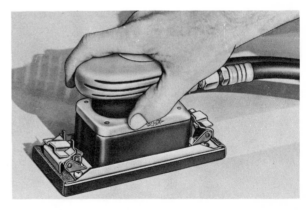

Fig. 5-6. For finish sanding of metal and paint surfaces, a sander with a reciprocating or orbital motion may be used.

have a straight reciprocating motion, while others, known as the orbital type, have a slight rotary motion.

Such sanders are used primarily for removing scratches left by the grinding operation. Many mechanics also use them for featheredging, that is the paint surrounding the damaged area is tapered back, so that there will be no sharp edge or ridge between the original paint and the area which is to be refinished.

Power sanding of this type is preferable to hand sanding methods which are time consuming. Only slight pressure should be applied when using the reciprocating or orbital type of sander. Sanders of this type can be used for either wet or dry sanding.

The pneumatic types operate at normal shop air pressure of approximately 75 psi, and are normally used for featheredging with abrasive paper of No. 60, 80 or 120 grit. The most popular is No. 80.

## BELT SANDERS

A belt sander may also be used to remove paint, sand, solder and plastic and for finished sanding. As shown in Fig. 5-7, it will produce a flat surface, and can also be used on sharp curved surfaces by using just the "toe" of the tool. Abrasive belts of various grits are available. One of the major advantages of the

belt sander is that it is equipped with a dust collector which greatly improves working conditions for the body mechanic, Fig. 5-7.

When using a belt sander, it is moved back and forth across the surface of the work. Care must be taken that the sander is kept moving and not held in one position, as that would tend to burn the metal. Also when locating high and low spots on a panel be sure to keep the strokes of the sander parallel. Then after further dinging, cross sand in opposite direction from the first sanding to recheck for high and low spots.

## SELECTING THE CORRECT ABRASIVE

In order to keep the time required to repair an auto body to a minimum and at the same time turn out high quality work, it is important that the correct abrasive be used at each stage of the reconditioning procedure.

Coated abrasives is a general term for all abrasives used in refinishing automobiles. In their various forms they may be known as sandpaper, waterproof paper, grinding disks, grinding combs, grinding belts, and many others.

The quality of the final finish is largely de-

Fig. 5-7. Belt sanders can be used on either flat or curved surfaces and have the added advantage that a vacuum attachment will carry away the dust.

pendent upon the proper selection and use of these coated abrasives. Although there are many types of coated abrasives, all are a combination of minerals, backing and bonds.

While the term sandpaper is still frequently used, it is not correct, as sand is not used. Of the five different minerals used as cutting agents in coated abrasives, three are natural, being mined or quarried, and two are artificially produced in electrical furnaces.

Flint quartz, commonly called "flint" is generally off-white when seen on the finished sheet of paper. Flint paper is commonly sold in hardware stores, but has almost no use in industry and auto body repair shops as other grains are far superior.

Emery consists of crystals of natural aluminum oxide, a good cutting agent, imbedded in iron oxide, which has no abrasive quality. Emery has been largely superceded by other types of abrasives.

Garnet of the same name as a semi-precious jewel and coming from the same source is sharp and hard. This is largely used in wood finishing.

Crocus is basically not an abrasive but a polishing agent of iron oxide.

Aluminum oxide is reddish brown in color, and is made in electric furnaces by fusing the mineral bauxite at extremely high temperatures. This comes from the electric furnace in large lumps, which are then crushed and separated for size. Special adhesives and processes are then used to secure the abrasive crystals.

Silicon carbide also is an electric furnace product and is produced by high temperature fusing of silica sand and coke. The result is a crystalline abrasive which is very hard and sharp.

Aluminum oxide and silicon carbide abrasive materials are the ones commonly used in auto body reconditioning and refinishing. Some authorities recommend the silicon carbide abrasive particularly for finishing primer-surfacer coats, as the crystals keep fracturing and thus continually provide a sharp cutting area to the work surface. On the other hand, aluminum oxide is extremely tough with a high resistance to fracturing, and, therefore, is capable of penetrating the surface. Because of such qualities some authorities recommend it particularly for metal finishing.

The two most frequently used materials for bonding the abrasive to the backing material are glue and resin. In general, glue bonds are not waterproof and less resistant to heat than resin.

Paper, cloth, fiber and combinations are the usual materials used for backing. Combinations either paper and cloth, or fiber and cloth are frequently used.

## SELECTING SANDING DISKS

Basically there are two broad types of sanding disks used in the auto body reconditioning field:

1. Open-grain abrasive disks.
2. Closed-grain abrasive disks.

On the open-grain disk, as the name implies, the grains of abrasive are separated so that there is appreciable space between the individual grains. The backing is only fifty to seventy percent covered with abrasive grains, leaving open space between grains. Such grits are available from 16 to 120 grit. The 16 grit has very coarse heavy grains of abrasive which are widely separated. The 120 grit disks are made up of much finer abrasive particles more closely spaced. The open-grained disks are designed for paint removal, and for cutting down welds and solder and other coarse material, which would tend to adhere to the abrasive particles on the disk, and in that way tend to reduce their cutting qualities.

The closed-grain abrasive disks are designed for work where the ground off particles are very fine and there is no tendency for these particles to adhere to the disk. On closed-grain disks, the abrasive particles are as close together as possible and there are no open areas which are not covered with abrasives. Closed grain abrasives are available in grains from 16, very coarse, to 320, extremely fine.

The grit of abrasive papers is marked on the back. Abrasive paper of various grits are shown full size in Figs. 5-8, 5-9, and 5-10.

Coarse grades remove more materials faster and fine grades produce smoother surfaces. In automobile body repair work to re-

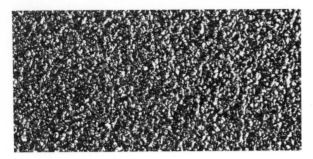

*Fig. 5-8. Twenty-four grit abrasive (full size).*

move paint, and the tool marks made during the straightening operation, a coarse grade, open-grain disk is used first. Then after the paint has been removed, the contour restored, and the heavy tool marks removed, a closed-grain fine grade disk should be used to provide surface smoothness. A still finer disk, usually 80 to 320 grit, is then used for feather-edging and final smoothing. Undercoats and finished lacquer, and occasionally synthetic enamel coats are sanded to produce the desired smooth surface. Such sanding may be done either dry or with water or gasoline. Dry sanding will produce a smooth surface more quickly, but wet sanding produces a smoother surface. Abrasive paper for sand-

ing undercoats and lacquer is available in types designed specifically for wet or dry sanding. In addition, some abrasive paper manufacturers produce a single paper which can be used for either wet or dry sanding.

Abrasive paper for wet sanding is usually available in grits ranging from 60 to 180, while 60, 80 and 100 grit paper is available for dry sanding.

## GRIT TO USE

There is some difference in opinion among auto body men regarding the use of specific grits for the various phases in auto body reconditioning. Some favor coarse grits, while others insist on using fine grits. It must be remembered that coarse grits, while cutting faster also produce deeper scratches which have to be removed before the actual painting; otherwise the scratches will show through the primer and color coats.

The accompanying tables show recommendations made by abrasive manufacturers for grits to be used in preparing the metal for painting, and also those to be used during the painting operation.

### TABLE OF ABRASIVE GRITS
### USED IN METAL PREPARATION

| REFINISHING OPERATION | TYPE OF ABRASIVE | RECOMMENDED GRIT | |
|---|---|---|---|
| | | WET | DRY |
| Removing rust, scale, old paint, etc. | Open coat | . . | 16 or 24 |
| | Closed coat | . . | 16 or 24 |
| Removing welds | Open coat | . . | 16 or 24 |
| | Closed coat | . . | 16 or 24 |
| | Fabric abrasive wheel | . . | 24 |
| Grinding Solder | Open coat | . . | 24 |
| | Closed coat | . . | 24 |
| Metal conditioning first step | Closed coat | . . | 24 or 36 |
| Metal conditioning second step | Closed coat | . . | 50 or 60 |
| Featheredging primary | Open coat | . . | 80 or 100 |
| Featheredging final | Closed coat | 220 or 320 | 220 or 320 |
| | Open coat | . . | 220 or 320 |
| Sanding primer coat | Closed coat | 280 or 320 | . . |
| | Open coat | . . | 280 or 320 |

REPAINT SANDING RECOMMENDATIONS

| TYPE OF FINISH | TYPE OF WORK | HAND SANDING | | RECIPROCATING SANDER | | DISK SANDER | |
|---|---|---|---|---|---|---|---|
| | | WET | DRY | WET | DRY | WET | DRY |
| Enamel | Quality | 320 | 240 | 320 | 280 | . . | 240 |
| | Fast | 280 | 220 | 280 | 220 | . . | 220 |
| Nitro Cellulose Lacquer | Quality | 360 | 320 | 400 | 400 | . . | 280 |
| | Fast | 320 | 280 | 320 | 280 | . . | 220 |
| Acrylic Lacquer | Quality | 400 | 320 | 500 | 400 | . . | 320 |

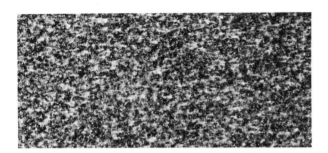

Fig. 5-9. Forty grit abrasive (full size).

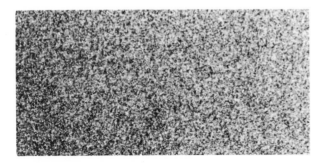

Fig. 5-10. Eighty grit abrasive (full size).

## INSTALLING ABRASIVE DISK

In some designs the abrasive disk is attached to the soft backing by means of a screw, which passes through to the motor driven plate. In another design the soft backing is coated on both sides with pressure sensitive adhesive, so that the abrasive disk will adhere to it, and the soft backing in turn will stick to the motor driven plate. The disk type sander is used for virtually all types of sanding, from heavy sanding required to cut down welds, to featheredging. The soft backing, plus the fact that it is a rotating disk, permits its use on many different types of contoured surfaces. As previously pointed out, open-grain disks are used for cutting down welds, solder, and for sanding of paint. However, even the open-grain disk will at times load up or become impacted with lead. The condition can usually be overcome by stopping the sander from time to time and striking the disk a few sharp blows with a metal bar or other tool. This will usually loosen the lead adhering to the abrasive grains so that they will again cut.

When using a rotary disk sander, it is the outer edge of the abrasive disk that becomes worn and will no longer cut. However, the remainder of the disk will generally still be in good condition. To avoid throwing the disk away, the outer used edge can be trimmed from the disk which is then mounted on a smaller sander pad. By first using a 9 in. abrasive disk, then cutting to 7 in., then to 5 in., considerable savings will result. The sander pad should always be the same size as the abrasive disk. Special machines for cutting the disks are shown in Fig. 5-11.

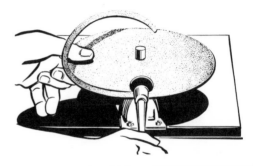

Fig. 5-11. After considerable use, the outer edge of the abrasive disk can be cut off, and the remainder of the disk installed on a smaller pad.

FIRST SECOND THIRD

Fig. 5-12. Attaching grinding disk on one type of sander.

When disk sanding close to a bead, there is a possibility of the disk cutting into the bead. To avoid that possibility, it is advisable to sand such areas by hand.

Burned spots will result if the disk grinder is held in one spot too long. They will also result if too much pressure is used on the grinder, or by using a worn or glazed disk. Burned spots can be avoided by a faster working rhythm, lighter pressure, better timed strokes, and the use of proper grits in good condition.

Loose metal or dirt on the sanding area will cause scratches. A worn or filled disk will also cause scratches. Failure to cross grind, especially when changing from a coarse to a finer grit is another cause of troublesome scratches.

Cross grinding especially under strong direct light will help the mechanic to see that the entire surface is uniformly finished.

## ATTACHING GRINDING DISK

While the procedure for attaching the grinding disk to the spindle of the grinder may vary slightly with different makes of grinders, the usual procedure is as follows: As shown in Fig. 5-12, first attach the flexible backing pad by threading the metal nut on the sander, spindle A. Do not thread by running the motor, but spin and tighten by hand.

Second, attach the sanding disk by laying disk B on the backing pad A, Fig. 5-12. Place the clamp nut C on the spindle, with the flange out. Give the clamp nut a turn or two into the backing pad hub.

Third, tighten the assembly by holding the backing pad with one hand and the sanding disk with the other. Turn the disk clockwise until the clamp nut draws up tight (the clamp nut will turn with the sanding disk due to the

adhesive stripping action on the nut). A spanner available as an accessory can also be used for tightening or removing the sanding disk.

## SANDING PITS, DENTS AND HAMMER MARKS

While it has been repeatedly emphasized that all dents, pits, sand and hammer marks should be removed before applying primer to the panel, there are occasions when this is virtually impossible. However, such areas must still be sanded before any paint is applied, otherwise there will be poor paint adherence.

Such areas can be sanded by using an octagonal shaped disk. Such disks, Fig. 5-13, will remove paint, rust, tar, from such low

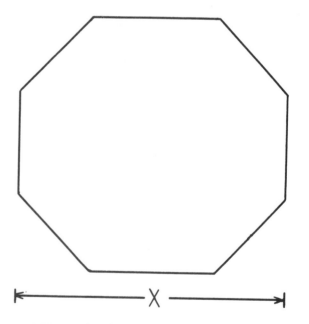

Fig. 5-13. Template for use in cutting abrasive disks to be used on rough surfaces. Dimension X is 5-1/2 in. for 7-in. disks, and 7 in. for 9-in. disks.

spots and inside curves without any difficulty. Octagonal disks are made by cutting up worn 7-in. and 9-in. disks. A pattern, such as shown in Fig. 5-13, can be made from sheet metal. In addition some of the abrasive companies will supply octagonal shaped disks on request.

## RUBBING COMPOUNDS AND POLISHES

Rubbing compounds are usually in paste form and contain a fine abrasive, such as pumice. In general, if the abrasive is relatively coarse, the material is known as a rubbing compound, and if the abrasive is of fine material it is known as a polish.

Rubbing compounds are used to eliminate fine scratches around a repair area and to smooth and bring out the gloss and luster in lacquer top coats. In addition, in some instances it is also used to "dress" acrylic enamel finishes which are to be finished with acrylic lacquer.

Compounding, like polishing, can be done either by hand or by machine. Small areas are usually done by hand. In such cases fold a soft cloth into a pad and apply a small quantity of rubbing compound to either the pad or the surface of the vehicle. Rub the area with the pad and compound in straight back and forth strokes.

In the case of larger areas, the operation is usually done by machine. Apply the rubbing compound to the surface and compound using a compounding pad on the machine polisher. Confine the operation to a small area at a time. Sand scratches around a feathered edge should be compounded until eliminated. A lacquer top coat should not be compounded until completely dry and the operation is completed when the desired luster is attained.

## QUIZ - Chapter 5

1. How many types of sanders are commonly used in auto body repair work?
    Three.
    Four.
    Five.
    Seven.
2. What gauge wire should be used in an extension cable 50 ft. long, when the current is 5 amperes?
    10 gauge.
    12 gauge.
    8 gauge.
    18 gauge.
3. Every electrically operated tool should be grounded.
    True.
    False.
4. When using an electric disk sander, it should be pressed firmly against the surface of the work.
    True.
    False.
5. Orbital sanders are used primarily for what type of work?
    Rough sanding.
    Finish sanding.
    When it is necessary to remove a lot of metal.
6. With what type of sander is it possible to use a dust collector?
    Orbital.
    Disk.
    Belt.
    Flexible shaft, disk sander.
7. Indicate two types of abrasive materials that are used on disks used in auto body repair work.
    Sand.
    Flint quartz.
    Emery.
    Garnet.
    Aluminum oxide.
    Crocus.
    Silicon carbide.
8. What type of abrasive is used for paint removal and cutting down welds.
    Open-grain.
    Closed-grain.
9. Which type of abrasive is the coarser?
    16 grit.
    120 grit.
10. What grit is usually recommended for removing paint?
    16 grit.
    320 grit.
    400 grit.
11. What grit is usually recommended for featheredging?
    16 grit.
    80 grit.
    400 grit.

# Chapter 6
# REMOVING DENTS
# WITH POWER TOOLS

Body mechanics in up-to-date shops use not only the conventional dolly blocks and dinging hammers to remove dents and straighten damaged panels, but also use power-operated sheet metal hammers, such as shown in Fig. 6-1. The advantage claimed

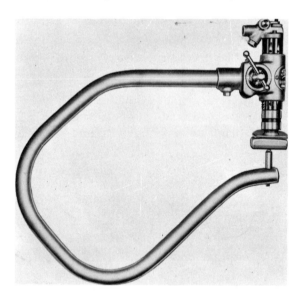

Fig. 6-1. Typical pneumatic fender hammer.

for power hammers is first of all, a considerable saving in time. That is a natural result as a power hammer can strike many more blows per minute than can be done by hand. Another major advantage is that sheet metal is not stretched as much as with the hand method.

When originally introduced, the power hammers, because of their design, could only be used on damage close to the edge of a panel. However, tools of more recent design have a deeper throat so that even the center of a roof panel can be straightened, Fig. 6-2.

The basic procedure in using a power dinging hammer is similar to that followed by the hand method. In some cases it may be desirable to rough out the panel with hand roughing tools. However, in many cases the power tool is used immediately.

After removing the dirt and sound deadening material from the underside of the panel, the straightening operation can begin. Select a frame which will permit the tool to reach the damaged area, and apply a light coating of oil to both sides of the panel. Starting at an undamaged section of the panel, the power is turned on and the tool is advanced to the ridge farthest away from the center of the damage. The tool is operated along this ridge

Fig. 6-2. Note the deep throat on this pneumatic fender hammer which is being used to straighten a roof panel.

until it is straightened. The work is continued around the outer edge of the damaged area in a circular manner until the center is reached. Some mechanics instead of following the circular method of starting at the outer edge and gradually pushing to the center, will use the diagonal method. They work directly across the damaged area. Then having beaten a straight path across, another path will be straightened at right angles to the first. However, this method requires more frequent adjustments of the tool, and as a result more time will usually be consumed in completing the job.

Just as when using a hammer and dolly to straighten a panel, mechanics will use a body file or power sander to locate spots which require further straightening.

## QUIZ - Chapter 6

1. What is the major advantage of using a power-operated sheet metal hammer?

Does better work.

Saves time.

Easy to use.

2. When using a power-operated sheet metal hammer, where should the work be started?

At the center of the damaged area.

At the ridge farthest away from the center of damage.

Any place on the damaged area.

3. What is the preferred procedure when using a power-operated sheet metal hammer?

Work in a circular manner until center of damaged area is reached.

Work diagonally across damaged area.

# Chapter 7
# USING
# PULL RODS

When removing dents and creases from auto body panels, considerable time is often required to remove the interior trim. Also the work is complicated when the damage is located in certain areas such as doors and rear deck lids, because of metal braces and other structural members which make it difficult to use the conventional dolly and hammer method.

On many jobs, the use of pull rods makes it unnecessary to remove upholstery or interior trim, as the work is done from the outside of the damaged panel. The procedure is to drill a series of 9/64-in. holes in the deepest part of the creases. These holes should be about 1/4 in. apart. The crease is then worked up gradually by inserting the hooked ends of the pull rods in the holes and pulling on the handles. Depending on the type of damage, as many as four pull rods, two in each end, may be used. The repair is started in this case, Fig. 7-1, at the front edge of the door. Work to the rear, then start

at the front again. At the rear edge of the door, two pull rods and a hammer with a taped face, Fig. 7-2, are used to prevent chipping the paint. Pull on the rods should

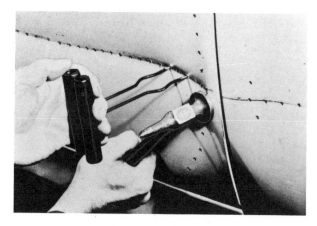

Fig. 7-2. As pull is exerted on the pull rods (hooked in the holes) a hammer is used to force the ridge back into place.

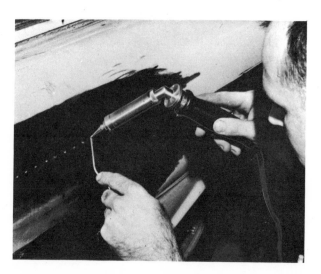

Fig. 7-3. After surface is smooth, holes are filled with solder. Note shape of point of soldering iron.

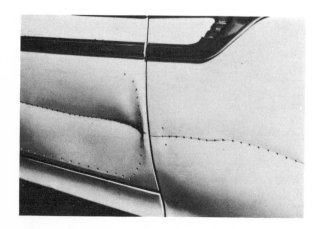

Fig. 7-1. Note the series of 9/64-in. holes drilled along the peak of the ridge.

Fig. 7-4. A damaged rear deck lid.

Fig. 7-5. Power pull equipment being
used initially to straighten damage.

be at right angle to the surface of the panel. Be sure to pull and not pry.

In this method of repair, light reflection of the paint helps to locate low spots. To increase reflection of the paint, it is advisable to clean the surface with a wax remover before starting the repair. Place the light at an angle to take full advantage of light reflection on the paint. In a final check use a file to locate low spots.

After the dent or crease has been removed the holes are filled with solder, Fig. 7-3. With special equipment that is available, as many as 30 holes can be filled in one minute. Tip of the soldering iron should not be blunt, but have a long rounded taper so it will enter the hole easily.

Using the same method to repair a damaged rear deck lid, Fig. 7-4, the procedure is as follows: Initial pulling should be done with a

set of pull hooks, channel bar, and power pull equipment, Fig. 7-5. The hooks are inserted through holes drilled as shown, which permit the deck lid to be pulled back into proper alignment, at the same time the damage is being removed. This set up takes about one minute to make. The next step, Fig. 7-6, shows some work with a hammer and pull hooks. The creases which appear here are finished without filling of any sort except for plugging the drill holes.

A slide hammer and the same pull hook used with the channel bar set up as in Fig. 7-7, may be used to finish roughing out and shaping the deck lid lower sections. After roughing, and because of metal stiffness in this area, the damaged portion is skinned over with lead to fill the low spots. Note the excellent fit of lower deck lid along the back quarter section,

Fig. 7-6. Using pull rods and hammer to further straighten
deck lid.

Fig. 7-7. A slide hammer being used to remove
some of the damage.

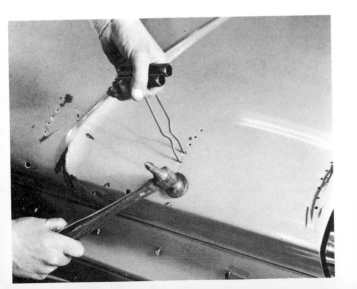

and rear quarter panel, and compare with Fig. 7-4. The repair is completed by filling the holes with solder, Fig. 7-8.

## QUIZ - Chapter 7

1. Is it necessary to remove interior trim when using pull rods to straighten damaged area?

    Yes.

    No.

2. What size holes are drilled in panel when using pull rods?

    9/64 in.

    9/32 in.

    3/16 in.

3. What is the preferred shape of the tip of the soldering iron used to fill the holes drilled in the panel?

    Blunt.

    Conventional pyramid.

    Long rounded taper.

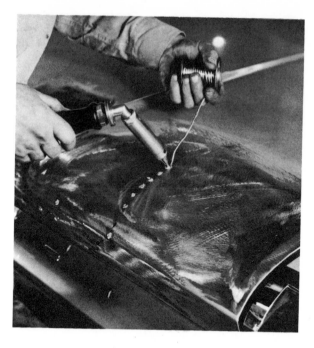

Fig. 7-8. The job is completed by filling the holes with solder.

# Chapter 8

# STRAIGHTENING PANELS
# WITH POWER TOOLS

## CHECKING FOR DAMAGE

In many cases of damage to auto bodies, the damage is so extensive that the entire body has become distorted. If the vehicle is of separate frame and body construction, the frame will have been bent, and if the vehicle is of unitized construction, the structural members will have been distorted. In other words, the damage is more than simple dents to individual panels of the body.

It then becomes the job of the auto body repairman to restore the body and frame to its original shape and condition. To do so it is necessary to know how far or how much the individual members of the body and/or frame must be straightened. This can only be done by accurate measurements.

In the event of extensive collision damage, major underbody repairs may be required to re-establish proper alignment. Extensive damage may include twist, side-sway, complicated sags, or a combination of these conditions in the underbody area. In most cases, the most practical method is to employ body and frame power straightening equipment to correct the condition. Such equipment offers a variety of controlled pushing and pulling operations as well as accurate frame and levelling gauges which are especially helpful in checking these conditions.

It must be remembered that misalignment of the frame and underbody can affect the fit of doors, hood and trunk lid. Even more important, such misalignment can influence the suspension system and adversely affect drive shaft alignment.

Underbody alignment must therefore be correct within plus or minus 1/16 in. of the specified dimensions. Such dimensions are supplied by car manufacturers and manufacturers of frame straightening equipment.

An actual car diagram is shown in Fig. 8-1. The dimensions are calculated on a horizontal plane parallel to the plane of the underbody. Measurements are made with a tram gauge, which must at all times be parallel to the plane of the underbody.

## PRINCIPLES OF TRAMMING

As indicated in Fig. 8-1, all diagonal dimensions are of equal distance to the same matching reference points, unless otherwise specified. It must be remembered that all measurements must be made in a horizontal plane. Specifications as shown, give the differences in vertical height of reference points.

In the absence of specialized tramming equipment an adequate job of alignment can be accomplished with the following procedure:

Place the car on a clean level floor and set the parking brake. Select several points along one frame side rail as shown in Fig. 8-2, and very carefully transfer these points to the floor by means of a plumb bob. Locate the corresponding points along the opposite side rail or members and very carefully transfer these points to the floor in the same manner. Carefully measure the distance from the floor, vertically to the check points on the frame.

Move the car away from the marks on the floor and measure distance between points as shown in Fig. 8-2. Corresponding measurements should be the same within 1/16 in.

To isolate certain conditions of frame

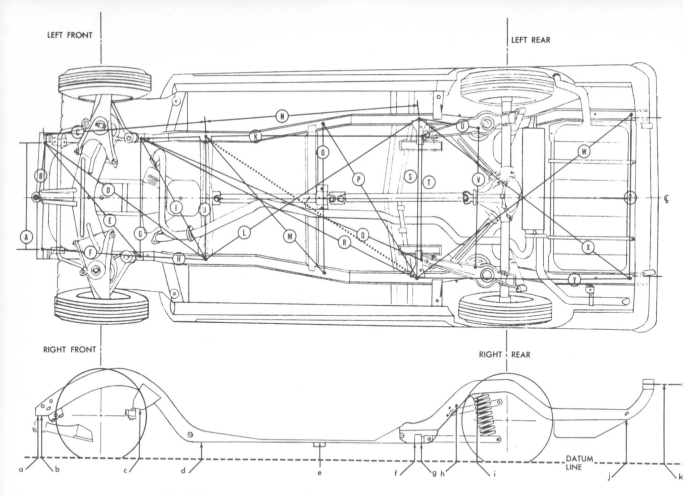

LEFT FRONT

LEFT REAR

RIGHT FRONT

RIGHT REAR

DATUM LINE

a    b      c      d      e      f    g h    i      j    k

*Fig. 8-1. Distances on frame to be measured when checking for misalignment.*

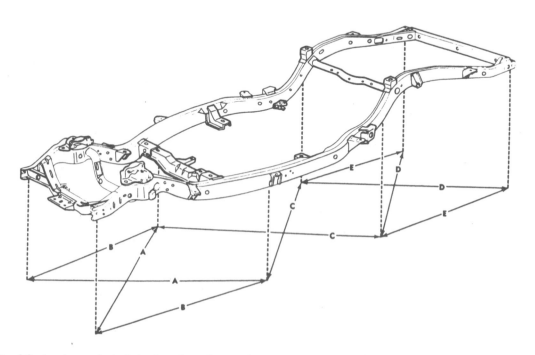

*Fig. 8-2. Another method of checking frame for misalignment. A plumb line is used to project points of frame to the floor and the distances as indicated are then measured.*

42

misalignment and also on different frame designs, it may be necessary to set up diagonal check points covering other areas than those shown in the illustration. If additional points are selected, be sure they are symetrically opposite.

In addition to checking the frame misalignment, as shown in Fig. 8-2, the body should also be checked by measuring and comparing diagonals as illustrated in Fig. 8-3.

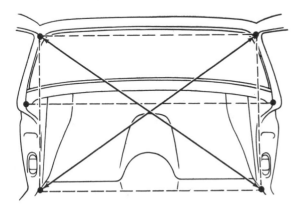

*Fig. 8-3. Typical points within body to be measured when checking for misalignment.*

## MISALIGNMENT CORRECTION

Frame misalignment can be corrected by straightening the out-of-line parts and/or by replacing cross members, braces, brackets, etc.

To prevent internal stresses in metal, frame straightening should be limited to parts that are not severely bent. If heat is needed to straighten a frame member, the temperature should be kept below 1200 deg. F. Excessive heat may weaken the metal and cause permanent damage. This is particularly true in the case of heat treated members.

If a frame member is replaced, use the same method of attachment as on the original frame members.

The plumb bob method of checking a frame for misalignment is dependent for accuracy on having a level floor.

## TYPES OF FRAME DAMAGE

There are many different ways in which a frame can be bent. The damage can occur as the result of a collision along the side, from the front or from the rear. Also the car can be rolled.

As the result of a front or rear end collision, the frame may develop a sag in the center, much like a hammock. When struck from the side, the frame will be bent inward and is described as having a "sway." Some types of front or rear end collision will cause the front or rear of the chassis to be bent upward or downward. The frame can assume a diamond shape when struck obliquely. The frame can also become twisted and have any combination of the foregoing.

## USING FRAME GAUGES

There are many different types of frame gauges available for determining whether a frame is misaligned. Their use will quickly tell whether the frame is twisted, swayed, sagged or diamond-shaped.

One type of frame gauge is basically a set of sighting points, Fig. 8-4. The points are

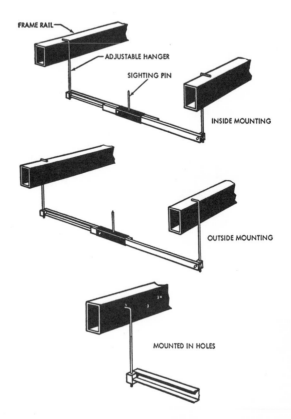

*Fig. 8-4. Points on frame for attaching gauges when checking frame for misalignment.*

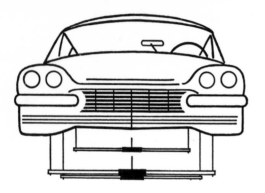

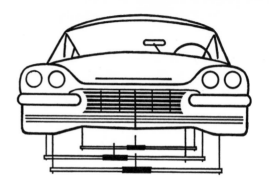

Fig. 8-5. Gauges should all be in alignment as shown, if frame is not distorted.

Fig. 8-6. Pins on gauges will not be in alignment if the frame is bent.

hung on the chassis at various points, Fig. 8-5. They can be hung directly on the side rails or in holes in the frame. Such gauges are adjustable to frames of different widths, and the side pieces are adjustable as to length. The center of the gauge is provided with a sighting pin which is always centrally located. A minimum of three gauges should be used. The more gauges used the greater the accuracy and the easier it is to determine the exact location and degree of misalignment.

As an example, when using such gauges to check for misalignment, install one gauge at the point where misalignment is suspected. Install another gauge in front of that area, and a third gauge well behind the suspected

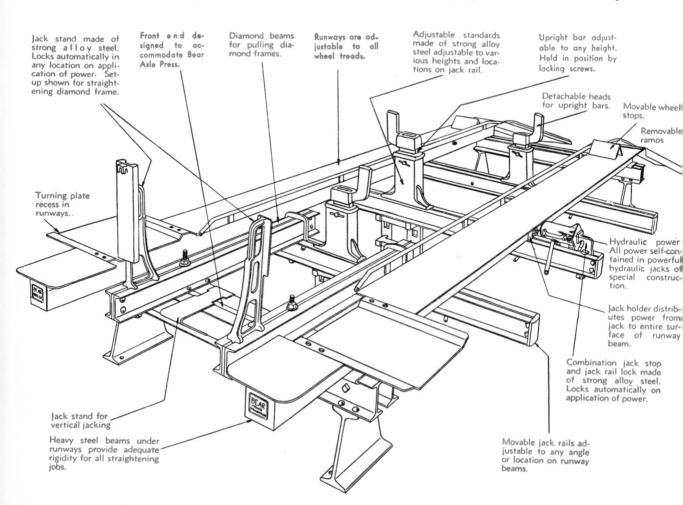

Jack stand made of strong alloy steel. Locks automatically in any location on application of power. Set-up shown for straightening diamond frame.

Front end designed to accommodate Bear Axle Press.

Diamond beams for pulling diamond frames.

Runways are adjustable to all wheel treads.

Adjustable standards made of strong alloy steel adjustable to various heights and locations on jack rail.

Upright bar adjustable to any height. Held in position by locking screws.

Detachable heads for upright bars.

Movable wheel stops.

Removable ramps

Turning plate recess in runways.

Hydraulic power. All power self-contained in powerful hydraulic jacks of special construction.

Jack holder distributes power from jack to entire surface of runway beam.

Combination jack stop and jack rail lock made of strong alloy steel. Locks automatically on application of power.

Jack stand for vertical jacking

Heavy steel beams under runways provide adequate rigidity for all straightening jobs.

Movable jack rails adjustable to any angle or location on runway beams.

Fig. 8-7. Stationary type of frame straightening equipment on which the vehicle is placed for straightening.

Fig. 8-8. Using portable type frame and body straightening equipment.

area, Fig. 8-5. If one gauge must be lowered to clear an obstruction, the other gauges must be lowered an equal amount.

If one of the sight pins is lower than the others, Fig. 8-6, there is a sag at that point. In the case of a twisted frame, none of the sight pins would be in alignment and one or more of the horizontal bars of the gauges would be tilted.

For a diamond-shaped frame, the diagonal dimensions of the frame are measured with a tram gauge. To determine whether the rear wheels are tracking the front, place the front wheels in the straight ahead position and compare the wheelbase on both sides of the vehicle.

## REPAIRING FRAME DAMAGE

There are two basic types of equipment used for straightening frames of automobiles. One type, Fig. 8-7, is stationary and the vehicle is driven on to the equipment for straightening. The other type, Fig. 8-8, is moved to the vehicle. Both methods use hydraulic jacks as power for straightening.

As shown in Fig. 8-7, the stationary equipment consists of heavy members to which the vehicle is fastened with chains and clamps. These same members are used as a base for the hydraulic jacks to force the damaged frame members back into their original positions.

In the portable type of equipment Fig. 8-8, the equipment is attached to the damaged car in such a way that the car frame or chassis members are used as a base against which the force of the hydraulic jacks is exerted.

Fig. 8-9, shows correcting sag in a car frame. As shown in the illustration, the

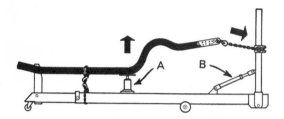

*Fig. 8-9. Diagram showing how to correct sag in car frame. Operation of the jacks A and B, straighten the frame.*

main beam of the equipment is placed under the car and the beam is chained to the frame. A hydraulic jack, A, is placed between the beam and the frame at the center of the sag area. As this jack is raised, jack B, Fig. 8-9, is also operated. The combined affects of pushing with jack A and pulling with jack B will straighten the frame.

The method of correcting sway damage such as would result when a car is struck on the side, is shown in Fig. 8-10. Note the side

*Fig. 8-10. Diagram showing how portable equipment is used to correct sway damage.*

anchoring from the anchor post of the equipment which is required when correcting center sway damage.

Note how in both of these examples, the car frame itself is used as an anchor to push and pull against. Similar arrangements can be made for correcting other types of frame damage with this type of equipment.

## SAFETY PRECAUTIONS

When using chains to anchor the chassis, several safety precautions must be remembered. First of all, do not pull chains around sharp corners as that will result in nicking the chain which in turn will develop a crack and eventually cause the chain to break. Chains should never be heated with a torch as this will destroy any heat treatment and seriously weaken the chain. It is also poor practice to bolt chain links together as the bolt may not be strong enough to withstand the force being exerted. When chains break, the ends will fly with a whiplike action and may cause severe damage or injury. To be on the safe side, it always pays to cover the chains with an old tarpaulin or other cover. In that way any snapback of the chain will be smothered.

## USING STATIONARY EQUIPMENT

An example of how the stationary type of frame straightening equipment is used is shown in Fig. 8-11, to Fig. 8-18 inclusive.

*Fig. 8-11. Corvair Monza coupe (rear engine) was hit at left front corner, heavily damaging hood, front panel, fender, luggage compartment floor and causing door misalignment. Right front also damaged.*

Fig. 8-12. Note gauges mounted on lower side of chassis. Gauges show 1/8-in. side-sway and 3/16-in. twist.

In this case a Corvair, Fig. 8-11, was hit at the left front fender, heavily damaging the hood, front panel, fender, luggage compart-ment floor, causing door misalignment. The right front door was also damaged.

The arrangement of the tramming gauges is shown in Fig. 8-12. A sidesway of 1/8 in. and a 3/16 in. twist is indicated. The gauges, as placed in Fig. 8-13, show a mash of 4-3/4 in., front cross member pushed back to the gas tank, steering gear shaft bent, knee assembly back, and visual damage to inner panel and frame. The gauges were attached to car with magnets at front and screw-in stud at cowl.

Fig. 8-14 shows double holdback with pinch weld clamps and support tube holding against

Fig. 8-13. Mash was 4-3/4 in., front fender was pushed back to gas tank, steering shaft bent, knee assembly back, and visual damage to inner panel and frame. Gauges were attached to car with magnets at front, screw-in stud mounting at cowl.

Fig. 8-14. Double holdback with pinch weld clamps and support tube holding against stepbeam rear uprights. This hold-back was used for all pulls.

Fig. 8-16. Tower hookup to pull upper panel, fender and cowl while applying simultaneous lower body pressure at the frame rail with upright on sliding stepbeam. Independent pull can be made as varying pressures are required. Three-way pull brought cowl forward, lengthened frame side rail and inner panel.

Fig. 8-15. Note double hookup through headlight opening and center of luggage compartment, jacking at stepbeam. Also note wooden padding is used to protect sheet metal and permit wider, stronger pull.

Fig. 8-17. After roughing out to this point, inner floor panel, cowl and wheel housing panel were found to be repairable, and much expensive panel replacement cost was bypassed. No sheet metal was removed up to this point.

stepbeam rear uprights. This holdback arrangement was used for all pulls when straightening the damage.

Note double holdback through headlamp opening in Fig. 8-15, and center of luggage compartment, jacking at stepbeam. Wood padding was used to protect sheet metal and permit wider, stronger pull. Power tower at left is attached to stepbeam before first hookup to save time.

Tower hookup to pull upper panel, fender and cowl, while applying simultaneous lower body pressure at frame rail with upright on sliding stepbeam, is shown in Fig. 8-16. After roughing out to this point, inner floor panel, cowl and wheel housing panel are repairable, Fig. 8-17, and much expensive replacement

cost was bypassed. No sheet metal was removed up to this point. Fig. 8-18, shows the completed job. All upper and lower body parts match up.

Fig. 8-18. The completed job. Only replacement parts needed were hood, fender, front panel and damaged chrome.

## USING PORTABLE EQUIPMENT

In this example of correcting damage to a vehicle with a unitized body, the damage resulted from a collision at rear center, Fig. 8-20. As a result both rear quarter panels buckled out and entire rear end drooped. The roof developed a buckle and the trunk lid, left quarter panel and adjoining sheet metal were damaged beyond economical repair and had to be replaced.

As with all unitized body construction, special attention must be given to certain load bearing or structural members such as frame

the floor pan area as the result of front or rear end collisions. Underbody measurements may be made from 5/16-in. holes in the side rails. If, under unusual conditions, all key locations are unsuitable for reference points, begin repair operations progressively, starting with the floor pan area. If preliminary tram measurements indicate any misalignment of the horizontal and vertical reference dimensions of the central area of the floor pan, check driveshaft alignment before starting repairs.

In Fig. 8-19, note the rear frame rail area. The left rail is 1-5/16 in. farther from the

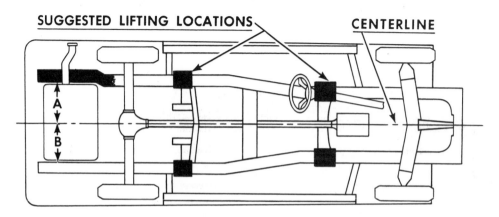

**SUGGESTED LIFTING LOCATIONS**      **CENTERLINE**

A

B

**NOTE: LENGTH "A" IS 1-5/16" GREATER THAN "B"**

*Fig. 8-19. Care must be taken when lifting unitized bodies. Illustration shows locations for lifting Buick Special. Note also that dimension A is greater than dimension B.*

side members, inner wheel-house panels, cowl areas, cross members, the floor pan and sections of floor pan that form part of the cross members or box sections. These must be brought back to their original position and condition. This may be done by: Replacing with new parts if the damage is severe, cutting out a strip of metal and replacing it with a smooth patch if the wrinkles cannot be removed, or welding on a reenforcing strip if necessary. All welding, as well as repairs must be structurally sound for both safety and strength.

Accuracy of reference points must be checked since a reference point measurement that originates from a damaged area will produce inaccurate results. The unitized type of construction used in the Buick Special seldom develops a diamond-shape or twist in

body centerline than the right rail. Fig. 8-20, shows damage caused by the collision at the rear center. As a result, both rear quarter panels buckled out and the whole rear end drooped. Note also the damage to the roof,

ROOF BUCKLE

DOOR MISALIGNMENT AND BUCKLE

UNDERBODY CLAMPS EK 130

ALIGNMENT GAGE EK 304

*Fig. 8-20. Indicating location of some of the damage. Note location of underbody clamps and alignment gauge.*

trunk lid, left quarter panel and adjoining sheet metal Fig. 8-21, shows the door misalignment, gauge location and the sharp crease at rear of quarter panel. The extent

Fig. 8-21. Note door misalignment and sharp crease at rear of quarter panel, also location of alignment gauge.

of damage to the trunk lid and rear sheet metal is indicated in Fig. 8-22. Alignment of the front of the car was checked with the floor pan area to be sure there was no hidden

Fig. 8-22. Illustrating damage to trunk lid and rear sheet metal.

damage. The gauges are located just ahead of the front wheel (not visible) and at the center of the car just below the door hinge pillar, Fig. 8-23.

The trunk interior is shown in Fig. 8-24. Notice the sharp crease in the quarter panel, the tilt in the rear cross rail, the extra creases in the trunk floor, and the disconnected brace.

Since measurement and inspection determined both rear frame rails were drooped and shortened, the problem was to pull them "up" and "out." A portable Damage Dozer was hooked up as shown in Fig. 8-25. The

Fig. 8-23. Another view showing location of gauges for checking alignment of front of car with floor pan area.

anchor post is shown pushing against the cross tube which connects the body anchor clamps. A clip is gripping the pinch weld of the damaged sheet metal. Whenever possible, the damaged sheet metal should be used to help pull the connecting members back into place. This is true even though the damaged metal is going to be replaced with a new panel. The buckles, discovered by measuring and inspection, were hammered out while the metal was under tension, whenever possible.

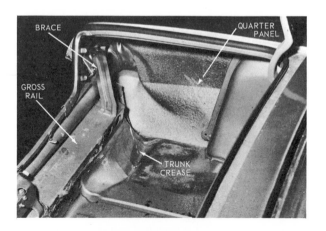

Fig. 8-24. Showing damage to interior of trunk.

Fig. 8-25. Hookup used for straightening. The anchor post is shown pushing against the cross tube. Clamp is gripping the pinch weld of damaged sheet metal.

## Straightening Panels With Power Tools

Fig. 8-26, is a close-up of the clamp hookup on the pinch weld. A hookup similar to that in Figs. 8-25 and 8-26 was also used to correct the right side; except the right

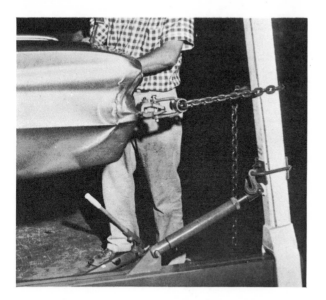

Fig. 8-26. Close-up of clamp hookup at pinch weld.

Fig. 8-27. After underbody dimensions were corrected, the damaged sections to be replaced were removed and the new trunk lid installed.

quarter did not have to be replaced. After the underbody dimensions were returned to specifications, the damaged sections to be replaced, were removed and the new trunk lid installed, Fig. 8-27.

The replacement parts were then clamped in place and tack welded in preparation for final welding, Fig. 8-28. At this and other

Fig. 8-28. Note how replacement panels were held in place, prior to being welded in position.

stages throughout the repair, additional measurements and checks were made to insure accuracy in the finished job. The results of final welding are shown in Fig. 8-29. Both gas and spot welding were used. A close-up of some of the metal-finishing work is shown in Fig. 8-30. The trunk lid alignment is now

Fig. 8-29. Both gas and spot welds were used to replace panels.

Fig. 8-30. A close-up photo of some of the metal-finishing work.

correct and all replacement sheet metal fits its mating parts. The tilting of the rear frame rail, damage in the trunk floor, crease in the quarter panel and the disconnected brace were repaired, Fig. 8-31. Completed job is shown in Figs. 8-32 and 8-33.

Fig. 8-31. The tilt in the rear frame rail, damage to trunk floor and crease in rear quarter panel were repaired.

Fig. 8-32. View of the completed rear.

Fig. 8-33. Side view of the completed car.

## USING SPECIALIZED STRAIGHTENING EQUIPMENT

The extent to which specialized straightening equipment can be used is limited only by the ingenuity of the mechanic. Some types of modern hydraulic equipment can be used for both pulling and pushing. By means of special clamps, hooks and accessories, the jacks can be applied to straighten almost any type of sheet metal damage.

Fig. 8-34, is particularly interesting. This shows the equipment removing a crease in the roof of a car. Note that the pull is being

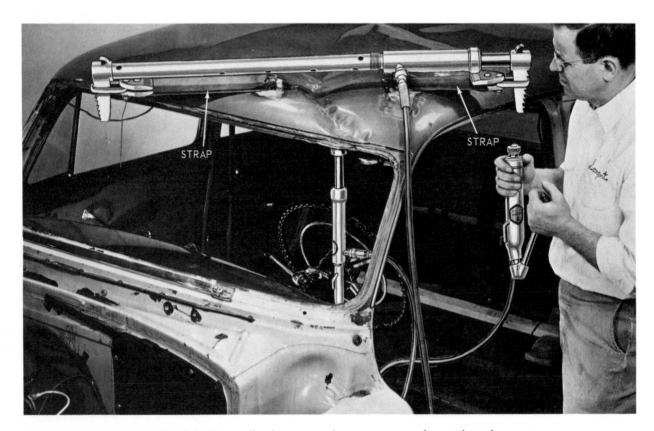

Fig. 8-34. Here pull is being exerted to remove crease from roof panel.

exerted on straps that have been soldered or welded to the roof panel. As the pull is exerted to pull out the crease, pressure is being applied on the underside of the crease. Using

Fig. 8-35. Stretching out a damaged hood.

Fig. 8-36. Hookup used for restoring window opening. Note wood blocks and rubber tipped equipment.

this procedure, it is possible to straighten the panel and avoid the lengthy procedure of complete replacement.

Fig. 8-35, shows a method of straightening a damaged hood. In this case, clamps were used to attach the equipment to the hood.

An arrangement for straightening a window opening of a door is illustrated in Fig. 8-36. Note the wooden blocking used to prevent the extended jack from slipping.

To push out a rear end that has been pushed in, an arrangement such as shown in Fig. 8-37, can be used. Fig. 8-38, shows the sides of a car body being pulled together.

Fig. 8-37. Damage such as this to the rear compartment is frequent. Here the outer edge of the trunk floor is being pulled out into position.

Fig. 8-38. Pulling the door lock pillars together.

Having one side of the front sheet metal-work pushed toward the center of the vehicle is a common situation. Fig. 8-39, shows how to push it back by fastening a clamp to the lamp housing. This clamp is then used as an anchor for the equipment, while it pushes out the damaged area.

Fig. 8-39. One method of moving a headlight and panel outward into position.

Fig. 8-40, shows how the front and rear edges of a fender panel can be pulled together with hydraulic equipment.

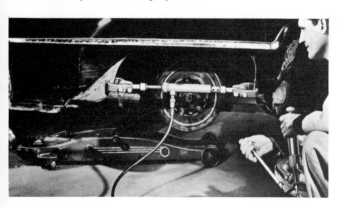

Fig. 8-40. Removing damage to a rear quarter panel.

One form of spreading equipment is shown in Fig. 8-41. In this case, the rocker panel was forced in, and the equipment is spreading it out to its original position. Fig. 8-42, shows a different type of spreading equipment. In this X-ray view, the spreader has been placed within the door to force out a dent. It can also be used as a dolly in this position.

When using portable hydraulic equipment to push out dents, the pressure is first applied

at the outer edges of the damaged area. Then you should work in a circle around the area, gradually approaching the center. After the work has been roughed out in that manner, it is then completed with a dolly block and hammer.

Fig. 8-41. Special spreader being used on a rocker panel.

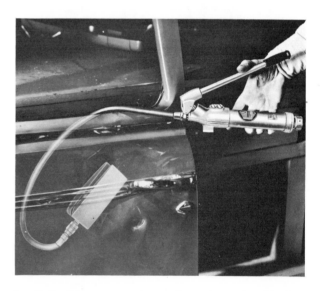

Fig. 8-42. Using a special spreader within a door panel to press out damage.

## KOREK STRAIGHTENING SYSTEM

A recently developed system for straightening auto bodies and frames uses a flat reference plane consisting of specially designed steel members set into the floor of the shop,

Fig. 8-43. These members provide firm anchorage for the necessary pushing and pulling required to straighten the damaged areas of the auto body and frame.

With this system it is possible to push, pull and anchor from 360 deg. around the vehicle and the force can be exerted upward, to the side, and downward. In addition, the straightening forces can be applied in several directions at the same time.

When straightening a vehicle by this system it is first placed on safety stands so that the extent of damage can be accurately gaged and also to place it at an efficient working height.

Proper anchoring of the vehicle to the base is important as any pulling force will have an opposite reaction on the anchoring system. Anchoring at or near the safety stands is recommended whenever possible. With anchors close to the supporting stands, downward bending of undamaged portions of the vehicle is avoided.

The pull forces are applied by 10 ton hydraulic rams which can be placed at any point around the vehicle as well as underneath it.

In Fig. 8-43 four separate pulls are being applied and the forces can be applied simultaneously or independently as desired.

A high pull setup, which is desirable when repairing roof damage, is also possible. By means of extension tubing the desired height is reached and pulls can be made from the base area to an effective height of 8 ft.

## QUIZ - Chapter 8

1. How do you determine the extent of damage to the structural members of the vehicle?
   By observation.
   Accurate measurements.
2. What is the usual tolerance for underbody alignment?
   1/4 in.
   1/16 in.
   .005 in.
3. When checking a frame for misalignment, how are the measurements made?
   Horizontally.
   Vertically.
   Diagonally.

Fig. 8-43. Details of Korek straightening system. Pull forces are applied by a 10 ton hydraulic ram.

4. If specialized tramming equipment is not available, how are points on the frame transferred to the floor?
   With a tape measure.
   With a plumb bob.
   With a carpenters square.
5. What is the limit of temperature that can be applied to a frame member to aid in straightening?
   2000 deg.
   1200 deg.
   1750 deg.
6. When using sighting points (gauges) to locate misalignment of frames, what is the minimum number that should be used?
   Two.
   Three.
   Four.
   Five.
7. If one of the sight pins of a tram gauge is lower than the others, what is indicated?
   Damage exists at that point.
   There is no misalignment.
8. What type of equipment is used for straightening frames?
   Hydraulic jacks.
   Steam hammer.
   Screw jacks.
9. When using chains to anchor a chassis, should the chains be passed around sharp corners?
   Yes.
   No.

# Chapter 9
# WELDING WITH OXYACETYLENE, ELECTRIC ARC

Welding is a metalworking process in which metals are joined by heating them to the melting point, and allowing the molten portions to fuse or flow together.

There are two basic methods used for welding in the auto body shop:

1. Oxygen acetylene.
2. Electric arc.

In the auto body shop, oxyacetylene welding equipment is used not only for welding, but also as a source of heat for soldering, shrinking metal and for softening the metal so that it can be more easily straightened. Oxygen acetylene is also used for cutting metal.

In oxyacetylene welding, the mixture of the two gases produces an intensely hot flame that will melt and fuse metals. When cutting metals with a special torch, a jet of oxygen striking a piece of iron or steel heated to its kindling temperature will cause the metal to burn away quickly. Chemically, oxygen cutting is similar to the eating away of iron and steel by ordinary rusting only much faster. In rusting, the oxygen in the air or water affects the metal slowly. Directing a jet of oxygen at metal heated almost to its melting point, actually speeds up rusting and burns away the metal. The iron oxide melts and runs off as molten slag and exposes more iron to the action of the oxygen. When welding, two pieces of metal are placed together. The edges are melted with the flame and the molten metals flow together. In most cases, welding rod or electrode is added to strengthen the joint.

## ELECTRIC ARC WELDING

Electric arc welding is a process whereby the heat necessary to bring the metal to a molten state is obtained by a continuous electric arc formed between a welding rod and the work. In electric arc welding, where a generator supplies the current in the shop, one terminal of the generator is grounded on the work and the other is connected to the welding rod or electrode. As the electrode is brought into contact with the work an electric arc is formed. This has sufficient heat to fuse the work.

The coating on welding electrodes is composed of a number of chemicals blended together and bonded to the wire or electrode. The object of the coating is to provide protection for the weld metal from oxygen and nitrogen in the air. As the coating burns it produces a gaseous shield which protects the metal as it flows from the electrode to the work. The coating contains alloys which combine with the weld deposit to form a slag or covering over the bead to protect it from the atmosphere and too rapid cooling. See Fig. 9-1. In auto body work, this method, arc welding, is frequently used when rewelding seams which have been spot welded originally, but cannot be spot welded again.

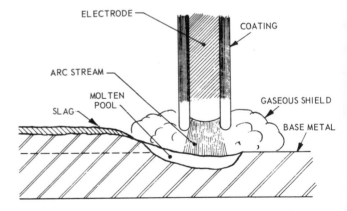

*Fig. 9-1. Close-up showing electric arc welding procedure.*

When using arc welding it is important that the two sections be brought into close alignment. Relatively large space between sections cannot be repaired satisfactorily by arc welding. In such cases gas welding becomes necessary.

## OXYACETYLENE EQUIPMENT

When welding with oxyacetylene the following equipment is needed:
1. Oxygen cylinder.
2. Acetylene cylinder.
3. Oxygen regulator.
4. Acetylene regulator.
5. Welding torch.
6. Connecting hoses.
7. Protective goggles.
8. Lighter.

In most cases the oxygen and acetylene are in tanks. However, equipment for generating acetylene is also available. Oxygen and acetylene cylinders must be kept away from heat. Never allow the flame of a torch to play on a cylinder as it might melt the safety fuse plugs. In storing and using cylinders always keep the valve ends up. During shipment the heavy cylinder cap is screwed over the valve to protect it from injury. If a cylinder valve should be broken off, the terrific pressure of the gas escaping from the cylinder would burn any material touched, and would give the cylinder jet velocity. It is essential that all cylinders be handled carefully, and be clamped or chained to a post or placed in a special cylinder truck, see Fig. 9-2, so there is no danger of being tipped over or dropped.

## SETTING UP ACETYLENE EQUIPMENT

With the cylinders correctly placed, remove the oxygen cylinder cap, then stand to one side of the valve outlet and open the valve slightly. When it hisses, close the valve. That procedure gets rid of any dust around the valve seat.

Attach the oxygen regulator, Fig. 9-3, to the oxygen cylinder, using an open-end wrench. The threads on the oxygen regulator are conventional right-hand threads. Be sure to keep oil and grease away from oxygen equipment. Do not lubricate the threads. In

Fig. 9-2. Oxygen and acetylene cylinders should be mounted vertically in a truck or chained to a post.

addition to having right-hand threads, the oxygen regulator can be recognized by noting the pressure range on the gauges. One of the gauges will indicate up to 4,000 psi. Also, oxygen regulators are usually painted green.

With the regulator attached to the oxygen cylinder, loosen the regulator handwheel. Stand away from the other regulator and open the cylinder valve. The lower gauge will indicate the cylinder pressure.

## INSTALLING ACETYLENE REGULATOR

Blow the dust out of the acetylene cylinder valve by opening the valve one-quarter turn. Then close it quickly. No flame or lighted cigarette should be nearby as acetylene is highly flammable. Attach the acetylene regulator (usually painted red), also shown in Fig. 9-3, to the cylinder. The connections have left-hand threads so it is not possible to install an acetylene regulator on an oxygen tank.

Loosen the regulator handwheel. Open the cylinder valve slightly, then one and one-half turns. Leave wrench in position on acetylene tank valve.

## CONNECTING HOSES

The oxygen hose is connected to the oxygen regulator, and the acetylene hose to the

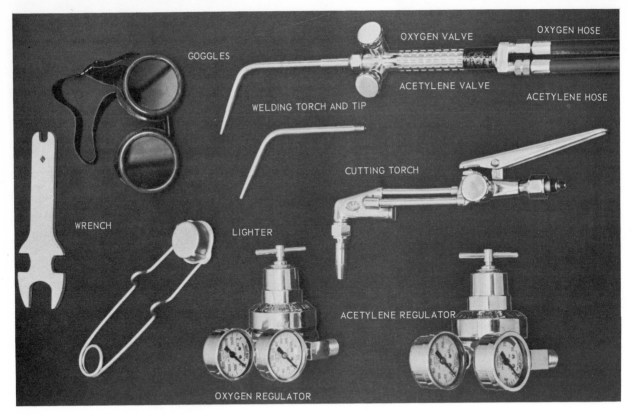

*Fig. 9-3. Basic accessories for welding with oxyacetylene.*

acetylene regulator. In the case of new hose, it is necessary to first blow out loose talc powder. This is done by attaching one end of the hose to the oxygen regulator outlet and opening the valve to 5 lb. pressure. Do the same with the acetylene hose.

## SIZE TIP TO USE

The size tip to use on the welding torch depends on the thickness of the metal to be welded. Most auto body sheet metal is approximately 20 gauge, or .032 in. Body men generally use a number two or number three tip. The tips recommended by Linde Air Products are as follows:

| METAL THICK-NESS | | WELDING HEAD SIZE ON TORCH | | | PRESSURE FOR OXYGEN AND ACETYLENE |
|---|---|---|---|---|---|
| IN. | GAUGE | W109 | W110 | W111 | |
| .. | 32 | 1 | 1 | 1 | 5-7 |
| .. | 28 | 1 | 1 | 1 | 5-7 |
| .. | 25 | 2 | 2 | 2 | 5-7 |
| 1/32 | 22 | 2 | 3 | 3 | 5-7 |
| 1/16 | 16 | 3, 4 | 4 | 4 | 5-7 |
| 1/8 | 11 | 4 | 5 | 5 | 5-7 |
| 3/16 | .. | 4, 5 | 7 | 7 | 5-7 |
| 1/4 | .. | 6 | 8 | 8 | 6-9 |

## LIGHTING TORCH

Different pressures are needed for welding different thicknesses of metal as noted in the preceding table. First open the torch oxygen valve one full turn, turn in the oxygen regulator handwheel until correct pressure for the job shows on the gauge. For auto body sheet metal this is usually 5 to 7 lbs.

Then close the oxygen valve. Next open the torch acetylene valve one full turn and turn on the acetylene regulator hand valve until the correct pressure shows on the gauge. Close the torch acetylene valve promptly.

After putting on protective goggles, Fig. 9-3, point the torch down and away from you. Open the torch oxygen valve about one-quarter turn, then the torch acetylene valve one full turn. Light the gas at the tip with a friction-type lighter, Fig. 9-3. Open both valves wide and adjust torch acetylene valve slowly until a neutral flame is obtained, Fig. 9-4.

## ADJUSTING THE FLAME

With the gas burning as outlined in the preceding paragraphs, open the oxygen valve slowly. The flame should gradually change

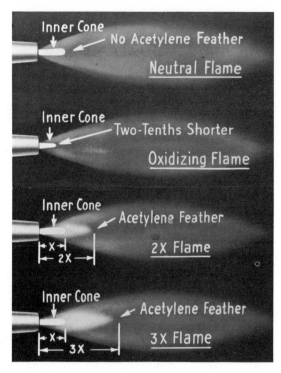

*Fig. 9-4. Illustrating method for indicating amount of excess acetylene used. After the flame has been adjusted to neutral, the torch acetylene valve should be opened, or the oxygen valve closed until the desired acetylene feather is obtained.*

from a yellow acetylene flame, to a blue carburizing, or reducing flame, Fig. 9-4. Starting with an excess acetylene flame, a neutral flame is obtained by slowly closing the pipe acetylene valve until the acetylene feather disappears.

To obtain an oxidizing flame, either increase the oxygen or reduce the acetylene.

## WHAT TO DO ABOUT BACKFIRE

Improper handling of the torch causes the flame to backfire; that is, go out with a loud snap. It may happen if you touch the work with the tip or nozzle, overheat the tip or nozzle, operate at incorrect pressures, if the head or nozzle is loose, or if there is dirt on the head or nozzle seat. The torch may be relighted as soon as the trouble is corrected.

## WHAT TO DO ABOUT FLASHBACKS

A flashback occurs when the flame disappears and gas burns inside the equipment.

This is usually accompanied by a squealing or hissing noise from inside the torch, sparks coming out the nozzle, heavy black smoke coming from the torch, blowpipe handle getting hot. In some cases the flame may go back far enough so that it will burst through the hose. When this happens, close the oxygen needle valve immediately. Then close the acetylene valve. After allowing time for the equipment to cool, relight the torch in the usual manner.

Flashbacks can usually be eliminated by using the correct pressures for each welding head or cutting nozzle. If flashbacks occur frequently there is a strong possibility that the torch and/or tip are defective.

## AT THE END OF THE JOB

Turn off the torch. First close the torch acetylene valve, then the torch oxygen valve.

If you are stopping work for only a few minutes:

1. Turn out oxygen regulator valve until loose.
2. Open torch oxygen valve.
3. Close torch oxygen valve.
4. Turn out acetylene regulator hand valve until loose.
5. Open torch acetylene valve.
6. Close torch acetylene valve.

If you stop work for more than ten minutes:

1. Close oxygen acetylene valve.
2. Open torch oxygen valve until all pressure goes down to zero.
3. Turn out oxygen regulator handwheel until loose.
4. Close torch oxygen valve.
5. Close acetylene cylinder valve.
6. Open torch acetylene valve until all pressure goes down to zero.
7. Turn out acetylene handwheel until loose.
8. Close torch acetylene valve.

## WELDING PRACTICE

To weld sheet metal, a neutral flame (flame obtained by burning approximately one-to-one mixture of acetylene and oxygen) should be used. Skill can be attained by practicing on strips of sheet metal. At first, do not attempt to weld two pieces of sheet metal together, but move the flame across the surface of the sheet metal, carrying the "puddle" along the surface, Fig. 9-5. Do not

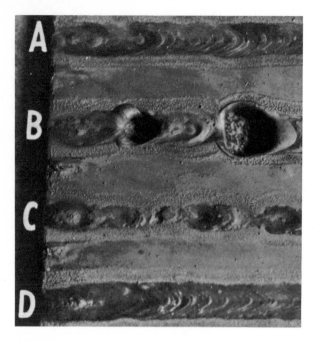

Fig. 9-5. A practice piece with good results shown at A and D. Excess heat caused holes to be burned as shown at B, while too little heat was used at C. No welding rod was used when making this practice piece.

use any welding rod. The purpose of this exercise is to obtain skill in carrying a puddle across the surface of the sheet. The torch should be held so that the flame points in the same direction that the weld will be made and at an angle of about 45 deg., Fig. 9-6. The

Fig. 9-6. Note angle of welding rod and torch.

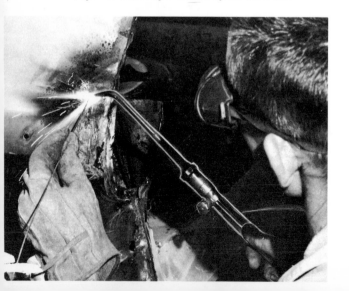

inner cone of the flame should be about 1 in. away from the surface of the sheet. Hold the torch in this position until a pool of molten metal about 3/16-in. to 1/4-in. in diameter is formed. Then move the torch slowly so as to move the puddle in the desired direction to obtain an even ripple effect. To do this, the torch should be swung from side to side in a small arc. If the torch is moved too slowly, holes may be burned through the sheet metal. If the torch is moved too quickly, the desired degree of melting and overlapping of the puddles will not be obtained.

After some skill is obtained without using a welding rod, repeat the preceding exercise, using a welding rod, Fig. 9-7. In this case, the addition of the welding rod will produce a slight ridge of metal above the surface of the sheet. The position of the welding rod should be similar to the welding torch, except that it is held in the left-hand and at an angle of slightly more than 45 deg. The spot on the sheet, and the tip of the welding rod should be brought to the melting temperature

Fig. 9-7. Examples of good and poor welds. Those at A and D are satisfactory, while the weld at B shows the effects of too much heat. Insufficient heat, little fusion and improper melting of the welding rod produced the weld shown at C.

at the same time. It will be found that the best position for the end of the welding rod is just inside the outer end of the flame while the flame is being concentrated on the spot at the start of the weld.

After practicing the use of the welding rod, place the edges of two pieces of sheet metal 1/16 in. apart and weld them together. In this case it is important that the welding action penetrate completely through to the inner side of the sheet.

# Welding

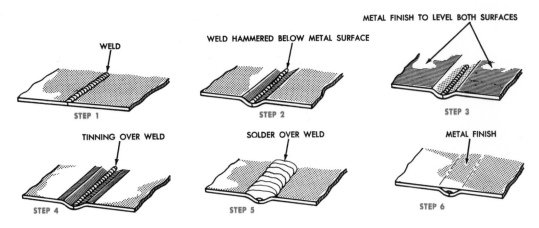

Fig. 9-8. *Typical welding operations used when replacing a body panel.*

During the welding action, the welding puddle must be controlled so that it will not fall through the gap. However, the metal added from the rod must be thoroughly fused with the base metal on both sides of the joint for the entire thickness of the sheet.

After sufficient skill has been attained on welding small sheets of metal together, work on an actual fender or body panel can be attempted.

## WELDING A PANEL

After welding two pieces of sheet metal together, there will be a slight ridge along the welded seam, Step 1, Fig. 9-8. This must be hammered below the contours of the surface approximately 1/16 in., Step 2. Using a disk sander, make the surface clean and smooth, Step 3. The groove and weld is then tinned, Step 4, and filled with solder, Step 5. The final step in preparation for painting is to sand the surface, Step 6.

## ELECTRIC WELDING

When two electrical conductors are brought together to form a contact, current will flow. Then when the conductors are separated a short distance an arc will be formed, and the current will continue to flow through the arc. This will produce such high temperatures that metal is melted. Under extreme conditions temperatures as high as 6300 deg. F. are obtained.

To maintain such an arc as used for weld-

ing, special equipment is needed. Such equipment will generate current of the correct specification, or transform it from a power supply line. A flux-coated filler rod or electrode is used to maintain the arc and to supply metal needed to fill the gap separating the metals being welded. Such welding is used extensively when rewelding seams which were originally spot welded.

A difficulty in the use of arc welding on sheet metal is that it cannot be used to fill wide openings or gaps. The intense heat of the arc tends to melt away exposed edges faster than the filler metal can be deposited.

It is not necessary to leave a gap between the edges being welded. Care must be exercised to avoid burning through the thin metal of which the auto bodies are made. When the electric arc is used on a lapped sheet metal joint, the surfaces must fit tightly together, otherwise holes will be burned in the work.

A big advantage of using electric arc welding on body sheet metal is that it causes less heat distortion than oxyacetylene. This is true because it progresses more rapidly, and without the blast of the heated gases. There is also reduced fire hazard when used close to flammable materials, such as upholstery and other interior trim. There is, however, still some hazard caused by sparks which are thrown off.

When welding the heavier section materials used in the frame of the automobile, electric arc has a big advantage of speed with reduced distortion.

## ARC WELDING EQUIPMENT

In arc welding, the metal being welded forms part of the electrical circuit. One terminal from the power source is connected to the work, and the other terminal is connected to the electrode holder. When the electrode is touched to the work, the circuit is completed, the arc is formed and a very heavy current flows. It is this heavy current which melts the electrode and causes it to stick to the work. Special procedure must therefore be followed when forming the arc.

## FORMING ARC

A difficulty experienced in forming or striking the arc, especially by beginners, is that the electrode fuses to the work. While there are several methods of striking the arc, the following is the method most frequently used.

First move the electrode toward the work, moving it downward and vertically, as shown in Fig. 9-9. Just as soon as the electrode touches the surface of the work, withdraw it to the correct arc length.

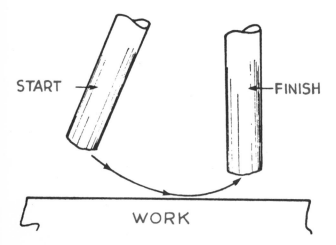

Fig. 9-9. One method of striking an arc is to move the electrode downward and vertically. As soon as electrode touches surface of work withdraw it to correct length of arc.

Another method, which is a variation of that just described, is to move the electrode at an angle to the work in a sort of scratching surface method. The electrode will scratch across the work to form the arc, Fig. 9-10.

When the arc is formed withdraw the electrode to form an arc of the proper length.

The second method may be easier for beginners, particularly when using an AC machine.

If the electrode fuses to the work, give the holder a quick twist. If this does not free the electrode, it will be necessary to open the

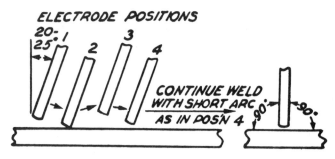

Fig. 9-10. In this method of striking an arc, the electrode is moved across surface of work in scratching motion.

circuit by letting go of the electrode with the holder. Never, try to free a fused electrode without the protective helmet on. Do all loosening of the electrode with the shield in front of your eyes. The student should practice the motion of striking the arc, with the current turned off. Then after having become familiar with the proper motion, the current may be turned on and the actual arc formed. The correct length of the arc work on sheet metal is approximately 1/8 in. to 3/16 in.

Fig. 9-11. Electric welding equipment which uses alternating current.

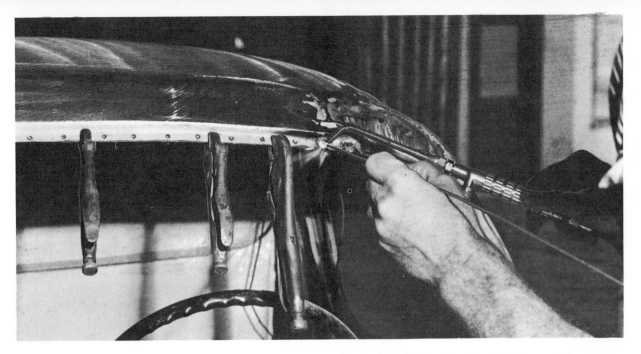

Fig. 9-12. This photo shows a mechanic brazing a car roof to the front header. Note the original spot welds.

## AC AND DC WELDERS

Both AC or DC welders may be used for auto body work. The DC welder can be used to do all types of welding, and in any position. However, the cost of the equipment is usually greater than an AC welder, see Fig. 9-11.

The direct current welder consists basically of a direct current generator with the necessary controls. The alternating current arc welder consists of a transformer which is connected to the commercial power lines.

## SPOT WELDING

Instead of having a continuous weld to join two pieces of sheet metal together, welding in spots less than an inch apart is often done. Such welding is used largely in production work. It is often used to weld the roof to the side panels, Fig. 9-12. Similar welding in spots can be done in the repair field by using an arc spot welding gun, as shown in Fig. 9-13. Such equipment produces a weld spot to join two pieces of overlapped sheet metal. It is designed for use in any position and on any seam which was originally welded by resistance type spot welding by the manufacturer. When using an arc spot welding gun, welding rod is also used so a slight hump is made at each weld.

As little heat is produced with arc spot welding, little distortion results. This method is therefore used frequently when the welds are made in close proximity to upholstery and other flammable materials.

## RESISTANCE SPOT WELDING

Many auto body panels are joined together at the time of manufacture by resistance spot welding. Panels are joined by a series of spot welds. The welds are placed about 1 in. apart instead of using a long continuous weld.

Fig. 9-13. Spot welder being used on rocker panel.

In this production type welding, the weld area is gripped between the electrodes of the spot welding machine and a high amperage low voltage current is passed through it. The electrical resistance of the overlapping layers of the joint is much higher than that of the electrodes, and consequently as the current passes through it, a high degree of heat is generated. This heat is sufficient to melt the metal at points of contact and welds are formed.

An example of this type of spot welding is shown in Fig. 9-12.

Fig. 9-15 shows the schematic drawing of an electric or resistant spot welding operation. The usual method of breaking these welds apart is to insert a cold chisel between the two sheets of metal and force it through with a hammer.

The use of resistance spot welding is difficult in the repair shop because of the problem of obtaining access to both sides of the panels being welded, as required in this type of welding.

## ARC WELDING SAFETY

When doing arc welding, it is important that a special helmet be worn to protect your eyes, see Fig. 9-14. Also important is the wearing of protective clothing and gloves to

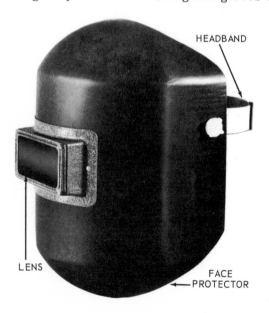

*Fig. 9-14. One type of arc welding helmet.*

prevent injury from flying sparks. The brilliant light given off by the arc will cause burning similar to sunburn on an exposed surface of the body, and it is particularly harmful to the eyes.

Special screens should also be provided to protect other workers in the shop. Welding

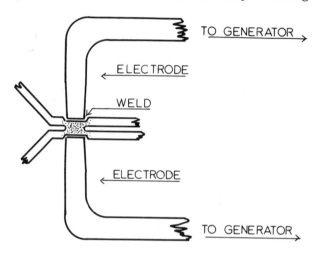

*Fig. 9-15. Schematic drawing of resistance spot welding operation.*

should not be performed in any area where there is any possibility of sparks falling on flammable material.

All electric cables should be examined periodically to make sure that the insulation is in good condition, so there will be no danger of electric short circuits.

### BRAZING

Brazing is another method of joining two pieces of metal by means of heat. In brazing a nonferrous (nonferrous means without iron) filler rod, which melts at 800 deg. F., is used. The 800 deg. temperature for brazing compares to 400 deg. F. for soldering, and 2800 deg. F. for welding steel.

In auto body repair work, brazing is sometimes used for repairing seams which were originally electric spot welded. In order to make a strong joint, it is essential that the two surfaces be close together. The usual recommendation is .003 in. to .005 in.

When brazing, the nonferrous filler rod actually diffuses and penetrates into the metals being joined to form an alloy. Brazing is done only on metals that have a higher melting point than the brazing material or filler rods. Metals being brazed should not be heated to the melting point.

In brazing the alloy formed on each of the two metals will join and intermix so that a joint of maximum strength is formed.

As in the case of soldering, a flux is needed when brazing. This flux is available in plastic, liquid and powder forms, and also as a solid coating on the nonferrous filler rod.

Many body men use a paste or powder form of flux, and apply it in the following manner. The filler rod is heated, and then is dipped into the container holding the flux. The end of the rod is coated with flux when it is withdrawn. Then as the filler rod is melted, the flux is also melted and runs ahead to clean the surface and prevent oxidation.

Filler rods that are coated with flux eliminate the necessity of dipping the rod into the can of flux, and in that way time is saved.

When brazing, molten brazing material flows back through the joint as the result of capillary action. This is caused by the attraction of the surface for any liquid that will wet it. Other examples of capillary action are oil running up a wick, and ink being drawn up by blotting paper.

An advantage of brazing is that it requires less heat and fusion welding and therefore there will be less distortion, particularly when the brazing is done on low crown sections of panels.

## QUIZ - Chapter 9

1. Is oxyacetylene welding equipment used only for welding?
   Yes.
   No.

2. How should oxygen and acetylene cylinders be stored?
   Valve ends up.
   Lying on side.
   Kept in cartons.

3. When setting up oxyacetylene welding equipment, how should you get rid of dust around the valve seat?
   Wipe away with clean cloth.
   Use camel's hair brush.
   Open valve slightly.

4. The threads on the oxygen regulator are right-hand threads?
   True.
   False.

5. What is the usual color for the connections on the oxygen regulator?
   Red.
   Green.

6. What color are the connections of the acetylene regulator?
   Red.
   Green.

7. Should threads of oxygen equipment be lubricated?
   Yes.
   No.

8. What size tip is usually used when welding auto body sheet metal?
   2 or 3.
   4 or 5.
   0 or 1.

9. When lighting the welding torch, what method should be used.
   Friction lighter.
   Match.

10. If there is an excess of acetylene, what color is the flame?
    Blue.
    Yellow.
    Red.

11. What color is a carburizing flame?
    Blue.
    Yellow.
    Red.

12. When welding sheet metal, what type flame should be used?
    Carburizing flame.
    Neutral flame.
    Oxydizing flame.

13. How far should the inner cone of the flame be from the surface of the work?
    2 in.
    1 in.
    3 in.

14. When arc welding sheet metal, is it possible to fill wide gaps?
    Yes.
    No.

15. Does electric arc welding cause much or little heat distortion?
    Much.
    Little.

16. Alternating current is never used when welding sheet metal.
    True.
    False.

17. What kind of rod is used when brazing?
    Nonferrous rod.
    Swedish iron rod.
    Nickel-steel alloy.

# Chapter 10
# CUTTING
# SHEET METAL

There are six principal ways of cutting sheet metal as used in the auto body shop.

A. Oxygen-Acetylene Torch.
B. Electric Arc.
C. Abrasive Wheel.
D. Power Saw.
E. Shears.
F. Impact Hammer and Cutter.

## CUTTING WITH OXYGEN-ACETYLENE

Cutting with the oxyacetylene is one of the fastest methods of cutting sheet metal. An objection to its use is that a relatively wide cut is made and consequently more metal is wasted than when an abrasive wheel or power saw is used. When cutting with oxyacetylene, a small area is heated with the flame until it is bright red and starts to melt. Then a jet of oxygen is directed against the preheated area and a narrow slit is quickly burnt through the metal, Fig. 10-1.

Oxygen is what does the cutting. It makes a liquid iron oxide as it joins with the hot steel. This flows out or is blown away, exposing more metal to the jet of oxygen. By moving the blowpipe or torch, Fig. 10-2, the jet of

Fig. 10-1. Cutting door inside panel with oxyacetylene torch.

oxygen is guided to cut a straight line, curved or irregular line as desired.

The nozzles for cutting have one center hole surrounded by four smaller holes, Fig. 10-3. The outer holes provide the small oxyacetylene flame to preheat the metal to start cutting, and to keep the cut going after it has started. The jet of oxygen is regulated by the cutting oxygen lever and comes from the center hole.

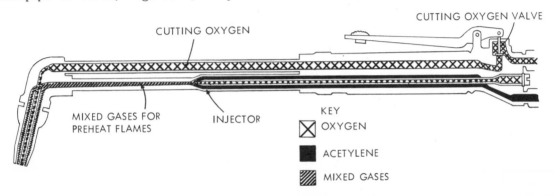

Fig. 10-2. Details of oxyacetylene torch construction.

For cutting sheet metal a #0 nozzle is normally preferred, with about 15 lb. oxygen and 4 to 5 lb. acetylene pressure.

When cutting with oxygen, the first step is to clean the area being cut, using a wire bristle brush, power sander or other suitable means. Then, mark the line to be cut. A soapstone pencil is usually recommended for drawing the line, although chalk is also used extensively. This line is then center punched every one-half inch so it can be seen while working.

Light the torch. Hold the nozzle so that the cutting oxygen hole is over the edge of the panel being cut and at the marked line. The preheat flame will heat both the top of the panel and the side edge. Keep the edges of the pale blue core for preheating flame about 1/16 in. away from the metal for best results. Also keep the nozzle of the blowpipe at right angles to the surface of the panel until a spot under the preheating flame starts to melt. Then tilt the nozzle so that the flame points toward the edge of the panel. Slowly open the cutting oxygen valve by pressing down on the lever. As soon as cutting starts, as indicated by a shower of sparks, slowly straighten the nozzle again and press the oxygen lever all the way down. When the cut has gone all the way through the panel, tilt the nozzle forward a little in the direction of cutting. If the blowpipe is moved too fast the cutting will stop. Should this occur, release the oxygen lever and start the cut over again with the preheat flame.

When using a cutting blowpipe, both hands are needed. The right hand is used to control the oxygen lever and guide the blowpipe, while the left hand is placed slightly forward of the right and is used to balance the weight of the blowpipe and support its weight. When cutting an arc, the left hand is used as a pivot or axis and the gun is swung about that point. To cut a straight line, simply roll the hand that supports the blowpipe.

When cutting thick sections of metal a somewhat similar technique is followed. However, larger size nozzles are needed and the rate of cutting is much slower.

When making a square cut, that is a cut that goes straight through the metal, set the nozzle so that the two preheating jets fall directly in

line to be cut - one in front and the other behind the cutting oxygen, Fig. 10-3. When making a bevel cut, as is sometimes neces-

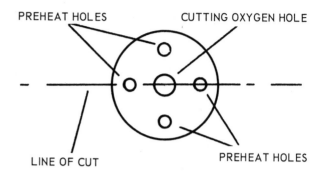

*Fig. 10-3. Cutting torch should be held as indicated when cutting straight through the metal.*

sary when cutting thick pieces of metal, such as the vehicle frame, set the nozzle so that the preheat holes are in the position shown in Fig. 10-4. This provides the additional preheating required when making a double cut.

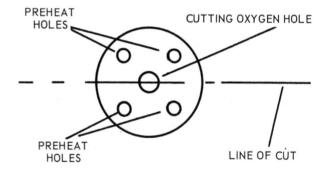

*Fig. 10-4. When making a bevel cut through thick metal, make sure preheat holes of torch are held as shown.*

## CUTTING WITH ELECTRIC ARC

When cutting sheet metal with an electric arc, usually a direct current machine, carbons are generally used. Electric negative should be used in all cases, and a current of 50 to 100 amps. is all that is needed for cutting the sheet metal used in auto bodies, Fig. 10-5.

The arc should be started at some point from which the molten metal will easily flow. By starting at the bottom and working up, the molten metal will flow out of the cut. Also the cut should start at the edge of the panel.

Fig. 10-5. Cutting a body panel with an electric torch.

## CUTTING WITH ABRASIVE WHEELS

A fast way to cut sheet metal is to use special abrasive wheels and saws designed especially for the purpose, Fig. 10-6. Very little metal is wasted by this method. With disks or circular saws of large diameter, it becomes difficult to cut curves of small radii, but in straight line cutting operations disks and circular saws are preferred by many mechanics. In addition there is no fire hazard when using grinding wheels or saws. The same equipment can be used for slotting

Fig. 10-6. Using a circular saw to cut a body panel.

Fig. 10-7. A jigsaw being used to cut a body panel.

sheet metal, cutting old bolts, removing welds, and for miscellaneous grinding.

Fig. 10-6, shows a truck trailer panel being cut by this method. When using an abrasive wheel or circular saw for cutting, care must be exercised that the saw is moved in a straight line. If curves are attempted, the saw will bind and quickly become dull.

## POWER JIGSAWS FOR CUTTING

There are several different types of equipment that are broadly classed as saws. One saw that is used for cutting sheet metal in the body shop is the jigsaw as shown in Figs. 10-7 and 10-8. This electric driven tool will cut arcs of small radii, and is also used for straight line cutting.

When using this method, the cut should not be forced but the saw should be moved along smoothly without attempting to cut too fast.

Fig. 10-8. Another type of saw designed to cut body panels.

## CUTTING WITH SHEARS

While power driven equipment is used for all major cutting of sheet metal in auto body shops, hand shears are still used extensively for small work and close fitting of panels.

## CUTTING WITH IMPACT HAMMER

An impact hammer, fitted with a cutting chisel is also used for cutting sheet metal. However, this frequently results in a rough ragged cut and as a result other methods are usually preferred.

### QUIZ - Chapter 10

1. Name four ways to cut sheet metal.
2. Cutting sheet metal with oxyacetylene is one of the quickest methods of cutting sheet metal.
    True.
    False.
3. It is not necessary to first clean the surface of the metal before cutting with oxyacetylene.
    True.
    False.
4. The edges of the pale blue cone for preheating flame should be kept how far away from the work when cutting with oxyacetylene?
    7/8 in.
    1/16 in.
    1/4 in.
5. When cutting with abrasive wheels, it is easy to cut an arc of small radius.
    True.
    False.

*Using machine with polishing compound to give a higher than normal lustre to finished surfaces.*

# Chapter 11

# HOW TO
# SHRINK SHEET METAL

In many cases, as a result of a collision, the sheet metal will become stretched. In addition, as a result of using a dolly block and dinging hammer, the metal will be reduced in thickness and will therefore tend to occupy a greater area than originally. When this occurs the metal will tend to bulge, as shown in Fig. 11-1.

![](Fig. 11-1 bulge illustration)

Fig. 11-1. As the result of either hot or cold working, sheet metal will become stretched, and will bulge as shown.

When metal becomes stretched or bulges, it is necessary to shrink it so it will occupy the same space as originally.

There are three major methods of shrinking sheet metal:

A. Using a special shrinking hammer.
B. Cutting slits in the bulged area.
C. Use of heat.

The hammer used for shrinking sheet metal is the same as a conventional dinging hammer, except that the face of the hammer is cross-grooved, Fig. 11-2. These grooves are quite deep and when used will mark the metal with a series of square dots. The hammer is used with a dolly in the usual manner, but instead of making the metal thinner, it will tend to shrink it as a result of the many tiny dents formed by the grooved face of the hammer. When using a shrinking hammer, care must be taken that the full face of the hammer strikes the surface of the panel.

A bulge or stretch can also be removed from the panel by cutting slits in the metal and allowing the edges of the slits to overlap. The overlapping surfaces are then welded together, after which the weld is countersunk and the surface smoothed with a disk grinder or a file. This method, however, is not considered good practice and is seldom used by skilled body men.

The best and most frequently used method of shrinking metal is by means of heat. The complete shrinking process is to heat a spot at the center of the bulge, as in Fig. 11-3.

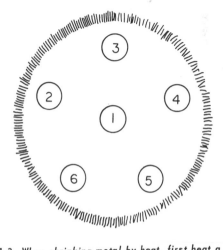

Fig. 11-3. When shrinking metal by heat, first heat a spot at the center of the bulge and continue as shown by the numbered spots.

Fig. 11-2. Face of hammer used for shrinking metal. Note that face is cross-grooved.

Using a dolly block and hammer, this is then hammered down, Fig. 11-4. In successive rim heats, Fig. 11-3, additional spots are heated and hammered down. This is a basic procedure, and an area being shrunk by this method is shown in Fig. 11-4.

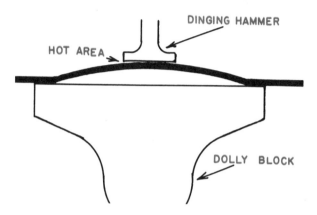

Fig. 11-4. After heating the area, the surface is worked with hammer and dolly.

Naturally, no attempt should be made to shrink a panel until the surface has been worked over and has been made relatively smooth. In addition, the lacquer or enamel should also be removed before starting the shrinking process.

Three different sizes of heat spots will be found sufficient to cover practically any type of shrinking. On compound curved surfaces a spot not more than 1/8-in. in diameter should be heated at one time. On plane flat surfaces, 1/4 to 5/8-in. heat spots can be used. Larger heat spots are used in cases of excessive bulge, but at no time should a heat spot larger than 5/8 in. be used.

It is well to remember that auto body sheet metal loses its temper or springing effect when heated to a cherry red. By heating small spots, the natural spring and resiliency of sheet metal is retained in the metal between the spots.

Most body panels have at least a slight curve. Therefore, if the metal is shrunk too much it will cause a flat area at that point and sometimes causes buckles to appear elsewhere in the panel. The flat area would then have to be stretched to the proper degree with a hammer and dolly.

The first heat should be applied in the approximate center of the bulge, heating a spot to a cherry red about 1/8-in. to 1/4-in. in diameter, depending on the size and height of the bulge. This spot is then hammered down while red hot, directing the blows against the red spots with the flat face of a dolly underneath. After this initial heating and hammering operation, the bulge assumes a crater like shape, Fig. 11-5. The next step is to

Fig. 11-5. Shrinking an area with a torch.

shrink the rim of this crater in successive stages, Fig. 11-3. Selecting the highest point of this rim, the heating operation is then repeated, and hammer and dolly used as on the first spot.

On the next high spot, which is No. 3, Fig. 11-3, the preceding operations are again repeated. It will be observed the bulged surface is being brought down and begins to assume its former shape and contours. The procedure is continued, taking five successive steps, until the entire bulged area is brought down to the level of the first spots.

Due to the expansion of the metal while hot, the surface will be slightly bulged after the last spot is hammered down, but will continue to shrink until the metal is thoroughly cool. It is very important to allow the metal to become thoroughly cool before any final dinging is done, after which it can be determined whether the surface is at its proper level. Should there be one or more high spots remaining, these should be shrunk again, using very small heat spots.

The panel surface is then ready for final sanding and preparation for priming. It is always good practice to clean and paint the underside of the area that has been shrunk too, otherwise rust will quickly form.

In the case of a long narrow stretch, the shrinking is started at either end instead of the center.

Aluminum shrinking follows the same general procedure as steel, except that care must be used to avoid burning through the metal at point of contact with the flame because aluminum absorbs heat much more rapidly than steel, and does not change color under heat. It also cools more quickly. Just as soon as the metal starts to blister where the flame contacts the metal, the flame must be removed and hammering done quickly with a wood or fiber mallet.

## QUIZ - Chapter 11

1. How does a shrinking hammer differ from an ordinary dinging hammer?
   Has a heavier head.
   Has a longer handle.
   The face is cross-grooved.
2. When shrinking metal with a torch, where should the heat be first applied?
   At the center of the area.
   At the edge of the area.
3. When shrinking an area on a plane flat surface, how large should the heat spots be made?
   1/8 in.
   1/4 to 5/8 in.
   1 in.
4. When shrinking sheet metal, what should be the color of the heated spot?
   Red hot.
   White hot.
   Straw color.

# Chapter 12
# REPLACING
# PANELS AND FENDERS

In many cases the damage to fenders and other panels can be repaired by dolly block and hammer, or other straightening methods. However, in other cases, considerable time can be saved by removing the damaged panel and installing a new one, or by cutting out the damaged area and inserting a new section.

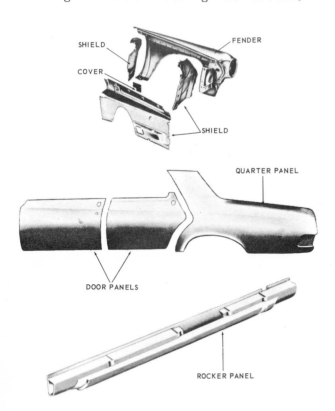

Fig. 12-1. Typical replacement panels.

Whether to repair the original panel or install a new one depends on the extent of the damage, and which repair method would cost the least. This can be determined only as the

result of experience and accurate estimates of the time involved in making repairs and replacements, together with the cost of parts.

Some of the frequently replaced panels are shown in Fig. 12-1. Some others are illustrated in Chapter 1, on Auto Body Construction.

At this point it should be emphasized that great accuracy is required in straightening work in order that doors and windows will operate correctly, and in the case of front end work the front suspension cross member is made to unusually close limits. This is necessary to insure proper front wheel alignment. Therefore, in many cases it is better practice to replace a member than to attempt to straighten it.

## REMOVING A FENDER PANEL

When it is desirable to replace a complete panel, it is necessary to remove the bolts securing it to the rest of the structure, or cut through the spot welds as the case may be.

In most cases the front fender panel is bolted to the rest of the structure, Fig. 12-2. Other panels may be spot welded, Fig. 9-13, or fusion welded, Fig. 12-3. In the case of spot welds, Fig. 12-4, most mechanics usually drill through the spot welds and then use a power chisel to completely separate the panel from the rest of the body structure.

Installation of a new panel is not difficult provided the rest of the body has not been damaged. The alignment of a new front fender, Fig. 12-2, is simplified, for in most cases the bolt holes are elongated so that the position of the panel can be shifted and correctly aligned. In general, only front fender panels

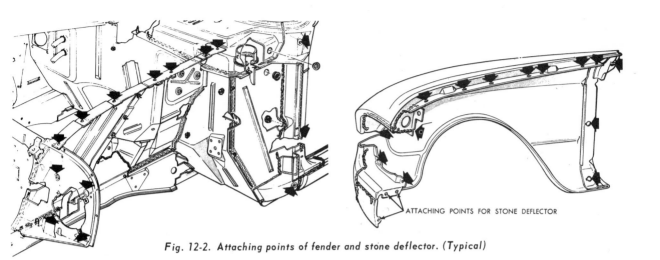

Fig. 12-2. *Attaching points of fender and stone deflector. (Typical)*

are bolted in position, while rear fender panels, or rear quarter panels, as these are known, are generally welded in position, Fig. 12-3.

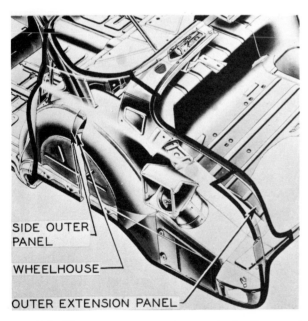

SIDE OUTER PANEL

WHEELHOUSE

OUTER EXTENSION PANEL

Fig. 12-3. *Illustrating outer extension panel, wheelhouse and side outer panel.*

## REPLACING A COMPLETE PANEL

Typical service panels are shown in Fig. 12-1. If the complete panel is to be replaced, the old panel should be removed by cutting

along the weld, if fusion welded in place, or by drilling out the spot welds, if it is spot welded in place. Car and body manufacturers have the panels welded at different places, and it is necessary to examine the body to determine where the welds are located in each case. In addition, collision manuals will give diagrams of the panels for the different makes and models of cars which indicate where these welds are located.

Before cutting out the old panel, it is important that the damage to the area be restored to its original shape and alignment. This can be checked by comparison with the other side of the vehicle.

After removing the old damaged panel, the inner panel, such as the wheelhouse, rocker and other inner panels are carefully checked and straightened or replaced, as the case may require. The new outer panel is placed in position by means of vice-grip pliers, or by

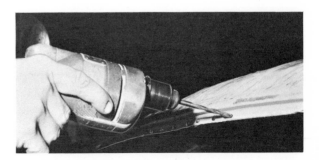

Fig. 12-4. *Drilling out spot welds at front edge of roof.*

C clamps. The welder then starts at the center, and proceeds first in one direction, then the other. In order to reduce distortion due to heat, it is advisable to weld a space of only 2 or 3 in. at a time. Leave a gap and weld another short length. In that way temperatures are kept down, and distortion kept to a minimum. When the weld is complete, it is hammered down, filled and finished as described in the chapter on Welding.

## REPLACING PARTIAL PANELS

In many cases it is desirable to replace only the damaged area of a fender or panel. In general, the decision on whether to replace a panel or repair the existing panel depends on the length of time required to straighten the damaged area. Such a decision is dependent on the availability of a replacement panel, its cost, and also the cost of labor.

When only a portion of a panel is to be replaced, the first step is to straighten the area so that it is in alignment with the body. Then outline the damaged area with chalk making sure the undamaged area is not sprung out of proper contour. Take measurements carefully from the edge of the panel, the molding, or beading, and transfer these measurements to the replacement panel, scribing lines where the panel is to be cut.

Cut along these lines to obtain the desired area of the replacement panel. There are several different methods of cutting a panel, and these were described in the chapter on Cutting Sheet Metal.

After straightening the cut edges of the replacement panel, position it over the damaged

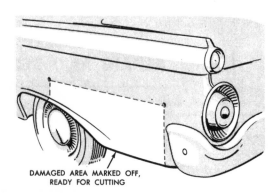

DAMAGED AREA MARKED OFF,
READY FOR CUTTING

*Fig. 12-5. Damaged area is carefully marked off before it is cut out.*

area. Scribe a line on the damaged panel, outlining the new replacement panels, Fig. 12-5. Then cut out the damaged area.

Straighten the cut edge of the damaged area, and fit the service panel portion into the cut out area in the body panel. Be sure that two parts do not overlap at any point. The new section can be held in position by C clamps, or by vise-grip pliers, Fig. 12-6.

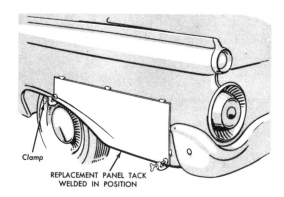

Clamp

REPLACEMENT PANEL TACK
WELDED IN POSITION

*Fig. 12-6. Section of service panel is then held in position with clamps while it is welded in place.*

Tack weld at intervals, starting at the center and working toward each end. Then make a continuous weld around the two pieces. By welding at intervals, and only about 4 in. at a time, the possibility of distortion due to heat is minimized.

Details on welding and hammering the weld below the surface are given in the chapter on Welding.

## DOOR PANEL REPLACEMENT

If a door outer panel is severely damaged and the door inner panel is undamaged, or is in a repairable condition, a door outer panel is available for service as well as a complete door.

If the outer panel is to be replaced, first remove the door assembly and the exterior moldings and hardware. It is not necessary to remove the window regulator, and remote control mechanisms, lock and runs.

Place the door on a flat surface with its edges extending over the edges of the surface, Fig. 12-7. Remove the hem flange by grinding, and repair any damage to the inner panel. Position the new outer repair panel, and bend the end flange over the inner flange. Spot braze the hem flange to the inner panel. Metal finish the exterior surface, paint it and assemble the interior trim and hardware.

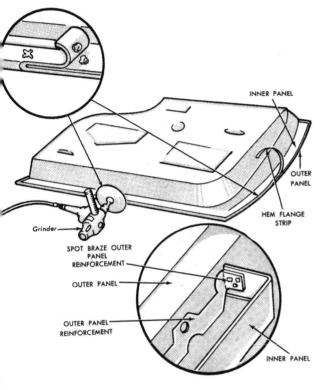

Fig. 12-7. Removing hem flange of door, prior to replacing the outer panel.

It will be necessary to break the weld on the door with an outer panel reinforcement. Spot braze the reinforcement when assembling the new panel.

## TOP PANEL REPLACEMENT

Before replacing a top it is important to have the basic body dimensions correct. These can be determined by triangular measurements as shown in Fig. 8-3. Also try the new top panel in position and use it as a template to check for any distortion of the body. After making sure the body is in alignment and not distorted, the new top panel is

carefully positioned on the car, and a line is scribed around the edge of the panel.

The old roof is then cut out with one of the methods described in a previous chapter. The new panel is again positioned on the body and is tacked in place with an occasional weld. After again checking for accurate alignment of the new panel with the body, the welding is completed. As in the case of welding other panels in position, only a few inches should be welded at a time.

### QUIZ - Chapter 12

1. How is the front fender usually attached to the rest of the vehicle?
   By means of bolts.
   Spots welds.
   Sheet metal screws.
2. Is the position of the front fender panel adjustable?
   Yes.
   No.
3. Before replacing a damaged panel, what should be done?
   Clean the damaged area.
   Straighten the area so it is in alignment with the body.
   Obtain a replacement panel.
4. When welding a replacement panel in place, where should the welding start?
   At the right edge.
   At the left edge.
   At the center.
5. When welding a replacement panel in place, it should first be tack welded in place.
   True.
   False.
6. Door outer panels are available for replacement.
   True.
   False.
7. The basic body dimensions should be checked by triangulation, before installing a new top.
   True.
   False.

# Chapter 13

# FILLING DENTS
# WITH SOLDER, PLASTIC

On certain areas of an auto body it is difficult to remove all the dents. This is particularly true in the case of doors, deck lids and hoods, as such panels are built-up sections and it is difficult to back up the dinging hammer, dolly block or spoon. Even when using the pull rod system some fill-in is required. Therefore, after making the area as smooth as possible, the remaining dents are brought up to the level of the undamaged panel by filling in with either solder or plastic.

Both methods are popular. Lead is faster as an appreciable amount of time is required for plastic fillers to dry.

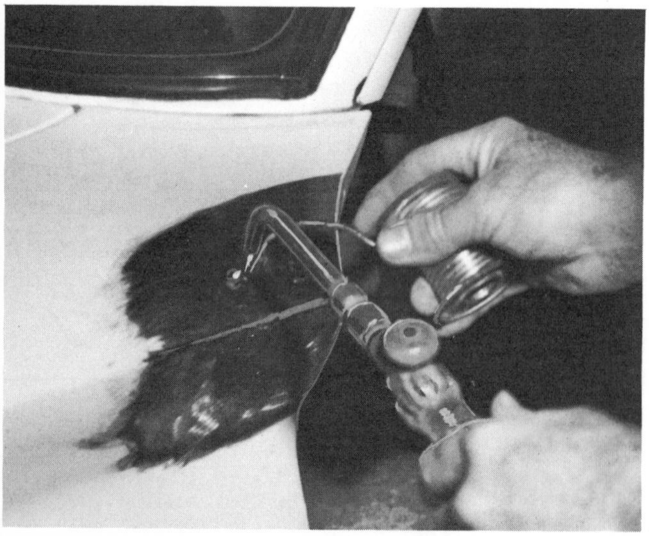

mer and dolly or other means. The metals are joined without melting the base metal.

When filling dents on auto body work, the air-acetylene torch is used. Oxygen is not necessary. The melting point of the solder used to fill dents is 361 to 437 deg. F. Solder flows at 469 to 543 deg. F. The composition of auto body solder varies with different manufacturers. The tin content may range from 15 to 35 percent and the lead content from 65 to 85 percent. The higher the percentage of tin, the lower the melting point.

In order to get the solder to adhere to the sheet metal of the body, it is first necessary

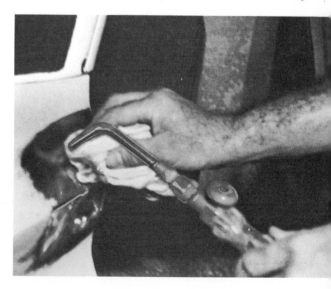

Fig. 13-1. Using acid core solder and torch to tin an area to be filled with solder.

Fig. 13-2. Either a clean cloth or steel wool can be used to spread the solder over the surface being tinned.

## SOLDERING

In auto body work, tin-lead mixture, known as solder, is melted and is used to fill indentations that cannot be removed by ham-

to clean and tin the surface. The paint can be burned off with the torch and the surface is then further cleaned by sanding. The next step is the application of the flux. This can be either a liquid or a paste type. Its purpose is to still further clean the surface by removing any oil or oxides that may be present. Commercial fluxes in both paste and liquid form are available for soldering all types of metals. After the application of the flux, following the manufacturer's instructions, the surface is tinned. That is, the surface is heated and then solder is melted onto the area by means of the acetylene torch. Instead

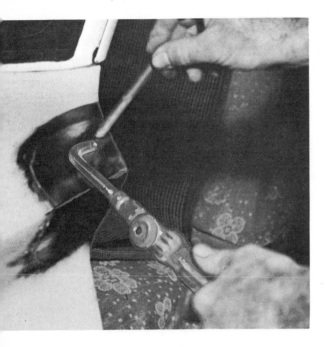

Fig. 13-3. Melting solder on tinned surface.

of using a paste or liquid flux, some mechanics will use an acid core solder for tinning, Fig. 13-1. The melted solder is then spread over the area by means of some steel wool, or a cloth, Fig. 13-2. When the tinning is completed the surface will have a bright shiny appearance and there will be a strong bond between the tin and the sheet metal of the body. Also when additional solder is added to fill the dent, there will be a strong bond between this filler solder and the tinned surface.

After the tinning operation, the body solder (usually in bar form) is melted onto the area, Fig. 13-3. Care must be exercised so that just enough heat is applied to keep the solder plastic, but not molten. Keeping the solder in this plastic condition, it is then smoothed with a maple wood paddle, Fig. 13-4. Suffi-

cient solder must be applied so that it is slightly higher than the surrounding panel. When cool, the surface of the solder is sanded with an open-coat No. 24 grit abrasive, or with a body file.

## SOLDERING ALUMINUM

Some automobiles and some truck bodies are made of sheet aluminum. Such bodies can be soldered, although welding is usually used to join aluminum parts. For filling dents special plastics are often used. Aluminum solders are generally self-fluxing, and when using such solders instructions provided by the manufacturer should be followed.

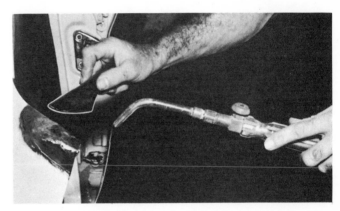

Fig. 13-4. Spreading soft solder over the surface with a wooden paddle.

The reason why aluminum and aluminum alloys are hard to solder is that they conduct heat away rapidly, and they oxidize faster than most metals. The most difficult part of the operation is tinning the surface. Once that has been accomplished, the remainder of the job is easy. In many cases, the special aluminum solders can be used for tinning and conventional solders for the remainder of the job.

## HOW TO FILL DENTS WITH PLASTIC

Instead of solder, special plastic materials are frequently used to fill depressions in auto bodies. There are many different makes of such plastics available. The method of applying the plastic varies somewhat with different manufacturers.

Before attempting to apply any plastic to a

rusted or dented area, it should be carefully sanded, with a disk sander to remove paint and rust, Fig. 13-5. A coarse grit such as

*Fig. 13-5. Before applying plastic filler to a car body, it should be carefully sanded.*

No. 24 open grit should be used to make the surface slightly rough and provide "bite" for the plastic. In addition the area surrounding the damaged area should be cleaned with a grease and wax remover. Also featheredge

*Fig. 13-6. If necessary, shrink the area with torch and then use hammer and dolly.*

the area with a No. 80 feathering disk to taper back the paint around the area.

If the metal has been stretched and a bulge is present, heat the area until it is red hot, Fig. 13-6, and shrink it with a dolly and shrink hammer.

Then mix the plastic in accordance with instructions on the container. In most cases, two materials are provided, a resin and a catalyst. Both materials are mixed with a putty knife, Fig. 13-7. Instead of using a box lid, some mechanics prefer to mix the ingredients on a sheet of glass.

*Fig. 13-7. Mixing plastic resin and catalyst.*

The plastic is then applied to the surface with a rubber squeegee, Fig. 13-8. If the dents are deep and a thick application is necessary, it is advisable to apply several thin layers and allow each layer to dry before applying the next coat.

*Fig. 13-8. Applying plastic with rubber squeegee.*

Fig. 13-9. Heat lamp being used to speed drying of plastic.

in progressively larger sizes so each succeeding patch will overlap the preceding patch. Wadded newspaper can be used to support the fiber glass when covering large

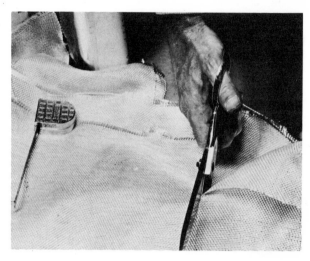

Fig. 13-10. Cutting fiber glass cloth prior to application on rusted area.

To hasten the drying, heat lamps may be used, Fig. 13-9. Or if heat lamps are not available, the flame of a welding torch can be played over the surface. However, care must be taken not to apply too much heat at one time by this method.

Plastic patches can be cured in about 30 minutes if a battery of infrared lamps is used.

After the plastic filler is dry, it is sanded in the usual manner and then primed and painted.

Fig. 13-11. Area is first sanded and then heated with heat lamps, prior to application of fiber glass cloth.

## FILLING RUSTED AREAS

A somewhat different procedure and materials are used to repair rusted areas. In general, the materials include fiber glass cloth, epoxy resin, and hardener.

The procedure is to first sand the surface in the usual manner to remove rust, dirt and paint. Then wipe the surface with an oil-free, wax-free cleaning solvent.

Drill a series of small holes through the metal all around the damaged area. This will insure quicker adhesion of resin to the metal.

Cut the fiber glass cloth. The cloth should be large enough to lap two or three inches over the damaged area, Fig. 13-10. If the rusted area is depressed below the surrounding surface, several layers of fiber glass cloth should be applied. These should be cut

holes and bridging deep dents. At this point, direct the rays from a heat lamp on the surface, Fig. 13-11. This will provide better adherence and reduce curing time.

Fig. 13-12. Before applying the fiber glass patches, they are impregnated with epoxy resin and hardener.

Wearing rubber gloves to protect the hands, mix enough epoxy resin and hardener to impregnate all patches. Care must be taken to use correct proportions of materials for if the mixture is too liquid, it will run when used on a vertical surface. The resin should be mixed in a glass tray.

Dip each of the fiber glass patches in the mixture, Fig. 13-12. When the patch is saturated apply it to the rusted area, Fig. 13-13.

Fig. 13-13. Applying the fiber glass cloth patches to the rusted area.

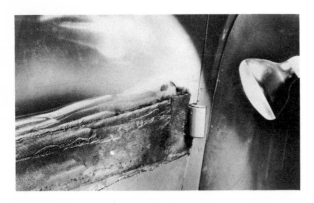

Fig. 13-14. The patch is first dried and then sanded. Paint is sprayed in the usual manner.

Use heat lamps, Fig. 13-14, to hasten drying time. And then sand and refinish the surface in the usual manner.

## QUIZ - Chapter 13

1. Which method of filling dents is faster, lead or plastic?
   Lead.
   Plastic.
2. Solder is a mixture of what two metals.
   Zinc and tin.
   Lead and zinc.
   Lead and tin.
   Copper and zinc.
3. What is the melting point of solder used to fill dents on auto bodies?
   361 to 470 deg.
   500 to 570 deg.
   560 to 670 deg.
4. What is purpose of soldering flux?
   Help clean the surface.
   Roughen the surface.
5. When applying solder to the tinned surface, in what condition should it be?
   Molten.
   Plastic.
6. When using a disk sander to smooth the surface of solder, what grit should be used?
   No. 24 grit.
   No. 240 grit.
   No. 180 grit.
7. When using plastic to fill a dent it is not necessary to featheredge the area.
   True.
   False.
8. Plastic is usually applied to the surface with what type of tool?
   Wooden paddle.
   Rubber squeegee.
9. When covering a rusted area with fiber glass cloth, what is the purpose of drilling holes through the metal?
   Provide better adhesion.
   Necessary for the pull rods.
   Used to attach the fiber glass.

# Chapter 14

# REPAIRING
# FIBER GLASS BODIES

Fiber glass car bodies are formed from chopped fiber glass preforms and fiber glass mats fused together with a polyester resin. Fiber glass is a fiber made by drawing out molten glass into long thread-like fibers. When resin cures or hardens, it binds fiber glass filaments together to form a solid reenforced panel having unusual strength. A reenforced fiber glass body has a high resistance to impact, which means it will not dent. In most minor accidents the body would be undamaged. If damage does occur, it would tend to be localized, not transmitted through the body and cause damage at a point away from the impact (as in the case of metal bodies). Various replacement panels are available for service. Complete panels may be used, or sections may be cut from the panels to accomodate the repair necessary.

The following steps should be used in repair of reenforced fiber glass parts:

1. Study the repair to be made.
2. Remove the damaged material.
3. Fill the damaged area with the proper mixture of resin and fiber glass.
4. Allow the activated resin to cure and harden.
5. Finish and paint the repaired area.

In general the following materials are needed for repairing fiber glass bodies:

Polyester resin.
Polyester filler.
Catalyst.
Fiber glass cloth.
Fiber glass powder or chopped fibers.
Fiber glass bonding strip.

These items are readily available in kit form. In cases where the kit is to be used for repairing both fiber glass and metal bodies, epoxy resin rather than polyester resin should be obtained, as polyester resin does not stick to metal satisfactorily.

The resin is activated by the addition of a catalyst in proper proportions, as specified by the manufacturer.

## SAFETY PRECAUTIONS

In cases where resin tends to cause skin irritation, it is recommended to apply a protective cream to the hands, or preferably to use rubber gloves when working with the resin, or filler and hardener.

Any resin accumulated on tools, clothing or the hands may be removed with lacquer thinner before the resin starts to jell or harden. It is important to use caution when handling thinner because it is highly flammable.

Resin mixtures should be used only in well-ventilated areas, as the mixture produces toxic fumes. When grinding or polishing the resin repair areas, it is advisable to use a belt sander with a vacuum attachment for dust control, Fig. 5-7. If the use of a vacuum attachment is not practical, or possible, a respirator should be worn to avoid inhaling the resin dust.

Catalyzed resin should not be left standing too long, as the chemical action results in rapid heat buildup and therefore is a fire hazard. Keep a water container available that is large enough to provide ready disposal for such left over or unused mixed material. Do not leave mixed resin and catalyzed material for extended lengths of time in the shop or undisposed of when the shop is closed.

## RESIN PREPARATION

Typical instructions are as follows: Place one ounce of resin in a wax-free container, and add 10 drops of catalyst to the resin, and mix well. This formula will normally harden in 30 minutes. Ten ounces of resin to 1 tsp. of catalyst. Use the same proportion for larger amounts.

Mix only as much as you are going to use within 30 minutes. The addition of more of the catalyst will cause a faster chemical reaction, therefore, setting up time will be reduced accordingly.

The filler is activated by the addition of a catalyst in proper proportions.

## FILLER PREPARATION

Place the desired amount of the filler (powdered fiber glass) on a clean hard surface. Using a spatula or putty knife mix in the catalyst: (typical mixtures) 1/4 tsp. for a golf ball size lump, or 1 oz. of catalyst, to a 3 lb. 1 qt. can. If the putty-like filler hardens too quickly use less catalyst.

Wipe a thin coat of mixed material on the area to be repaired, assuring a good bond and then fill the entire hole with the filler mixture.

When the filler and catalyst are mixed as directed above, it will harden in about 10 minutes. For quicker hardening, use more catalyst while mixing. It is a good practice to mix a small quantity of the resin and catalyst, or the filler and catalyst, according to the basic formula, and note the hardening time required. The hardening time will vary according to temperatures and humidity conditions.

CAUTION: Never return mixed filler or resin to the stock can. Keep the can closed and in a cool place of storage. Do not take internally. Wash hands after using, and before smoking or eating.

## REPAIRING HOLES IN PANELS

The following procedure is for use on the reverse side of panel, when accessible.

First clean the surface around the damaged area with a good commercial grease and wax remover. Remove all paint and primer with No. 80 grit paper, to expose plastic material at least 3 in. beyond the damaged area. Grind or file all cracked or splintered material away from the hole on both the inside and outside of the area to be repaired, Fig. 14-1.

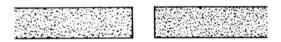

*Fig. 14-1. Grind or file edge of hole to remove splintered material.*

On the inner surface of the repair area, remove any dirt, sound deadener, etc., from the damaged area. Scuff the area around the hole with coarse No. 80 grit paper to provide a good bonding surface. Bevel the outside edge of the area to be repaired about 30 deg. to permit better patch adhesion, and the inner edge to about 45 deg. as shown in Fig. 14-2.

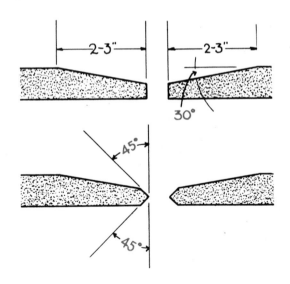

*Fig. 14-2. Bevel surface of edge of hole.*

Clean the repair surface well with mineral spirits, naphtha or a non-oily solvent.

Cut five pieces of fiber glass cloth large enough to cover the hole and the scuffed area. The amount may vary and the number of pieces should be determined by the thickness of the original panel. Prepare a mixture of resin and hardener (catalyst) following the mixture procedures previously outlined.

Using a small paint brush, saturate at least two layers of glass cloth with activated resin mix and apply to the inside or back surface of the repair area, making sure the cloth is in full contact with the scuffed area surrounding the hole.

Saturate three more layers of glass cloth with activated resin mix and apply to the outside surface, making certain that these layers are in complete contact with the inner layers, and in full contact with the scuffed outside repair area, Fig. 14-3.

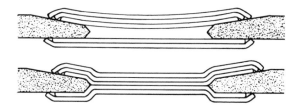

*Fig. 14-3. Apply fiber glass cloth and make saucer-like depression.*

After the layers of saturated glass cloth are in place make a saucer-like depression in them in order to increase the depth of the resin and glass putty-like repair material. Note: Immerse brush and all other tools in lacquer thinner immediately after use. Allow layer of saturated cloth to become tacky. To expedite hardening, external heat, preferably an infrared lamp, may be used. If external heat is used, do not heat area above 200 deg. F. Too much heat will distort the material.

Disk sand the patch area slightly below the contour of the panel, Fig. 14-4.

*Fig. 14-4. Sand hardened patch slightly below contour of panel.*

Mix patch material as outlined under Resin Preparation, and using a small spatula or putty knife, trowel this mix into the saucer-like depression in the repair area, leaving a sufficient mound of material to grind down smooth and flush when hardened. Before the patch begins to harden, waxed paper may be taped over the patch, then a rubber squeegee may be used to smooth out the patch, while keeping the patching material well above the surrounding contour of the panel. Allow patch to harden, Fig. 14-5.

*Fig. 14-5. Apply putty-like patching material.*

When patch is fully hardened, sand the excess material down to the basic contour with No. 80 grit paper and finish sanding with No. 120 or finer grit paper, using a sanding block or pad.

Then prime the surface and paint, using the same procedure as described for metal bodies.

The use of the bonding strip instead of the fiber glass cloth, cut to the desired size and shape, where contours permit, will expedite repair procedure. Cut a piece of bonding strip about 1-1/2 in. larger all around than the opening to be repaired. Rough sand or grind the contact surface of the bonding strip.

Rough grind the underside of the panel in the same manner. Position the bonding strip in place and drill several holes in the panel around the area to be patched and through the bonding strip. Press the bonding strip tight against the inside of the panel and install several sheet metal screws, Fig. 14-6. Re-

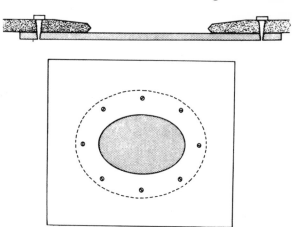

*Fig. 14-6. Fasten bonding strip with sheet metal screws.*

move the bonding strip and apply a liberal quantity of the resin mix to both of the cleaned and roughened surfaces. Reinstall the bond strip, then tighten the sheet metal screw securely and permit the bond to cure. Remove the sheet metal screws and fill the holes and cavity as previously outlined.

When the reverse side of a hole in a panel is not accessible, the following procedure may be used. Clean surface around damaged area with a good commercial grease and wax remover. Remove all paint and primer with No. 80 grit paper to expose plastic material about 3 in. beyond damaged area. Grind or file all cracked or splintered material away from the hole on the outside surface of the area to be repaired. Scuff the area around the hole with coarse No. 80 paper to provide a good bonding surface.

Bevel the outside edge of the area to be repaired about 20 deg. to permit better patch adhesion. Clean the repair surface well with mineral spirits, naphtha, or non-oily type solvent. Cut five pieces of fiber glass cloth large enough to cover hole and scuffed area. Prepare a mixture of resin and catalyst, following the procedure outlined previously. Using a small paint brush, saturate the five layers of glass cloth with activated resin mix and apply to the outside surface making certain that these layers are in complete contact with each other, and in full contact with the scuffed outside repair area.

After the five layers of saturated fiber glass cloth are in place, make a saucer-like depression in them in order to increase the depth of the resin and glass repair material. Immerse brush and all other tools in lacquer thinner immediately after use.

Mix patch material as outlined under Resin Preparation, and using a small spatula or putty knife, trowel this mix into the saucer-like depression in the repair area, leaving a sufficient mound of material to grind down smooth and flush when hardened. The remainder of the procedure is identical with that previously outlined, when both sides of the hole are accessible.

## REPAIRING SPLIT OR CRACKED PANELS

Clean the surface as previously described and then using a hacksaw blade, cut along the break line and remove the broken portion of the panel. On the inner surface of the repair area, remove any dirt, etc. from the damaged area. Scuff the area around the hole with coarse No. 80 abrasive paper to provide a good bonding surface. Remove all cracked and fractured material along the break, and bevel the edge of the break area to be repaired approximately 30 deg. to permit better patch adhesion. The surfaces on each side of the split or crack should be brought into proper alignment by means of C clamps, or other suitable means. Clean the repair surface well with mineral spirits, naphtha, or similar dry solvent. Cut three pieces of fiber glass cloth large enough to overlap the repair area by approximately 2 in. Apply the mixture of resin and hardener with a small paint brush to the three layers of glass cloth to the inside or back surface of the repair area, making sure the cloth is in full contact with the scuffed area beyond the break. Allow a layer of saturated cloth to cure.

Then mix patch material as outlined under Resin Preparation.

Scuff the break area with abrasive in order to provide a good bonding surface. Using a small spatula or putty knife, trowel the mix into the break area on the external surface, leaving a sufficient mound of material to grind down smooth and flush when hardened.

## PANEL REPLACEMENT

Cut out damaged portion of panel with a hacksaw blade and then remove all dirt and paint from both sides of the panel for a distance about 2 to 3 in. back from the patching line.

Cut out section of panel from service replacement panel to be used. If section of panel does not fit closely to break line, reshape section of panel to suit.

Bevel all attaching edges approximately 45 deg. so a single V butt joint will be formed on the finished surface when the pieces are are jointed. Align section of replacement to adjacent panel. If C clamps cannot be used to align panel, use 3/16-in. bolts and nuts with large washer on inner and outer surface of panels to hold panels in alignment, or use bonding strips and sheet metal screws, Fig. 14-7. Clean the repair surface well with mineral spirits, or naphtha, or similar type non-oily solvent.

Cut three pieces of fiber glass cloth large enough to overlap the entire length of the joint area approximately two to three inches.

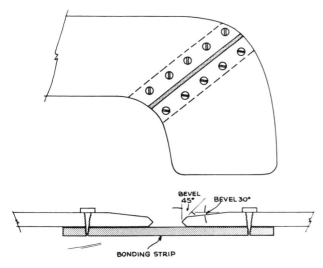

Fig. 14-7. Join panels with bonding strip and sheet metal screws.

Prepare a mixture of resin and hardener in the manner previously outlined. Saturate the three layers of glass cloth with activated resin mix and apply to the inside or back surface of the repair area, making sure the cloth is in full contact with the scuffed area surrounding the joined areas. Allow inner layers of saturated cloth to cure.

Mix patch materials as outlined under Resin Preparation. Scuff joint line area with abrasive paper. Using a small spatula, trowel the mix into the joint line area on the external surface, leaving a sufficient mound of material to grind down smooth and flush when hardened. After allowing the patch to harden, remove the C clamps, or sheet metal screws, as the case may be. The repair is completed as outlined previously.

## QUIZ - Chapter 14

1. A fiber glass body has high resistance to impact.
   True.
   False.
2. Fiber glass panels are not available for replacement.
   True.
   False.
3. The resin used in making fiber glass repairs may cause skin irritations.
   True.
   False.
4. Why is it advisable to use a belt sander when sanding fiber glass?
   It cuts faster.
   A vacuum attachment can be used to draw in the dust.
   Conforms to the curves of the body more accurately.
5. Catalyzed resin should not be left to stand too long, because -
   It dries and hardens quickly.
   Chemical action results in rapid heat build-up and is therefore a fire hazard.
   It evaporates quickly.
6. It is not necessary to clean the surface before applying fiber glass repairs.
   True.
   False.
7. After fiber glass patch has hardened, what grit abrasive should be used first?
   No. 80 grit.
   No. 180 grit.
   No. 16 grit.

# Chapter 15

# ALIGNING HOODS, DECK LIDS, PANELS

The accurate alignment of hoods, rear deck lids and panels is important, not only from the standpoint of appearance, but also unless correctly installed in relation to adjacent panels, hoods and deck lids will not close properly, and in addition will tend to squeak and rattle. In the case of rear deck lids, or trunk lids, there will also be a strong tendency toward rain and dust leakage.

In order to provide adjustment the hinges of such panels are usually provided with elongated holes, and in addition the position of latches are also made adjustable to insure proper operation. In many cases also, panels are adjusted by means of shims.

Taking up the subject of correct installations of hoods, the clearance or spacing between the edge of the hood and the adjacent side panels, Fig. 15-1, should be the same on both sides of the hood, and should measure approximately 5/32 in. In addition to having

Fig. 15-1. Space between hoods and deck lids at arrow should be 5/32 in.

the same clearance on the sides the hood should not be lower on one side than the other, so that the surface of the hood is flush with adjacent panels.

If the sheet metal (fenders, hood, cowl, door) are not in proper alignment adjustments must be made. While the procedure on different makes of bodies varies somewhat, the adjustment of front fender and bumper on recent models of Fisher bodies is typical.

## FISHER BODY ADJUSTMENTS

If the front end of the sheet metal assembly is too high, or too low, resulting in objectionably uneven vertical spacing between the front fenders and doors, it will be necessary to add shims at front support location, Fig. 15-2. Whenever shims are to be added or removed at the front support location, it will be necessary to loosen the lower rear attachment bolts, both at the shimming location, and at the inner skirt to body mount bracket.

Slight adjustment of fender to door spacing can be made by loosening the lower rear shimming bolts and also skirt body mount bracket and inserting a screwdriver between the rocker panel and fender to pry opening wider at lower edge. Or have helper lean on front fender to lessen gap at the bottom.

Rear height of the front fender is adjustable at rear location, Fig. 15-2. When shimming for rear height, it will be necessary to loosen lower rear attaching bolts, and the inner skirt to body mount bracket.

In and out adjustment of the lower rear edge of the front fender is accomplished by shimming at the two fender to body attaching bolts, Fig. 15-2.

The fender line should be flush with the rocker panel. Whenever adjustment is made at that location, the inner skirt to body mount bracket bolts must be loosened.

The bumper attaching bolt holes in frame cross member, anchor brackets, back bars, and bumper faceplate are slotted to permit movement of the bumper and permit proper alignment of adjacent parts.

The hood upper latch is adjustable and the procedure is to loosen the upper latch mounting bolts and tighten finger tight. Close the hood, causing the latch to shift to correct alignment. Then open hood and tighten bolts.

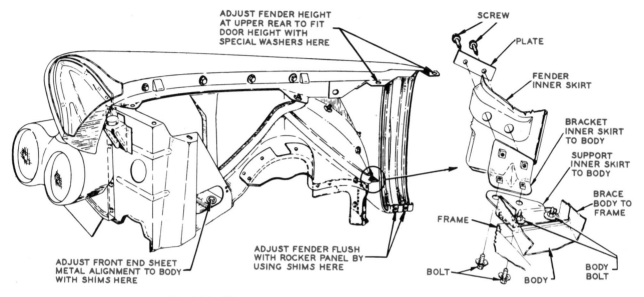

ADJUST FENDER HEIGHT AT UPPER REAR TO FIT DOOR HEIGHT WITH SPECIAL WASHERS HERE

SCREW

PLATE

FENDER INNER SKIRT

BRACKET INNER SKIRT TO BODY

SUPPORT INNER SKIRT TO BODY

BRACE BODY TO FRAME

FRAME

BODY BOLT

ADJUST FENDER FLUSH WITH ROCKER PANEL BY USING SHIMS HERE

BOLT

BODY

ADJUST FRONT END SHEET METAL ALIGNMENT TO BODY WITH SHIMS HERE

*Fig. 15-2. Illustrating adjustment points on typical Fisher body.*

## HOOD ADJUSTMENTS ON FISHER BODIES

Rear height of hood is determined on late model Fisher bodies by special washers between hinge and hood, Fig. 15-3. Removing or adding washers will shift rear of hood up or down with respect to hinge.

If the rear of the hood tends to flutter, it indicates too little tension. To increase tension add special washers between the hood and the hinges at the front bolts, Fig. 15-3.

Front height of the hood is determined by two adjustable rubber bumpers. However, the front of the hood may not contact these bumpers unless the hood latch is correctly adjusted.

When the hood to fender spacing is out of adjustment, minor adjustment can be made by means of slotted holes, to space the hood properly between the fenders, Fig. 15-3.

Fore and aft movement of the hood is allowed by slotted holes in the hinges. Before adjusting, scribe a reference line along the edge of each hinge flange. Then loosen the hinge to hood bolts and shift the hood from this line as required.

## FENDER ADJUSTMENTS (FORD)

The fenders on recent model Ford built vehicles are mounted in such a manner that either fender can be shifted fore or aft to increase or reduce the amount of clearance between the forward edge of the door and the rear edge of the fender. When installing a fender, this alignment is accomplished when all the fenders and cap screws are loose. Shift the fender the required amount and while holding the fender in the desired position, tighten the fender bolts and cap screws. The proper amount of clearance between hood and fender is 5/32 in., Fig. 15-1.

If the fender is installed and only a limited amount of fore or aft adjustment is required, the following procedure is recommended:

1. Loosen three cap screws that secure fender to fender apron, Fig. 15-4.

2. Loosen three cap screws securing fender and lock dowel support.

3. Loosen cap screw at fender to cowl bracket.

4. Loosen cap screw connecting fender to rocker panel.

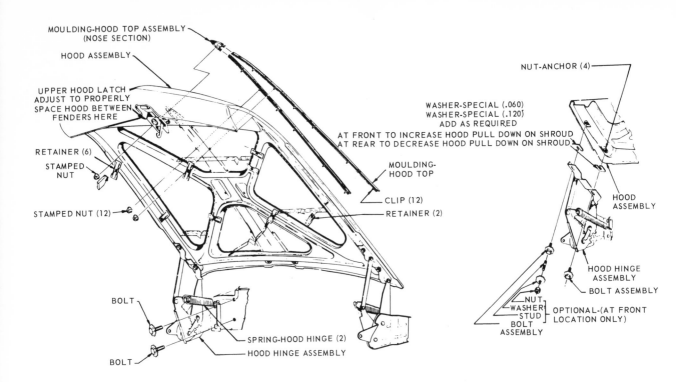

MOULDING-HOOD TOP ASSEMBLY
(NOSE SECTION)

HOOD ASSEMBLY

UPPER HOOD LATCH
ADJUST TO PROPERLY
SPACE HOOD BETWEEN
FENDERS HERE

RETAINER (6)

STAMPED
NUT

STAMPED NUT (12)

BOLT

BOLT

SPRING-HOOD HINGE (2)

HOOD HINGE ASSEMBLY

NUT-ANCHOR (4)

WASHER-SPECIAL (.060)
WASHER-SPECIAL (.120)
ADD AS REQUIRED
AT FRONT TO INCREASE HOOD PULL DOWN ON SHROUD
AT REAR TO DECREASE HOOD PULL DOWN ON SHROUD

MOULDING-
HOOD TOP

CLIP (12)

RETAINER (2)

HOOD
ASSEMBLY

HOOD HINGE
ASSEMBLY

BOLT ASSEMBLY

NUT
WASHER
STUD
BOLT
ASSEMBLY

OPTIONAL-(AT FRONT
LOCATION ONLY)

*Fig. 15-3. Details of hood adjustments on Fisher body.*

*Fig. 15-4. Method of attaching fenders on Ford built bodies.*

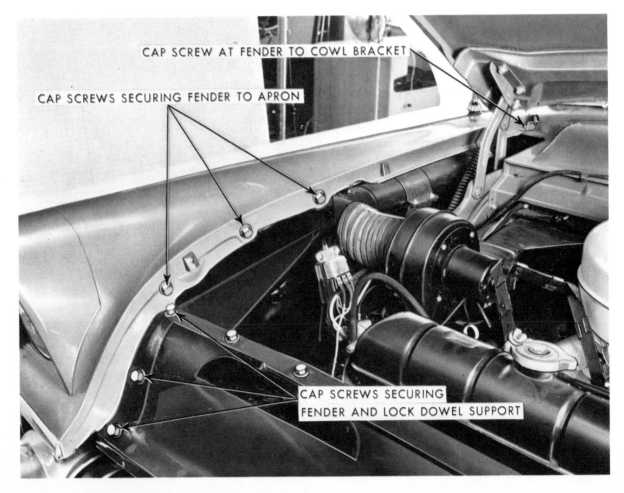

CAP SCREW AT FENDER TO COWL BRACKET

CAP SCREWS SECURING FENDER TO APRON

CAP SCREWS SECURING
FENDER AND LOCK DOWEL SUPPORT

5. From inside of car, remove cowl trim panel and loosen nut connecting front fender to cowl. Move fender fore or aft as required and while holding fender in desired position, tighten all cap screws and nuts.

To parallel the rear edge of fender with front edge of door the following procedure is recommended:

1. Underneath fender at rear, loosen 8 cap screws securing apron and deflector to body at dash to frame brace, apron and deflector to splash shield, and splash shield to body cowl side flange.

2. Loosen one cap screw at fender to cowl bracket, and one cap screw securing fender to body rocker panel.

3. Loosen the two attaching bolts located at bottom center of radiator support.

4. If more clearance is desired between fender and door at top, remove shims at radiator support. If more clearance is desired between the fender and door at bottom, add shims at radiator support.

The curve of the rear edge of the fender may be increased or reduced to bring it into conformity with the curvature of the door by inserting or removing shims between fender and cowl side panel, and between fender and rocker panel.

## HOOD ADJUSTMENTS

The hood on recent model Ford and Maverick cars can be adjusted fore and aft and side to side by loosening the hood-to-hinge attaching screws, and repositioning the hood, Fig. 15-5. To raise or lower the hood, loosen the hinge-to-fender reinforcement attaching screws, and raise or lower the hood as necessary.

On Mustang and Torino models, the hood is provided with fore and aft, vertical and side-to-side adjustments and the following directions refer to the position of the hood when it is fully lowered. The elongated bolt slots in the hinge and hood provide the side-to-side and fore and aft adjustments, Fig. 15-6. The enlarged holes at the fender apron provide for up and down adjustments. Hood bumpers, located on the top left and top right surface of the radiator support, can be adjusted up and down to provide a level surface

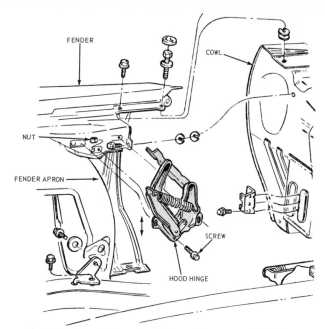

Fig. 15-5. Hood hinge installation of recent model Ford cars.

alignment of the hood panel and the front fenders.

On Ford, Mustang and Thunderbird models the hood latch adjustment is as follows: Before adjusting the hood latch mechanism, make certain that the hood is properly aligned. The hood latch can be moved from side-to-side to align it with the hood latch hook and up and down to obtain a flush fit with the front fenders. Loosen the hood latch attaching bolts until they are just loose enough to move the latch. Move the latch from side-to-side to align it with the hood latch hook. Loosen the lock nuts on the two hood bumpers and lower the bumpers. Move the hood latch up or down as required to obtain a flush fit between the top of the hood and fenders when an upward pressure is applied to the front of the hood. Then tighten the hood latch attaching screws.

Fig. 15-6. Hood installation of recent Torino and Mustang cars.

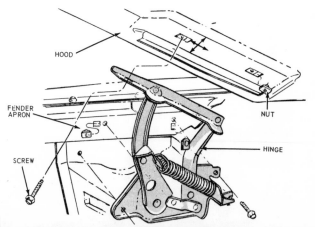

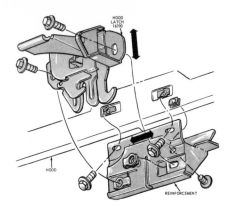

Fig. 15-7. Details of hood latch, typical of Ford, Torino and Mustang.

Raise the two hood bumpers to eliminate any looseness at the front of the hood when closed. Then tighten the hood bumper nuts.

Adjustment of the Mustang and Torino hood latches is similar and differs only in detail. The Maverick and Torino hood latch is illustrated in Fig. 15-7.

## TRUNK LID ADJUSTMENTS

To adjust compartment lid forward or rearward, or from side to side in body opening, loosen both hinge strap attaching bolts and adjust lid as required, then tighten bolts.

To adjust compartment lid at hinge area, up or down, install shims between lid inner panel and hinge straps as follows: To raise front edge of lid at hinge area, place shim between lid inner panel and forward portion of one or both hinge straps, at C, Fig. 15-7. To lower front edge of lid at hinge area, place shim between lid inner panel and rearward portion of one or both hinge straps at B, Fig. 15-8. Rear deck lid adjustment points on 1971 Fisher bodies are shown in Fig. 15-9, and are similar to the foregoing.

Fig. 15-8. Location of rear compartment lid adjustments.

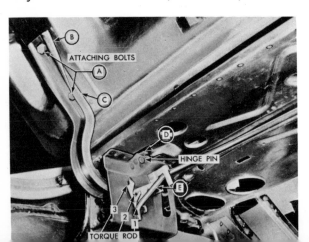

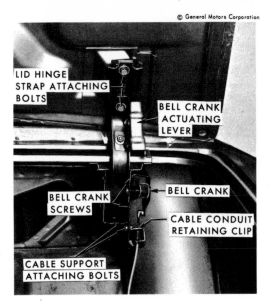

Fig. 15-9. Mechanical pull down unit and hydraulic cylinder cable attachment, 1971 Cadillac style, also rear compartment lid adjustments.

## QUIZ – Chapter 15

1. The position of hinges on deck lids is not adjustable.
   True.
   False.
2. On recent model Fisher bodies what means is provided for adjusting vertically the front end of the sheet metal assembly.
   Bolts in elongated holes.
   Shims.
   No adjustment provided.
3. How is rear height of hood on recent model Fisher bodies adjusted?
   Special washers between hinge and hood.
   Bolts and elongated holes.
   .005 in. shims.
4. Front fenders on recent model Ford Cars are adjustable, as to position, by what method?
   Elongated holes and bolts.
   Special washers.
5. What is the usual clearance between the hood and the fender?
   5/32 in.
   .001 in.
   .0025 in.
6. To correctly position the hood assembly on recent model Ford cars, how many adjustments are provided?
   Two.
   Three.
   Four.
   One.

# Chapter 16
# HOW TO
# ADJUST DOORS

It is important to adjust car doors accurately so that they will close easily and without undue force being exerted. When doors are not correctly adjusted, they are difficult to close and will rattle when driven over a rough road. In addition, they are apt to leak excessive amounts of rain and dust.

When doors are correctly adjusted, the clearance between the door and the surrounding frame should be approximately 1/8 in. to 5/32 in. However, along the bottom edge 1/4 in. clearance is often provided.

Adjustments are provided so that the door can be moved up and down, fore and aft, in and out.

## FISHER BODY DOORS

Typical front doors on recent model Fisher bodies are of the swing-out type with an integral door check on the top hinge assembly and a two-position hold open on the lower hinge. The hinges are attached to the front body hinge pillar and to the door assembly with bolts and anchor plates. Either of two methods can be used to remove the door from the body.

A. The door and hinge can be removed as an assembly from the body pillars.

B. The door can be removed from the hinge straps.

If door and hinges are to be removed from the body pillars, additional access may be obtained at lower hinge by loosening front fender lower rear attachment bolts. However, this may vary with different body designs.

Mark hinge locations on door or hinge pillar depending on method of removal being used.

On bodies equipped with electrically powered window regulators, proceed as follows: Remove door trim assembly and detach inner water deflector sufficiently to gain access to wire connector at motor.

Detach wire harness from inner panel as required and disconnect motors from harness at the connectors. Remove electric conduit from doors and remove wire harness from between the door panels through opening in door hinge pillar.

With door properly supported, remove the bolts securing upper and lower hinges to front body hinge pillar, or door hinge pillars, Fig. 16-1. With the aid of a helper, move door assembly from body.

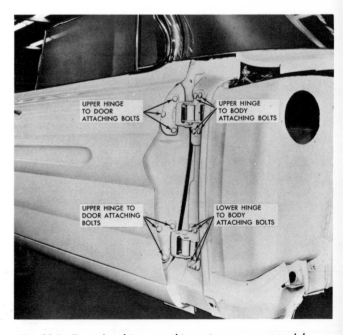

*Fig. 16-1. Front door hinge attaching points on recent model Fisher body (Typical).*

Replacement is accomplished by reversing the procedure. As an anti-squeak precaution, before installing the door, coat attaching surface of hinge with heavy bodied sealer.

In or out, or up and down adjustments are provided at door hinge pillars. Fore and aft adjustments are provided at front body hinge pillars.

For in and out or up and down adjustments, loosen hinge to door pillar attaching bolts, Fig. 16-1. Adjust door as required and tighten bolts. When performing in and out adjustments, adjust one hinge at a time so as not to disturb up and down adjustment.

To adjust door fore or aft, loosen hinge to body pillars attaching bolts, Fig. 16-1. Adjust door as required and tighten bolts. On some body models, one or more of the attaching bolts are not readily accessible due to inadequate wrench clearance. When fore and aft adjustments are made, the recommended procedure is to remove the obstructing attaching bolt and perform adjustments with the remaining three bolts. After satisfactory adjustments have been made, replace the previously removed bolt. Removal of the obstructing bolt and subsequent adjustments can best be accomplished with a ratcheting box end wrench.

## DOOR LOCK STRIKERS (FISHER)

The front and rear door lock striker on recent model Fisher bodies as installed on General Motors passenger cars consist of a single metal bolt and washer assembly that is threaded into a tapped, floating cage plate located in the body lock pillar, Fig. 16-2. With this design, the door is secured in the closed position when the door lock fork-bolt snaps over and engages the striker bolt.

The removal and installation procedure is as follows: Mark position of striker on body lock pillar, using a pencil. Procure a special tool or make a tool of the screw jack type and insert into the star shaped tool recess in the head of the striker bolt and remove striker, Fig. 16-2A.

To install, reverse the procedure. Make certain the striker is positioned within the pencil marks, touch up any unpainted surface on lock pillar adjacent to striker assembly.

Fig. 16-2. Lock to striker engagement on recent model Fisher bodies.

Torque striker bolt to 34-36 ft. lb.

Note: The door lock striker is an important attaching part in that it could affect the performance of vital components and systems, and/or could result in major repair expense. It must be replaced with one of the same part number or with an equivalent part if replacement becomes necessary. Do not use a replacement part of lesser quality or substitute design. Torque values must be used as specified during reassembly to assure proper retention of part.

When a door has been removed and reinstalled or realigned, the door should not be closed completely until a visual check is made to determine if lock fork-bolt will correctly engage striker.

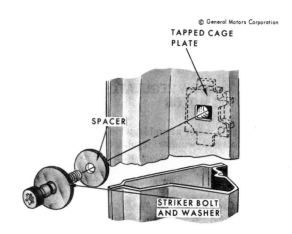

Fig. 16-2A. Door lock striker installation on recent model Fisher bodies.

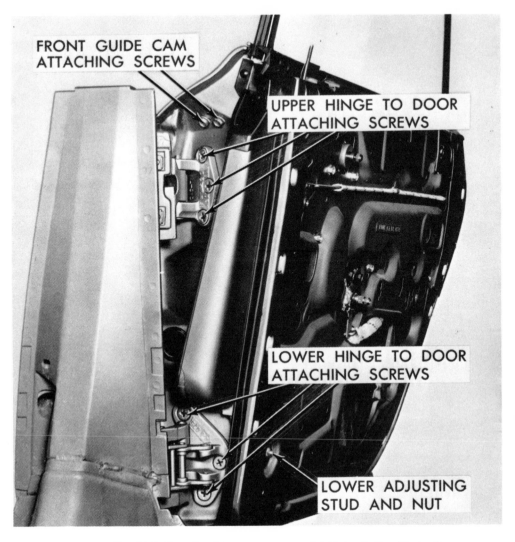

*Fig. 16-3. Rear door hinges on recent model Fisher bodies (Typical).*

To adjust striker up or down, in or out, loosen striker bolt and shift striker as required, then tighten striker.

To determine if striker fore and aft adjustment is necessary on recent model Fisher bodies, proceed as follows: First make sure door is properly aligned. Apply modeling clay or body caulking compound to lock bolt opening as shown in Fig. 16-2. Close door only as far as necessary for striker bolt to form impression in clay as shown in Fig. 16-2. Note: Do not close door completely. Complete closing may make clay removal very difficult.

Measure striker impressions as follows: Striker head should be centered fore and aft as shown, some tolerances are allowed. In any alignment, it is important that minimum dimensions as indicated in Fig. 16-2 be strictly maintained. Spacers are available to achieve the desired alignment.

## REAR DOOR HINGES (FISHER)

Typical rear door hinges differ slightly from those described as used on the front doors. The rear door hinges are attached to the center pillar with two butt type hinges. The hinges are attached to the center pillar and door hinge pillar by screws and anchor plates, Fig. 16-3. The lower hinge incorporates an integral door check and hold open.

To remove: (On 4-door sports sedan models lower the door window). Clean off excess

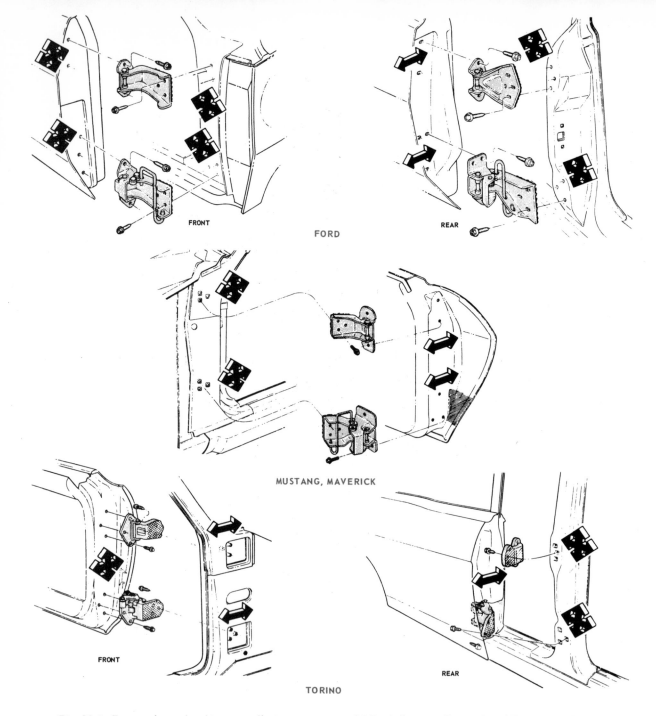

FORD — FRONT — REAR

MUSTANG, MAVERICK

TORINO — FRONT — REAR

*Fig. 16-4. Front and rear door hinge installation on recent model Ford, Mustang, Maverick and Torino models.*

sealer around each hinge strap and mark location on door hinge pillar, or center pillar, depending on whether hinge is being removed with door, or is being left on the pillar. On bodies equipped with electrically operated windows, it is necessary to remove the door trim assembly and water deflector. Then disconnect wiring from motor and remove conduit from door and harness from between door panels.

With door properly supported, move the three upper and lower attaching screws at door hinge pillar, or center pillar. On the four door sport sedan model, the rear door lower hinge to center pillar middle attaching bolt is also the rear door jamb switch. Be sure to disconnect wire before removing door. Door can then be removed.

When replacing the door, first with a scraper and mineral spirits, clean off the old sealing compound at hinge attaching areas. Take care not to soil adjacent trim material. Then apply a coat of heavy body sealer to attaching hinge straps. Lift door into position. Install screws loosely, align strap inside, scribe marks on pillar, and then tighten bolts. Check door for proper alignment. Install wiring harness.

In or out, or up and down, adjustments are provided at door hinge pillar. Fore and aft and slight up and down adjustments are provided at center pillar. When checking door for alignment, remove door lock striker from body pillar, and allow door to hang free on its hinges.

When performing in and out, or fore and aft adjustments, adjust one hinge at a time so that up and down adjustment is maintained.

Door should be adjusted so that when in the closed position its edges are evenly spaced around the door opening.

After performing any adjustment, the rear door window on four door sport sedan model should be checked for proper alignment with the side roof rail weatherstrip. In addition, door lock extension should be adjusted if necessary.

## FORD DOOR ADJUSTMENTS

The door hinges on Ford cars provide sufficient adjustment latitude to correct most door misalignment conditions. The holes of the hinge and/or the hinge attaching points are enlarged or elongated to provide for door alignment, as shown in Fig. 16-4. Do not cover up poor door alignment with a latch striker adjustment.

Alignment procedure: Determine which hinge bolts must be loosened to move the door in the desired position. Remove the side cowl trim panel and/or door trim panel and hinge access covers, Fig. 16-4. Loosen the hinge bolts just enough to permit movement of the door with a padded pry bar. Move the door the distance estimated to be necessary. Tighten the hinge bolts and check the door fit. Repeat the operation until the desired fit is obtained. Check the strike plate alignment for proper door closing. On two door hardtop models, check the quarter glass to door glass fit. Adjust quarter glass if necessary.

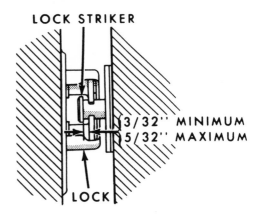

*Fig. 16-5. Door lock striker adjustment (Ford).*

## FORD LOCK STRIKER ADJUSTMENT

The striker pin can be adjusted laterally and vertically, as well as fore and aft. The lock striker should not be adjusted to correct door sag. The lock striker should be shimmed to get the clearance shown in Fig. 16-5, between the striker and the lock. To check this clearance, clean the lock jaws and the striker area and then apply a thin layer of dark grease to the lock strikers. As the door is closed and opened a measurable pattern will result. Move the striker assembly laterally to provide a flush fit at the door and the pillar or quarter panel.

## CHRYSLER TYPE
## FRONT DOOR ADJUSTMENT

There are two general types of front door hinge attachments, as shown in Figs. 16-6 and 16-7. Up or down adjustment of the door

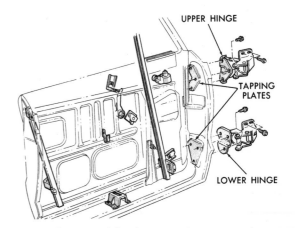

*Fig. 16-6. One type of door hinge attachment as used on some Chrysler models.*

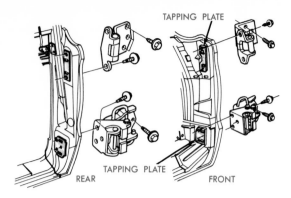

*Fig. 16-7. Details of door hinge attachment. The rear is shown at left and the front on the right (Chrysler).*

can be made at the front pillar or in the door itself, as shown in Figs. 16-6 and 16-7. First, scribe a line around upper and lower hinge straps. Place a wood block on the lifting plate of a floor jack and position it under door (support door near center of balance when attaching bolts are loosened). Loosen upper and lower door hinge attaching bolts. Observing scribe mark, raise or lower jack until door is in desired position. Tighten attaching bolts and remove jack. Open and close door several times and inspect clearance around all edges of door. Repeat procedure until door is centered in opening.

The fore and aft adjustment of the front door is made as follows: With the door in the full open position (trim panel removed) scribe a line around upper and lower hinge straps. Place a wood block on lifting plate of floor jack and position it under outer end of door. Loosen door upper hinge attaching bolts only. Observe scribe marks and raise or lower door to desired position (raising outer end of door moves upper part of door forward when in closed position).

Tighten attaching bolts. Loosen door lower hinge attaching bolts and raise or lower door to desired position (lowering end of door moves lower part of door forward when in the closed position).

Tighten attaching bolts. Open and close door several times and inspect clearance around all door edges. Repeat procedure until door is centered in door opening.

## ADJUST DOOR LOCK STRIKER

The in and out adjustment of the front door is made as follows: With the door in the full open position, place a wood block on lifting

plate of a floor jack and position it under outer edge of door. Loosen upper hinge to pillar attaching bolts. Raise or lower jack until upper part of door has moved in or out desired amount (raising the outer end of the door will move upper part of door into the door opening). Tighten upper hinge to pillar attaching bolts.

Loosen lower hinge to pillar attaching bolts. Raise or lower jack until lower part of door is in desired position (lowering jack moves door into door opening). Tighten attaching bolts.

Close door and observe alignment of door panel with body sill, fender, cowl and "B" post. Adjust door lock striker.

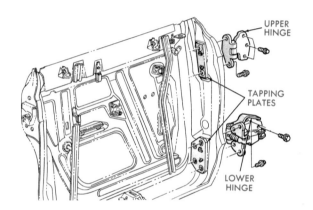

*Fig. 16-8. Details of rear door hinge, Fury models.*

## CHRYSLER TYPE
## REAR DOOR ADJUSTMENT

There are two general types of rear door hinge attachments. These are shown in Figs. 16-7 and 16-8. Up and down adjustment of the rear door is made as follows: With the rear door fully closed and front door open, scribe location of both upper and lower hinges on frame of door, Figs. 16-7 and 16-8. Then with the door slightly ajar, position floor jack under center of door. Loosen hinge to door attaching bolts. Observe scribe marks and raise or lower door to the desired position. Tighten attaching bolts. Close door and check alignment of door in opening. Adjust door lock striker.

To make the fore and aft adjustment, first remove "B" post trim panel and scribe around pillar post hinge plate. Loosen both upper

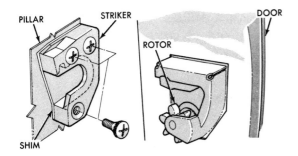

*Fig. 16-9. One type of striker and rotor used on some Chrysler, Dodge and Plymouth models.*

and lower pillar post hinge screws. With door slightly ajar, push door forward or back to desired position. Tighten pillar post hinge screws.

Close door and inspect alignment in door opening. Adjust door lock striker and install "B" post trim panel.

To adjust the rear door in or out, first scribe a mark on door around the door hinge plate. Loosen upper hinge attaching bolts. Grasp front edge of the door at the hinge and push door in or pull out to the desired position. Tighten hinge attaching bolts. Adjust one hinge at a time to prevent door dropping in door opening.

## STRIKER AND ROTOR ADJUSTMENT

On doors with striker and rotor type of door striker, Fig. 16-9, the door strikers are attached to the pillars. Oversize holes permit up-and-down and in-and-out movement. Fore and aft adjustment is made by adding or removing shims between the striker

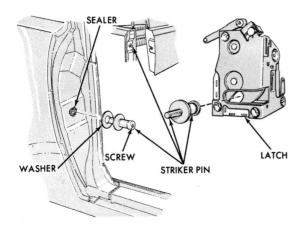

*Fig. 16-10. Pin type of striker used on some Chrysler built cars.*

and the post. The striker plate should be adjusted to lift the door slightly.

## LATCH AND STRIKER PIN ADJUSTMENT

On cars with latch and striker pin construction such as the Valiant, the front door cannot be locked until the door is completely closed. The silent type door latch, Fig. 16-10, features a rubber isolation of the round striker pin on the door frame and those surfaces acting as stops inside the latch. The latch assembly is built into a sheet metal pocket on the door face. The striker pin is attached by a single screw which also allows for adjusting.

## QUIZ - Chapter 16

1. What is the usual clearance between the door and the surrounding frame?

   3/8 in. to 1/2 in.

   1/8 to 5/32 in.

   .005 to .010 in.

2. Adjustments are provided so car doors can be moved up and down, fore and aft, in and out.

   True.

   False.

3. Before removing door lock strikers on Fisher bodies, the usual procedure is to first mark the position of the striker on the body with a pencil.

   True.

   False.

4. Will door misalignment result from improper tightening of body bolts on Ford cars?

   Yes.

   No.

5. On Ford cars, should the lock striker be adjusted to correct door sag?

   Yes.

   No.

6. Up and down adjustment of the Chrysler door can be made at the front pillar.

   True.

   False.

7. On Chrysler doors with striker and rotor type of door striker, the door strikers are attached to the doors.

   True.

   False.

# Chapter 17

# DOOR HARDWARE
# SERVICE

Window regulators (devices to raise and lower windows), together with the various control handles and door locks, are generally classified as door hardware. The door striker plate is also considered door hardware, but this was discussed in the chapter relating to the adjustment of doors.

It is important that auto body service men become familiar with the various types of mechanisms used on present day cars. Typical job procedures will be discussed in this chapter.

ROUND ALL EDGES
1/64" RADIUS EXCEPT
ON UP-TURNED LIP

8½"    1¼"
1¼"    1"
1⅝"    ¼"    ⅛"
¾"    ⅞"
¼"
GRIND    BRAZING

MATERIAL: 1/8 INCH STEEL

*Fig. 17-1. Details of tool for removing door and window regulator handles.*

## REMOVING DOOR INSIDE HANDLE (FISHER)

Door and inside quarter handles on Fisher bodies are retained by either screws or clips. On styles equipped with screw retained handles, the screws are either exposed or covered by a remote control cover plate. When a cover plate is used, it is generally held in place by short tabs and pressure, and can be

removed by prying on the edge.

On styles with clip retained handles, the clip is either exposed when the arm rest is removed, or else is hidden by the handle. Exposed clips can be disengaged from remote control spindle with a screwdriver.

Clips hidden by a window regulator or remote control handles can be disengaged by depressing the door trim assembly sufficiently to permit inserting a forked tool between the handle and the plastic bearing plate. Then with the tool in the same plane as the inside handle, push tool to disengage clip, Fig. 17-1. Plier type tool, Fig. 17-2, can also be used for this purpose. Pull the handle inboard to remove from spindle.

ROLL SPRING OUT.
DO NOT FORCE!

*Fig. 17-2. Plier type tool for removing door and window regulating handles.*

To install ventilator and window regulator handles, engage retaining clip on handle. Position handle at same angle as opposite side handle and press handle outboard until clip engages regulator spindle. On remote control spindles, install handle in horizontal position.

When Fisher bodies are equipped with what is called a paddle handle, Fig. 17-3, the removal procedure is to remove the door arm rest, then remove handle-to-remote attaching bolt. The handle can then be removed from the door.

## HOW TO REMOVE DOOR OUTSIDE HANDLES

On recent model Fisher bodies, the first step in removing the front or rear door outside handle is to raise the door window. Re-

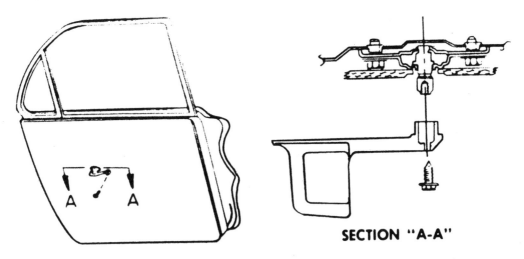

**SECTION "A-A"**

*Fig. 17-3. Details of paddle-type handle used on some Fisher bodies.*

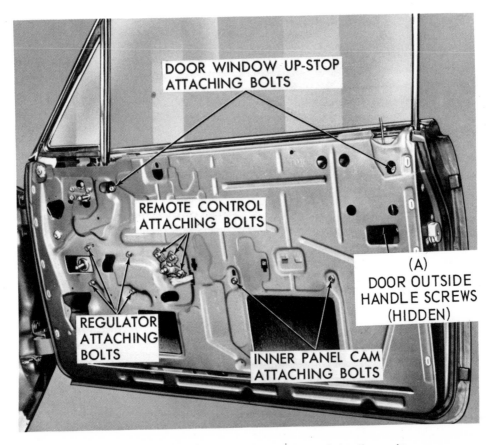

*Fig. 17-4. Inside of door. Note A, location of door outside handle attaching screws.*

move the door trim assembly and detach upper rear corner of inner panel water deflector sufficiently to gain access to door outside handle attaching screws, Fig. 17-4. Remove screws and door lock handle and gaskets from outside of body, Fig. 17-5.

To assemble, reverse the procedure.

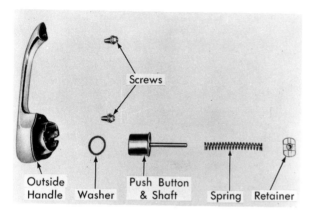

Fig. 17-5. Details of typical door handle used on many Fisher bodies.

## FRONT DOOR LOCK CYLINDER (FISHER)

To remove typical front door lock cylinders, Fig. 17-6, from a Fisher body, first raise the door window. Remove the door trim assembly and detach inner panel water deflector sufficiently to expose large access holes, as shown in Fig. 17-4. Through access hole, with a screwdriver, disengage door lock cylinder to lock connecting rod from door lock. A spring clip is used to secure remote control connecting rods and inside locking rod connecting links to door levers. A slot in the clip provides for disengagement of the clips.

With a suitable tool, slide lock cylinder retaining clip forward from door lock pillar facing, sufficiently to permit removal of lock cylinder with attached connecting rod.

To disassemble lock cylinder, remove pawl retaining clip, pawl and lock cylinder retaining clip, Fig. 17-6.

## FRONT DOOR LOCK ASSEMBLY (FISHER)

Locks on recent model Fisher bodies are the rotary bolt type lock with a safety interlock feature. With the safety interlock feature

it is important that the lock extension and housing engage properly in the door lock striker, and that, when necessary, striker emergency spacers of the proper thickness be used to obtain proper engagement.

To remove the front door lock assembly, first raise the window. Remove door trim assembly and detach inner panel water deflector. Through access hole, Fig. 17-4, disengage spring clips securing lock cylinder rod, remote control connecting rod, and inside locking rod to lock and disengage rods from lock. On some body models it is necessary to remove door window rear glass run channel, lower attaching screw and loosen upper attaching screws on lock pillar facing of door and at top of door inner panel to permit removal of lock.

On other body models, from inside of door, remove rear glass run channel, lower attaching nut or screw, and pull channel forward to permit removal of lock.

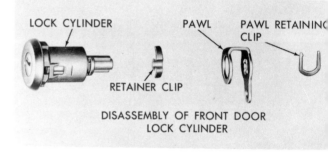

Fig. 17-6. Disassembled door lock cylinder (Fisher bodies).

Remove door lock attaching screws from lock pillar facing of door, and remove lock assembly from door, Fig. 17-7.

To install, reverse removal procedure. Prior to installation, apply a ribbon of medium body sealer across face of lock frame. Check unit for proper operation and, if necessary, adjust glass run channel for proper alignment prior to installation of inner panel water deflector.

## REAR DOOR LOCK ASSEMBLY (FISHER)

Locks are the rotary bolt type with safety interlock feature. With the safety lock feature, it is important that the lock extension engages properly in the door lock striker notch.

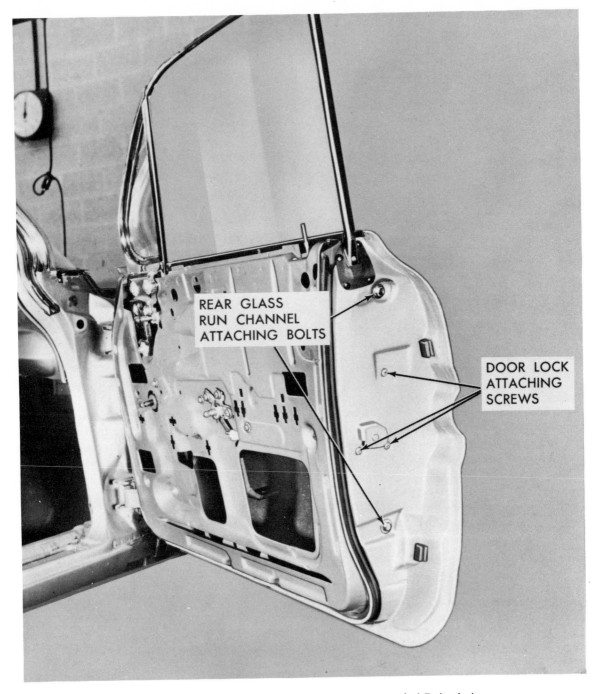

REAR GLASS
RUN CHANNEL
ATTACHING BOLTS

DOOR LOCK
ATTACHING
SCREWS

Fig. 17-7. Location of door lock attaching screws. Typical of Fisher bodies.

Where necessary, striker emergency spacers of the proper thickness can be used to obtain proper engagement. Typical removal procedure is as follows: Raise door window. Remove door trim assembly and detach inner panel water deflector. On most models through large access hole, remove screw securing lower end of glass run channel at door lock pillar, and raise end of channel to expose lock assembly, Fig. 17-8.

Through access hole disengage spring clips and detach inside lock connecting rod and remote control connecting rod from lock assembly. At lock pillar facing, remove door lock attaching screws and remove lock assembly through access hole.

To install rear door lock, reverse removal procedure. Check all operations of door lock before installing door trim and inside hardware.

## FRONT DOOR REMOTE CONTROL ASSEMBLY (FISHER)

On late model Fisher bodies, to remove typical front door remote control assembly and connecting rod, first raise the door

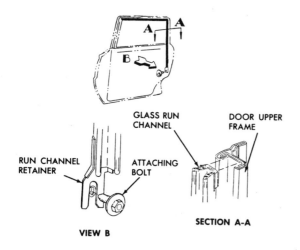

GLASS RUN CHANNEL

DOOR UPPER FRAME

RUN CHANNEL RETAINER

ATTACHING BOLT

SECTION A-A

VIEW B

*Fig. 17-8. Rear door window glass run channel.*

window. Remove door trim assembly and detach inner panel water deflector. Remove remote control attaching screws and disengage remote control from connecting rod, Fig. 17-4. To remove remote control connecting rod, carefully disengage spring clip securing rod to lock and remove rod from lock. Disengage rod from spring clip on door inner panel where necessary and remove rod.

To install, reverse removal procedure. Check door lock and remote control assemblies for proper operation prior to reinstallation.

## FRONT DOOR VENTILATOR (FISHER)

To remove the typical front door ventilator regulator on Fisher bodies, first raise the window. Remove door trim assembly and detach inner panel water deflector sufficiently to gain access to regulator attaching bolts, Fig. 17-9.

On styles equipped with electric ventilator regulators, disconnect regulator wires at connector. Remove ventilator T-shaft attaching bolt and ventilator regulator attaching bolt, Fig. 17-9. Disengage ventilator regulator shaft from ventilator T-shaft and re-

move regulator motor assembly from door through access hole.

To install reverse the procedure. Excessive play or flutter of ventilator at pivot shaft when ventilator is in the open position can be corrected by tightening ventilator T-shaft to regulator attaching bolt, Fig. 17-9. Bolts should be tightened carefully to avoid stripping threads in regulator spindle gear shaft.

To remove the front door ventilator on late model Fisher bodies, first remove the door trim assembly and detach inner panel water deflector. Lower the door window. Remove ventilator to door outer panel return flange attaching screw, Fig. 17-9. At front of ventilator assembly, break cement bond securing front door pillar sealing strip (at belt) to ventilator assembly.

Remove ventilator division channel lower adjusting stud and nut, Fig. 17-9. On styles with electrically operated ventilators, remove motor and ventilator assembly. Remove ventilator lower frame attaching bolt, and ventilator lower frame adjusting stud nut, Fig. 17-9. Remove ventilator regulator. Lift ventilator upward and remove from door.

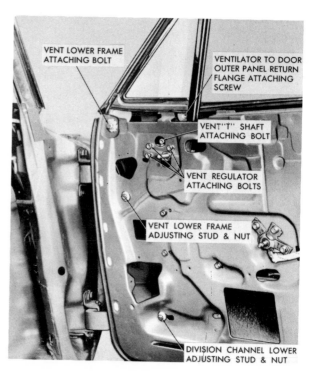

VENT LOWER FRAME ATTACHING BOLT

VENTILATOR TO DOOR OUTER PANEL RETURN FLANGE ATTACHING SCREW

VENT "T" SHAFT ATTACHING BOLT

VENT REGULATOR ATTACHING BOLTS

VENT LOWER FRAME ADJUSTING STUD & NUT

DIVISION CHANNEL LOWER ADJUSTING STUD & NUT

*Fig. 17-9. Details of ventilator hardware (Fisher).*

To replace, reverse the procedure. Prior to installation, apply a bead of body caulking compound to door outer panel return flange along area contacted by ventilator assembly.

## FRONT DOOR WINDOW ASSEMBLY (FISHER)

To remove front door window assembly on late model Fisher bodies, first raise the door window. Remove door trim assembly and detach inner panel water deflector. Through holes in inner panel, remove screw attaching window assembly front and rear stops to lower window shaft channel. Then lower window slightly and remove stops, Fig. 17-4.

Lower door window to expose window lower sash channel cam attaching screws. On styles equipped with electric window regulator, Fig. 17-10, disconnect wiring harness from motor connector. It may be necessary to loosen the ventilator frame and tilt it forward to facilitate removal of door window.

Remove window lower sash channel cam attaching screws and disengage cam from window sash channel. Then lift window assembly upward and remove from door. Do not operate motor after window assembly is disengaged as this will damage motor.

To install, reverse the procedure.

## DOOR INSIDE HANDLE (FORD)

When removing the door inside handle on Ford cars, a plier type tool is usually employed, Fig. 17-2. The procedure is to press the trim panel inward to provide access to the door handle retaining clip. Engage the clip with pliers, Fig. 17-2. If such a tool is not available, you can improvise one by grinding a hook on the end of a hacksaw blade. Engage the clip with the hook and pull out the clip. The handle and spacer can then be pulled from the shaft.

When installing the handle, first install a retainer clip on the handle. Point the handle in a forward direction approximately 45 deg. above horizontal, and press the handle and clip into position until clip snaps into its groove on the remote control shaft.

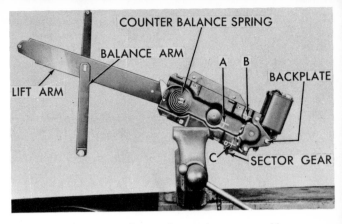

Fig. 17-10. Door window regulator and motor assembly (Fisher bodies).

## FRONT DOOR LOCK CYLINDER (FORD)

When a lock cylinder is replaced, both door lock cylinders and the ignition lock cylinder should be replaced in a set. This will avoid carrying an extra key which will fit only one lock.

Remove the trim panel and position the water shield away from the access holes. Disconnect the lock control-to-door lock cylinder rod at the lock cylinder arm. Remove the door lock cylinder retainer and remove the lock cylinder from the door. Transfer the lock cylinder arm to the new lock cylinder. Position the lock cylinder in the door, and install the lock cylinder retainer. Connect the lock control-to-door lock cylinder rod at the lock cylinder. Carefully position the water shield to the inner panel and install the trim panel.

## DOOR OUTSIDE HANDLE

To remove the door outside handle on Ford and Mustang models, first remove the door trim panel and water shield. Remove the four screws attaching the door weatherstrip at the belt line. Disconnect the door latch actuator rod from the door outside handle, Fig. 17-11. Remove the two nuts retaining the handle to the door. Remove the door handle and the pad from the door. Transfer the actuator rod clip and the pad to the new handle, if the handle is to be replaced. Insert the handle into the door and install the two retaining nuts. Connect the door latch actuator rod to the door latch. Position the weatherstrip at the belt line and install the outside handle and the door latch. Check the operation of the handle and the door lock and

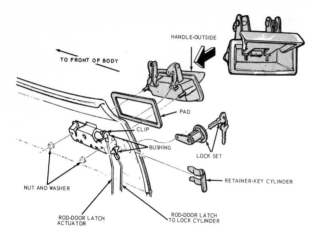

*Fig. 17-11. Door outside handle. Typical of Ford, Mustang and Torino.*

then install the water shield and door trim panel.

## VENT WINDOW REGULATOR REMOVAL (FORD)

First remove the door trim panel. Remove the cap screw and lock washer that secures the vent glass regulator to the vent glass lower pivot, Fig. 17-12. Remove the two cap screws that fasten the regulator to the door inner panel. Remove the regulator to the opening in the inner panel. When replacing

regulator, first rotate the vent regulator handle shaft until the flap on the regulator shaft is at a 90 deg. angle to the handle shaft.

Hold the regulator in place on the door inner panel and install but do not tighten the two attaching screws. Secure the regulator shaft to the vent window pivot with a cap screw and lock washer. Tighten the regulator to panel attaching screws. Install the door trim panel and hardware.

## REMOVING FRONT DOOR REGULATOR

On Ford and Mustang models with ventless glass (1971) the procedure for removing the front door regulator is as follows: Remove the door trim panel and water shield. Disconnect the window regulator arms from the glass channel and the door inner panel at the pivots, Fig. 17-13. Disconnect the glass channel bracket from the glass channel. Disconnect the remote control rod from the door latch. Remove the rear weatherstrip cap. Remove the upper rear stop and remove the belt weatherstrip and molding from the door. Remove the window regulator attaching screws and remove the regulator from the door. Installation is accomplished by reversing the

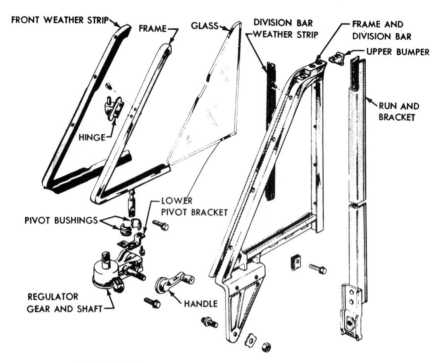

*Fig. 17-12. Details of vent window used on some Ford bodies.*

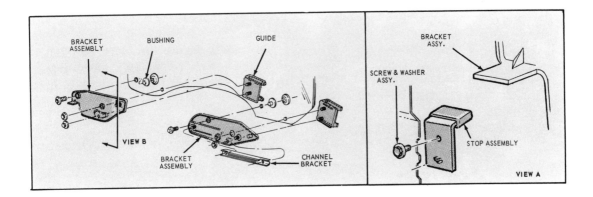

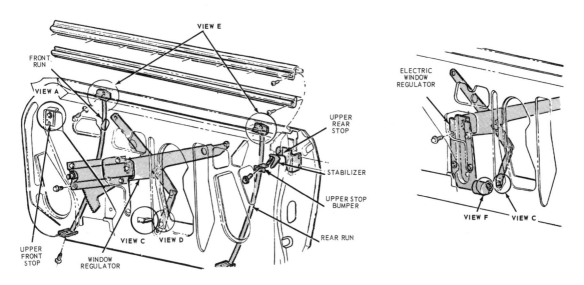

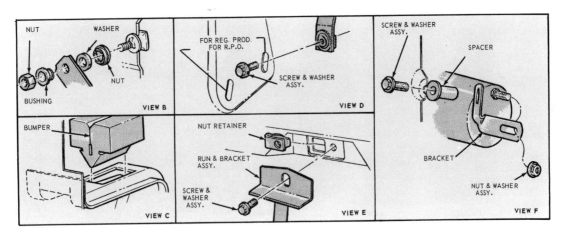

*Fig. 17-13. Front door ventless glass mechanism. Typical of recent model Ford cars.*

procedure.

To remove the front door regulator on 1971 Ford cars (not the ventless glass type) proceed as follows: Remove the door trim panel and water shield. Remove the retainer and nut attaching the glass channel bracket to the glass and prop the window in its up position, Fig. 17-14. Remove the equalizer bar bracket from the door. Remove the four regulator attaching bolts and remove the regulator.

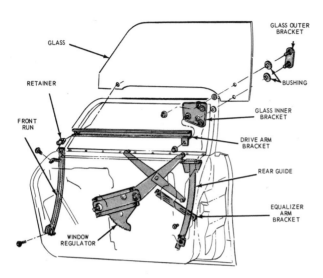

Fig. 17-14. Ford front door window mechanism (typical).

## DOOR INSIDE HANDLE REMOVAL (CHRYSLER)

On Chryslers (Dodge, Plymouth and Valiant), the door inside handles and window regulator handles are fastened with screws requiring an Allen type wrench for removal, Fig. 17-15. Removal of the screw permits the handle to be pulled from the shaft.

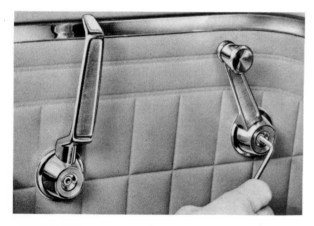

Fig. 17-15. Removing door handle from Plymouth.

## DOOR HANDLES (CHRYSLER)

To remove the outside handle from front door, first place door handle in up position, remove door handle attaching nuts from mounting studs, Figs. 17-16 and 17-17 and

link from handle to lock. Lift handle up and remove from door.

To install handle into door opening, engage link from handle to lock. Attach retaining nuts and check operation of handle.

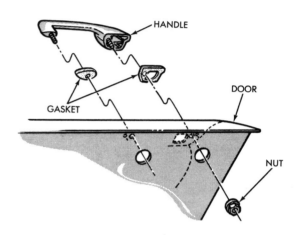

Fig. 17-16. Front door handle (Fury).

To remove outside handle of rear door, first open door and place glass in up position. Remove retainer from link at handle connector. Depress outside handle release button and remove link from handle connector. Remove nuts attaching handle to door and remove handle.

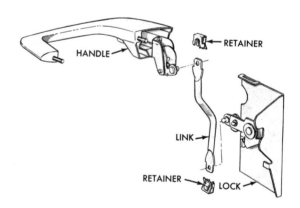

Fig. 17-17. Details of front door handle on Chrysler-Plymouth cars.

To install rear door handle, position handle in door and install mounting nuts. Depress handle button and position link over connector on handle. Install retainer over link and connector.

# Door Hardware Service

## LOCK CYLINDER (CHRYSLER)

To remove lock cylinder on late model Chrysler and allied cars, place window in top position. Disconnect cylinder link, Figs. 17-18 and 17-19, from clip on lock lever (four door only) and from cylinder. On two door models disconnect lock link from clip on lock lever, remove link control bracket mounting screws and remove cylinder link from cylinder. Remove retainer from cylinder body and cylinder from door.

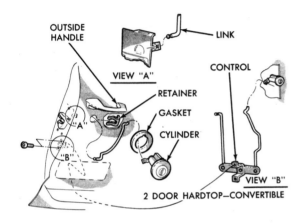

Fig. 17-18. One type of door lock used on Chrysler built cars.

To replace lock cylinder, position cylinder in door and install retainer on cylinder body. Connect the cylinder link to cylinder arm and to clip on lock lever (four door models).

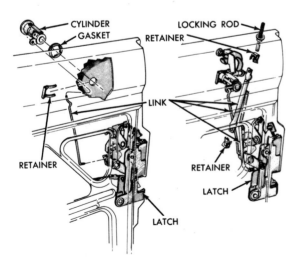

Fig. 17-19. Type of door lock used on some Chrysler built cars.

On two door models connect cylinder link to cylinder, position link bracket on door face and install attaching screws. Connect lock link to lock.

## ELECTRIC DOOR LOCKS (CHRYSLER)

Loosen the solenoid to mounting bracket screws. Push lock lever to down position and slide solenoid to full down position in mounting bracket. Raise lock lever to up position, extending solenoid rod to maximum position. Tighten solenoid to mounting bracket screws and test operation of the lock.

## REAR DOOR REGULATOR (CHRYSLER)

Fig. 17-20 is typical of the rear door regulators used on Chrysler built cars. To replace this type of regulator which is attached to the door inner panel by screw and washer assemblies, support the glass assembly when removing the regulator. The roller on the regulator front arm is retained by a spring nut. Lubricate outboard side of regulator sector gear tooth contact area approximately 1/2 in. wide along entire length of arc and studs on front and rear arms before installing.

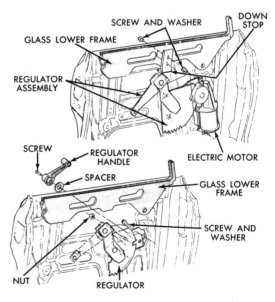

Fig. 17-20. Typical rear door regulator installation.

On some body models the rear door regulator installation is the same as that for front doors.

## DOOR EMERGENCY OPENING PROCEDURE

If a door latch is inoperative on Ford cars and cannot be opened from either inside or outside of the vehicle, a latch actuating tool can be made, as shown in Figs. 17-21 and 17-22. The actuating tool can be made of 1/8 in. welding rod or its equivalent.

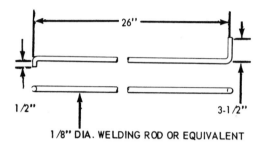

Fig. 17-21. *Details of tool used to actuate door latch.*

To actuate the latch, first lower the window glass of the inoperative door to its full down position. Insert the latch actuating tool in the glass opening at the rear edge of the door and engage the latch pawl lever, as shown in Fig. 17-22.

Apply a downward pressure on the latch pawl lever with the tool. This will open the door. When the door is open, inspect the latch assembly and rod attaching points to determine the cause of the trouble.

## QUIZ - Chapter 17

1. How are door inside handles attached on recent model Fisher bodies?
    Retaining clip.
    Screw.
    Tapered pin.
2. On recent model Fisher bodies, is it necessary to remove the door trim assembly before removing the door outside handle?
    Yes.
    No.
3. Locks on recent model Fisher bodies are

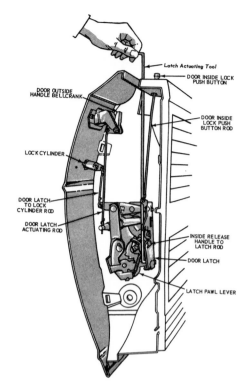

Fig. 17-22. *Releasing door latch with special tool.*

of the rotary bolt type.
    True.
    False.
4. What type tool is usually used to remove the door inside handle on Ford cars?
    Adjustable wrench.
    Plier-type tool.
    Screwdriver.
    3/8 in. end wrench.
5. How is the vent glass regulator secured to the vent glass lower pivot on recent model Ford cars?
    Cap screw.
    Bolt and nut.
    Spring clip.
    Press fit.
6. How are door outside handles attached on recent model Chrysler built bodies?
    Screws requiring Allen type wrench.
    Spring clip.
    Stud and nut.

# Chapter 18

# REMOVING INTERIOR TRIM, WEATHERSTRIP, UPHOLSTERY

When it becomes necessary to do work on door hardware, replace door glass and remove dents in certain panels, including the roof, it is usually necessary to remove interior trim and/or upholstery. When there is rain and dust leakage around the doors it is usually necessary to replace the door weatherstrip.

This chapter discusses typical procedures for removing trim, weather strip and upholstery from current auto bodies.

## REMOVING DOOR ARM REST ASSEMBLIES

Arm rests are attached to doors by means of screws located on the underside of the arm rest. Removal of these screws permits removal of the arm rest. A typical installation is shown in Fig. 18-1.

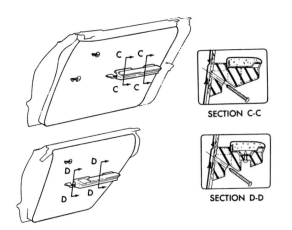

Fig. 18-1. Method of attaching arm rest assemblies to doors.

## DOOR TRIM ASSEMBLIES (FISHER BODIES)

There are two basic types of door trim assemblies used on recent model Fisher bodies,

a one piece assembly and a two piece assembly. The one piece assembly in most installations hangs over the door inner panel across the top and is secured by clips or nails down the sides and by screws across the bottom. Fig. 18-2 is a composite illustration of the various types of door trim panel fasteners.

On the two piece trim, the upper portion hangs over the door inner panel across the top and is secured by trim nails and screws across the bottom. The lower portion is retained by screws across the top and by clips down the sides and across the bottom.

The removal and installation of the door trim assemblies on recent model Fisher

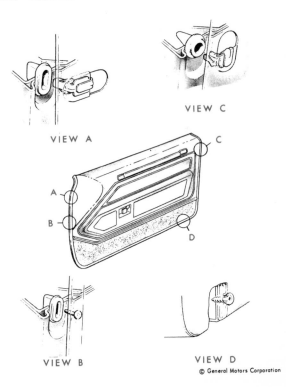

VIEW C

VIEW A

VIEW B

VIEW D

© General Motors Corporation

Fig. 18-2. Various types of door trim retention (Fisher body).

bodies is as follows: Remove door inside handles and door inside locking rod knob. Remove screws from door pull handles. On styles with remote control mirror assemblies remove remote mirror escutcheon and disengage mirror control cable from escutcheon. Also remove arm rests, remote control cover plates or other accessories that may be installed.

On cars equipped with two piece trim, remove attaching screws along upper edge of lower trim assembly. Then starting at lower corner, insert tool between door inner panel and trim assembly and disengage retaining clips from plastic cups down both sides and across bottom. On styles with courtesy lights in lower trim assembly, disconnect wire harness at lamp assembly. On some body styles it is necessary to remove all screws down both sides and across bottom of door trim pad. Then starting at a lower corner insert tool between door inner panel and trim assembly and carefully disengage retaining nails or clips from plastic cups inserted in door inner panel.

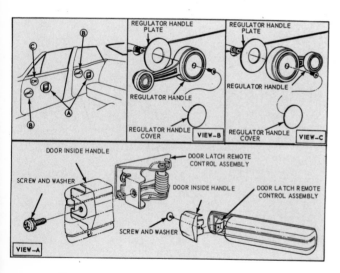

*Fig. 18-3. Typical Ford door and window regulator handle construction.*

To remove trim assembly, lift trim assembly upward and slide it slightly rearward to disengage it from door inner panel at belt line. On styles with electric switches located in trim assembly, disconnect wire harness and remove trim assembly from door.

To install door trim assemblies, reverse removal procedure.

On body styles with adjustable trim supports at belt line, the door trim assembly can be adjusted in or out so as not to restrict door window operation.

## FORD DOOR TRIM PANELS

To remove the door trim panels on recent models of Ford, Maverick and Torino cars, the same basic procedure can be followed. Unscrew and remove the door latch control knob. Pry the window regulator retaining screw access covers from the window regulator handles, Fig. 18-3. Remove the handle retaining screw and the handle. Remove any screws which retain the trim panel to the inner panel such as the arm rest retaining screws and the molding screws. Remove the screw which retains the door remote control handle to the latch mechanism and remove the remote control handle.

Front Doors: Remove the remote control mirror bezel nut if so equipped. With a putty knife, pry the trim panel retaining clips, Fig. 18-4, loose from the door inner panel. If the door has power windows, disconnect the switch lead wires from the switch and remove the trim panel. If necessary carefully loosen the door water shield.

Installation: Place a daub of special sealer over each retaining clip to seal the retaining clips when they are pushed into the door. Also apply sealer around the door handles, window regulator shafts and other existing holes. Fasten the water shield to the inner panel with sealer. Be sure that the water shield is securely fastened to the door inner panel.

If the trim panel is to be replaced, transfer the power window switch, ornamentation (if so equipped), and the retaining clips from the old trim panel to the new one. Also transfer the door pull handle which is fastened by two pop rivets.

The door pull handle covers, Fig. 18-4, are cemented in place. To remove the door pull handle pop rivets, carefully pry the covers away from the handle. Position the pull handle to the new trim panel and install the pop rivets. Clean old cement from the covers with naptha. Use a 1 3/4 x 3/8 in. tape and cement

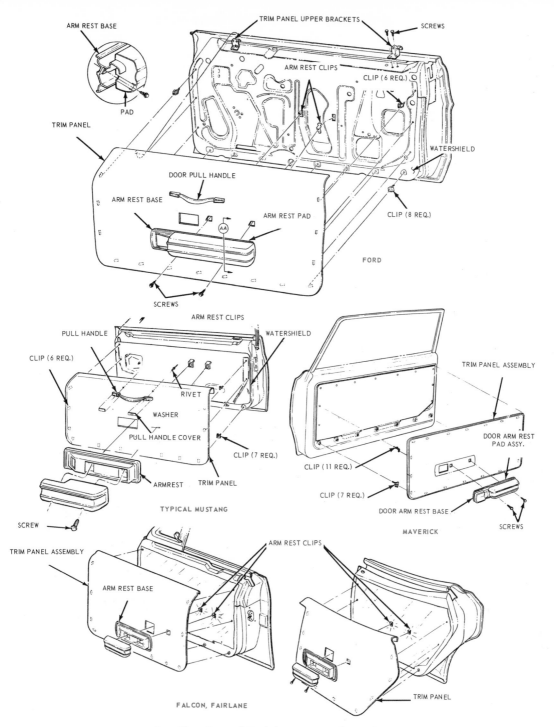

*Fig. 18-4. Typical Ford door trim panel installation.*

the covers back in place.

Position the trim panel to the door and connect the power window switch wires to the switch (if so equipped). Be sure that all the trim panel retaining clips are installed in the trim panel. Place the top edge of the trim panel over the trim panel upper brackets, and push the clips into place in the door inner panel, Fig. 18-4. Position the door remote control handle to the latch mechanism and install the retaining screw.

Position the arm rest to the door and install the arm rest retaining screws.

Front Doors: Install the remote control bezel nut if so equipped.

Position the window regulator handles on

their shafts. Install the handle retaining screws and press the retaining screw access covers into place. With the windows closed, the handles should be positioned as shown in Fig. 18-3. Install the door latch control knob.

Mustang Models: To remove the door trim, first remove the retaining screw from the window regulator handle and remove the handle from the shaft, Fig. 18-3. Remove the two retaining screws from the arm rest assembly and remove the assembly. Remove the two retaining nuts and remove the door remote control handle from the door. Remove the trim panel retaining screws. With a putty knife, pry the trim panel retaining clips out of the door inner panel and remove the panel from the door. Carefully remove the water shield if necessary. When replacing the trim panel on the Mustang, follow the same instructions as given for the Ford.

## FORD QUARTER TRIM PANEL REMOVAL

On Ford and Torino two door models, the removal procedure is as follows: Remove the

rear seat cushion and seat back from the vehicle. Remove the window regulator handle, if so equipped. Pry the handle retaining screw access cover from the handle and remove the retaining screw, Fig. 18-3. Remove any screws retaining the trim panel to the inner panel such as the arm rest retaining screws. On some models, the arm rest retaining screws are covered by an arm rest lower finish panel. For access to the screws, carefully pry the finish panel out of the arm rest. Remove the trim panel attaching screws. Then, unclip the trim panel retaining clips and pull the trim panel from the quarter panel, Fig. 18-5. Disconnect the power window switch wires, if so equipped from the switch. Installation is accomplished by reversing the procedure.

Fig. 18-6. Removing door trim from Plymouth bodies.

## DOOR TRIM ASSEMBLIES (CHRYSLER)

To remove the door trim on recent model Chrysler bodies, first remove the inside handles and arm rests. Remove screws attaching trim panel to door inner panel. Then insert a wide-blade tool or screwdriver between the trim panel and the door frame next to the retaining clips, and snap out the retaining clips around the edge of the trim panel, Fig. 18-6. The trim panel can then be removed from the door.

Before replacing the door trim panel, note the condition of the weather curtain cemented

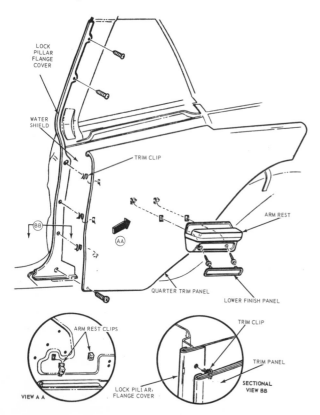

Fig. 18-5. Details of Ford quarter trim installation. Typical.

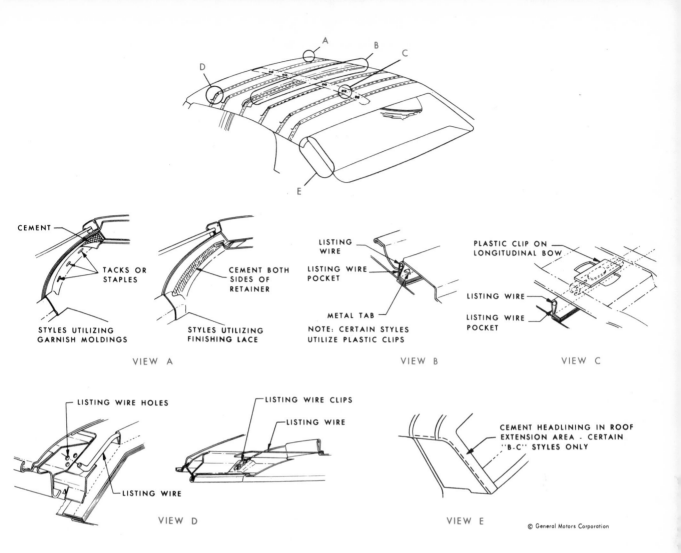

*Fig. 18-7. Typical cloth and vinyl headlining installations (Fisher).*

to the door frame. Make sure the escutcheon springs are placed on the regulator and remote control shafts. Align the trim panel retaining clips with the holes of the door frame and bump into place with the heel of the hand. The job is completed with the installation of the door handles and arm rests.

## HEADLINING ASSEMBLY (FISHER)

The headlining-cloth and vinyl coated (soft) headlining as installed on recent model Fisher bodies is contoured to the inner surface of the roof panel by listing wires. The listing wires are attached to the headlining by concealed listing wire pockets which are part of the headlining. The ends of the listing wires are secured in holes at the side roof rail or by use of clips which are attached to the side rail with screws.

On some body styles, the listing wires are further attached to the roof panel by snap-in type clips which are secured to the longitudinal roof bow, Fig. 18-7, view C.

When finishing lace is used at the windshield and back window opening, the headlining is attached at those areas with non-staining adhesive.

Where garnish moldings are utilized, the headlining is tacked or stapled in addition to being cemented at the windshield and back body openings, Fig. 18-7, view A.

The headlining is retained along the side roof rails by cement or the use of a pronged retainer. Depending upon the style, garnish moldings or finishing lace is also used to assist in retaining the headlining. The side roof rail garnish moldings are secured to the headlining retainer by clips which are located in the molding, Fig. 18-8.

115

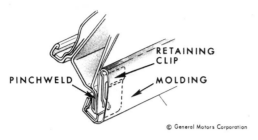

*Fig. 18-8. Side roof rail garnish moldings are secured to the headlining retainer by clips (Fisher).*

At the roof extension area, the headlining is secured either by cement to a metal retainer or by tacks or staples to a trim stick.

Quarter upper trim is removed after first removing arm rests or other accessory equipment.

To remove headlining-cloth or vinyl coated headlining, first place protective coverings over seat cushions and backs. Then remove all hardware and trim assemblies such as: Windshield side and upper garnish moldings or finishing lace, rearview mirror support, sun shade supports, dome or rear quarter courtesy lights, coat hooks, side roof rail moldings or finishing lace, back window garnish moldings or finishing lace, center pillar upper trim assembly, rear quarter trim where necessary, quarter upper trim finishing panel, back body opening garnish moldings or finishing lace, shoulder strap anchor plate and escutcheon.

Carefully remove tacks or staples securing headlining at windshield and back window opening or back body opening.

On styles using a pronged retainer, use a broad bladed tool and carefully disengage headlining from pronged retainers where present.

Carefully detach cemented edge of headlining around entire perimeter.

On some body styles, start at front of body and carefully disengage No. 1 and No. 2 listing wires from side roof rails and from plastic supporting clips on roof bows on styles so equipped, Fig. 18-7, view C. In like manner, working from the rear of the body, disengage listing wires from side roof rails and supporting clips on longitudinal bow. Exercise care to keep the headlining clean by gathering or folding listing wires on the outside.

On other body styles, start at the front of

the body, fully detach headlining and plastic supports from retaining slots in roof panel, Fig. 18-7, view A.

Depending on style, bend down tabs securing No. 3 listing wire or disengage No. 3 listing wire from plastic clips on structural bow and remove headlining from body.

On bodies using listing wires, make note in which holes listing wires are installed in side roof rails. Listing wires should be placed in same holes when replacing the headlining.

## REPLACING HEADLINING

If replacing headlining, remove listing wires from pockets of old headlining. Listing wires must be installed in corresponding holes in new headlining.

Check that plastic clips are installed in roof bow slots. Also that plastic supports are installed on headlining pockets after listing wires are installed in pockets.

Be sure trim cement is of the nonstaining type. Where finishing lace is used, be sure that cement is applied to both sides of retainers.

On most body styles (styles A, X and D) lift headlining assembly into body and install No. 3 listing wire and listing wire pocket over metal tabs at roof bow and bend up tabs to secure wire to bow. On styles that incorporate plastic clips in place of metal tabs, snap No. 3 listing wire into clips, Fig. 18-7, views B and C. Working toward rear from No. 3 listing wire, install listing wires in side roof rails and snap listing wires into plastic clips on roof bows. In like manner working forward install remaining listing wires, Fig. 18-7, view C. Listing wires may be adjusted up or down by utilizing appropriate holes in side roof rails. Listing wires should rest tight against roof panel after installation, Fig. 18-7, view D.

On other body styles (styles B, C, E and F) proceed as follows: Lift headlining assembly into body, then starting at rear listing wire and working forward install plastic supports with headlining attached into retaining slots in roof panel. Secure and stretch headlining at windshield first; then back window or back body opening. Stretch and secure headlining at rear quarters and side roof

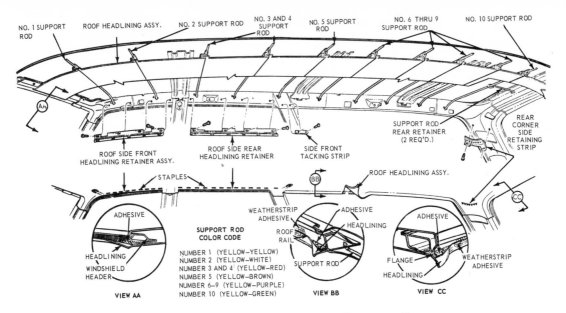

NO. 1 SUPPORT ROD · ROOF HEADLINING ASSY. · NO. 2 SUPPORT ROD · NO. 3 AND 4 SUPPORT ROD · NO. 5 SUPPORT ROD · NO. 6 THRU 9 SUPPORT ROD · NO. 10 SUPPORT ROD

SUPPORT ROD REAR RETAINER (2 REQ'D.) · REAR CORNER SIDE RETAINING STRIP

ROOF SIDE FRONT HEADLINING RETAINER ASSY. · ROOF SIDE REAR HEADLINING RETAINER · SIDE FRONT TACKING STRIP

STAPLES · ROOF HEADLINING ASSY.

WEATHERSTRIP ADHESIVE

ADHESIVE · HEADLINING · WINDSHIELD HEADER

SUPPORT ROD COLOR CODE

NUMBER 1 (YELLOW—YELLOW)
NUMBER 2 (YELLOW—WHITE)
NUMBER 3 AND 4 (YELLOW—RED)
NUMBER 5 (YELLOW—BROWN)
NUMBER 6—9 (YELLOW—PURPLE)
NUMBER 10 (YELLOW—GREEN)

VIEW AA

ROOF RAIL · SUPPORT ROD · ADHESIVE · HEADLINING

VIEW BB

ADHESIVE · FLANGE · HEADLINING · WEATHERSTRIP ADHESIVE

VIEW CC

Fig. 18-9. Details of Ford station wagon headlining installation.

## REMOVING FORD HEADLINING

rails. Permanently attach material removing draws and wrinkles and replace all previously removed inside hardware and trim assemblies.

The procedure for removing the headlining on recent model Ford cars in general applies to all models. If some of the steps do not apply to the particular model being serviced, proceed to the next step.

First remove the sun visor and bracket assembly. Remove the windshield upper garnish molding. Note: Visor center clip attached. Remove the upper screw from the two windshield side garnish moldings and position the moldings away from the "A" pillar. Remove the shoulder strap assemblies and the shoulder strap retainers and coat hooks.

Remove the roof side center garnish moldings. On all 4-door sedans, first remove the center cap from the junction of the front and rear side moldings at the center pillar. On some 4-door sedans, there is also a joint cover at the rear quarter. On 2-door hardtops, there is one joint cover at the rear quarter.

Remove the rear seat cushion and back. Remove the right and left quarter panels. Remove the roof side rear trim covers (right and left). Remove the back window garnish moldings. Bend the retaining tabs and re-

move the package tray and deadener. Bend up the tabs on all retaining strips and unhook the headlining from the tabs. Remove the dome light. Pry off the lens and remove four screws.

Remove the staples that fasten the headlining to the roof side retainer assemblies and around the back window.

Pull the headlining loose from the cemented area at the windshield header. Unhook the right and left retainers from the headlining rear support rod, disengage all support rods from the holes in the left and right roof rails and remove the headlining from the vehicle.

Installation: Unpack the new headlining and lay it out on a flat surface. Mark and trim the new headlining using the old one for a pattern.

Trim the listings on the new headlining to the approximate length of those used on the old lining. Remove the support rods from the old headlining and install them in the same relative rod listings of the new headlining. Roof headlining support rods are color coded at each end, Fig. 18-9. When ordering new rods be sure to note the color at each end of the rod. Position the headlining in the vehicle. To maintain the most driver headroom and wrinkle free headlining, insert the support rods into the upper holes in the left and lower holes in right roof rail except in the following cases. If the headlining is wrinkled (not taut enough) use the upper holes on both

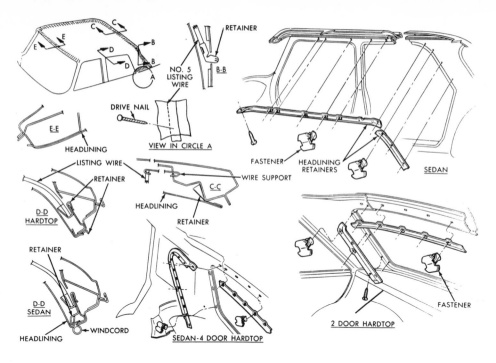

Fig. 18-10. Side rail retainers (Fury).

sides. If the headlining is too taut, use the lower holes on both sides.

Hook the rear retainers to the rear support rod. Staple the headlining to the retainer assemblies. Bend down the tabs on the retaining strips and hook the headlining to the tabs. Cement the headlining in place at the windshield header and trim the excess material

Install the roof side rear trim covers, package tray, the rear window garnish moldings and quarter trim panels. Cut a hole in the headlining material for the dome light and install the lens and bezel. Install all garnish moldings, shoulder harness assembly, retainers and sun visors.

## HEADLINING REPLACEMENT (CHRYSLER)

While the following applies particularly to Plymouth cars, it applies also in general to other Chrysler built cars and some of the illustrations and methods are also of use when working on bodies of other manufacturers.

The first step in removing the headlining is to remove the rear seat cushion, dome light, bezel and lens, sun visors, rear view mirror and coat hooks. Remove headlining from cemented areas at windshield header and rear window opening. Remove headlining

from under shelf panel. Using a dull bladed putty knife, disengage fabric from side rail header, Figs. 18-10 and 18-11, by gently forcing material up and off of retainers and while maintaining pressure on fabric, pull down and out. Work only small areas at a time.

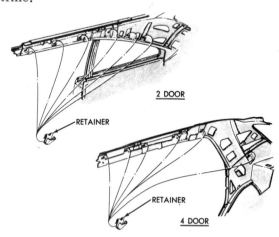

Fig. 18-11. Listing wire retainers (Plymouth Belvedere).

Remove headlining at windshield header and from fasteners at rear window area, Fig. 18-12. Remove listing wires from side rail retainers and support wire from rear listing wire, Fig. 18-13. Remove all foreign matter and cement from windshield header area and rear window opening areas. Remove

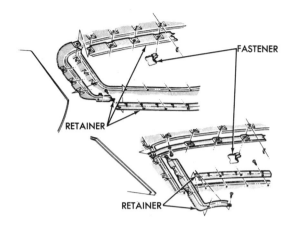

Fig. 18-12. *Rear window retainers (Plymouth Belvedere).*

listing wires from headlining and insert in comparable listing of new liner.

Installation: Trim excess listing material even with edges of headlining. Locate center line of lining at front and rear ends. Cut a small notch as an aid in maintaining headlining alignment during installation.

Locate and mark the center line points of windshield and rear window openings. Center headlining at rear window and insert rear listing wire to retainer clips on roof rail extensions. Hook rear listing wire to wire supports, Fig. 18-13, and stretch material sufficiently to remove all wrinkles while maintaining front and rear alignment. The same amount of material should hang down on both sides.

Insert remaining listing wires into roof side rail retainers, taking care that no wrinkles appear.

Apply cement to windshield header area and when cement becomes tacky, start at center line area of windshield and position headlining on cemented area.

Using a dull putty knife, secure liner on barbs at header area, do not install material at top of windshield posts, making sure there are no wrinkles and that fabric seam is straight.

Locate sun visor mounting bracket screw holes in header and cut holes in lining slightly larger than attaching screws. Install sun visors and tuck corners of headlining at top of windshield posts.

Locate rear visor mirror bracket screw holes, cut holes in fabric slightly larger than screws and install mirror. When installing headlining at side rail retainers, work only a small section at a time to make certain seams are straight and material is free from wrinkles.

Using a dull putty knife and working alternately from side to side, install headlining on side rail retainers. Apply cement at rear window opening and to quarter panel area. After cement becomes tacky, install head-

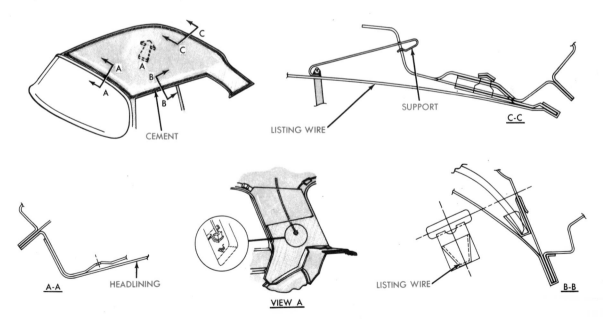

Fig. 18-13. *Headlining application (Plymouth Fury, Belvedere, Satellite).*

lining starting at top center and working outward and down the sides.

Install rear seat cushions and coat hooks. Replace accessories which have been removed.

In the case of Valiant and Barracuda models, the headlining is attached to the windshield header, roof side rails and quarter panel areas with cement only. Listing wire retainers are installed in slots in the roof side rail and quarter panel areas.

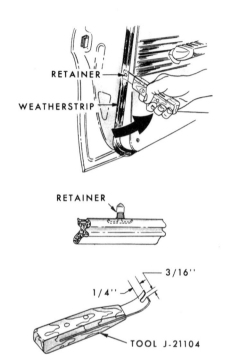

Fig. 18-14. Removing weatherstrip from Fisher bodies.

## FRONT AND REAR DOOR WEATHERSTRIP (FISHER)

Both front and rear door weatherstrips on recent model Fisher bodies use nylon fasteners to retain the door weatherstrip. The fasteners are a component part of the weatherstrip and secure the weatherstrip to the door by engaging piercings in the door panels. The serrations on the fastener retain the fastener in the piercing and also seal the openings from water entry, Figs. 18-14 and 18-15.

On closed styles, nylon fasteners are used below the belt line only. Weatherstrip adhesive retains the weatherstrip around the upper door frame. On all 1971 styles, in

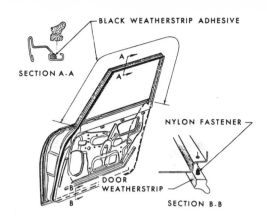

Fig. 18-15. Details of door weatherstrip as installed on Fisher bodies.

addition to the fastener, use weatherstrip adhesive at the belt line and down the front door pillar.

To disengage nylon fasteners from the door panel piercings use a tool illustrated in Fig. 18-14. This tool permits removal of the weatherstrip without damaging the serrations on the fasteners so that the weatherstrip can be reinstalled if desired.

Removal: On all hardtop and convertible styles remove door trim pad to gain access to weatherstrip fasteners hidden under trim assembly and remove fasteners. Use a flat-bladed tool to break cement bond between door and weatherstrip. On all 1971 styles, weatherstrip adhesive is used for a distance of 9 in. on door lock pillar and the entire length of the front door hinge pillar, Fig. 18-15. In addition, on closed styles, weatherstrip is retained by weatherstrip adhesive completely around door upper frame, Fig. 18-15. Use tool, Fig. 18-14, to disengage

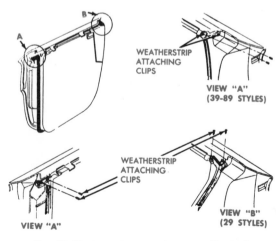

Fig. 18-16. Rear door weatherstrips (Fisher).

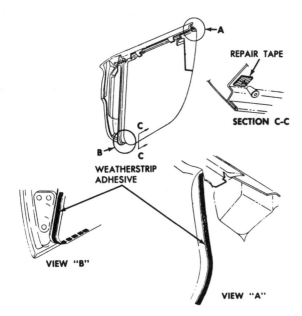

Fig. 18-17. Rear door weatherstrip adhesion application (Fisher).

weatherstrip from door where weatherstrip is retained by nylon fasteners.

When replacing weatherstrip, make sure all nylon fasteners are in good condition and replace any that are damaged. Use adhesive in all areas where it was used originally.

On some older model Fisher bodies, weatherstrip attaching clips were used, Fig. 18-16. These clips fit into individual sealing plugs, along door bottoms and sides. Cement usage was limited to door lock pillar panels at belt line and at the lower corners of doors, Fig. 18-17. Cement, however, can be applied at any area where additional retention is required.

Also on some older Fisher bodies, the rear door weatherstrip is a one piece mechanically retained type. Mechanical retention consists of a series of weatherstrip attaching clips which fit into individual sealing plugs along door bottom and sides. The weatherstrip is also mechanically retained by nylon snap fasteners at belt line of hinge and lock pillar panels. In addition, some body styles have the rear door weatherstrip further retained by a single weatherstrip attaching clip, and screw at upper radius of lock pillar panel.

## DOOR WEATHERSTRIP (CHRYSLER)

Door weatherstrip as used on recent model Plymouth cars and which is typical of other

Chrysler built vehicles is attached by means of cement and fastening clips. It can be easily removed by means of a dull bladed putty knife and careful prying.

Before attempting to install weatherstrip, make sure that all old weatherstrip particles and cement has been removed from the contact surfaces.

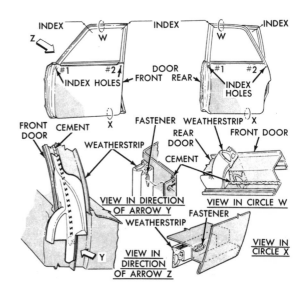

Fig. 18-18. Installing weatherstrip on Plymouth Fury models.

When installing weatherstrip on Fury models, apply lower half of weatherstrip, starting at number one index hole and using fasteners for locating and ending at number 2 index hole, Fig. 18-18. Apply a 1/8 in. bead of cement to weatherstrip seating area on door upper half. Install upper half of weather-

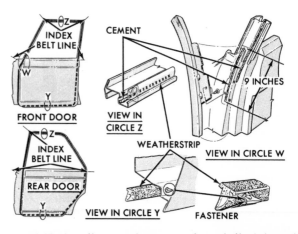

Fig. 18-19. Installing weatherstrip on lower half of door of some late model Chrysler-Plymouth models.

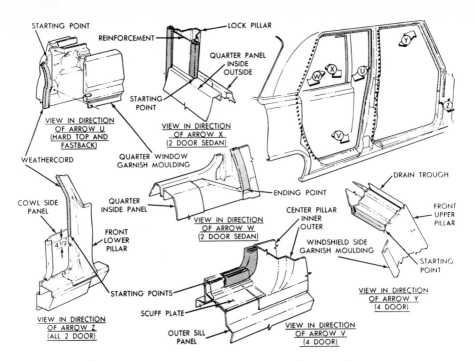

STARTING POINT

REINFORCEMENT

LOCK PILLAR

QUARTER PANEL
INSIDE
OUTSIDE

STARTING
POINT

VIEW IN DIRECTION
OF ARROW U
(HARD TOP AND
FASTBACK)

VIEW IN DIRECTION
OF ARROW X
(2 DOOR SEDAN)

WEATHERCORD

QUARTER WINDOW
GARNISH MOULDING

DRAIN TROUGH

COWL SIDE
PANEL

QUARTER
INSIDE PANEL

ENDING POINT

FRONT
UPPER
PILLAR

FRONT
LOWER
PILLAR

VIEW IN DIRECTION
OF ARROW W
(2 DOOR SEDAN)

CENTER PILLAR
INNER
OUTER

WINDSHIELD SIDE
GARNISH MOULDING

STARTING
POINT

STARTING POINTS

SCUFF PLATE

VIEW IN DIRECTION
OF ARROW Y
(4 DOOR)

VIEW IN DIRECTION
OF ARROW Z
(ALL 2 DOOR)

OUTER SILL
PANEL

VIEW IN DIRECTION
OF ARROW V
(4 DOOR)

*Fig. 18-20. Applying weatherstrip to doors of some Chrysler-Plymouth models.*

strip on door, indexing at the upper corners. Work weatherstrip from index points to a point midway between them. Avoid puckering or stretching of weatherstrip.

On other models apply weatherstrip to lower half of door, starting at hinge face at belt line, working fasteners into holes at door shut face, Figs. 18-19 and 18-20. Apply a 1/8 in. bead of cement to weatherstrip application surface on door upper section. Install weatherstrip around door frames, indexing at upper corners and working weatherstrip from index points to a point midway between them. Avoid puckering and stretching of weatherstrip.

## QUIZ - Chapter 18

1. How are door arm rests attached?
   Cap screws through door inner panel.
   Screws on underside of arm rest.
   Special type spring clips.
2. How is lower edge of door trim attached on most recent model Fisher bodies?
   By screws.
   Retaining nails.
   By grooved channel.
3. When removing door trim assemblies on recent model Ford cars is it necessary to remove garnish molding?

4. After removing inside handles and arm rests on recent model Chrysler bodies, how is the door trim panel removed?
   Use a screwdriver and snap out the retaining clips around edge of panel.
   Remove garnish molding and lift panel from retaining groove.
   Remove screws with Phillips type screwdriver.
5. On recent model Fisher bodies, how is the headlining made to conform to the contour of the roof?
   It is glued to the roof.
   By means of concealed listing wires.
6. Are roof lining support rods color coded on recent Ford models?
   Yes.
   No.
7. On recent model Chrysler built cars, how is the headlining attached to the windshield header?
   By means of small tacks.
   Listing wires.
   It is cemented in place.
8. What type fastener is used to attach the front door weatherstrip assembly on recent model Fisher bodies?
   Nylon component fasteners.
   Cement.
   Special adhesive tape.

# Chapter 19
# DOOR, WINDOW GLASS
# SERVICE

Replacement and adjustment of door windows form an important part of auto body work. Not only because it is frequently necessary to replace the glass, but also because it is often necessary to adjust the windows in order to eliminate rattles, and to make the windows raise and lower smoothly and easily.

There are many different types of window and regulator construction. The designs described and illustrated in the following pages are typical and should be studied to note their similarity as well as their differences. It is also important to remember that there will be some difference in the procedure with different body models.

When the windows become stuck and cannot be raised or lowered, the trouble is usually caused by misalignment. By following the instructions covering adjustment, the trouble can generally be overcome. In some cases, the trouble may be caused by worn channels or worn regulators. In such cases replacement of the worn parts will overcome the trouble.

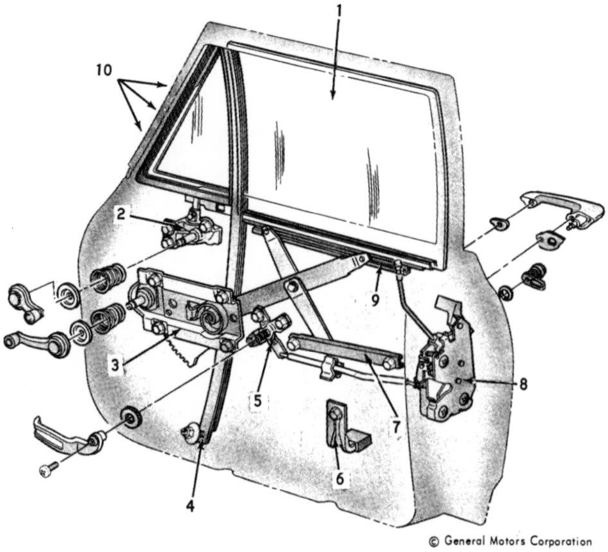

## WINDOWS AND REGULATOR SERVICE (FISHER)

To remove the front door ventilator on recent model Fisher bodies of the A type, first remove the door trim assembly and inner panel water deflector. With window in the up position, loosen down stop support attaching bolts and remove support, Fig. 19-1. Remove ventilator regulator, Fig. 19-2. Lower win-

© General Motors Corporation

*Fig. 19-1. Front door hardware A closed styles (Fisher). 1— Front door window assembly. 2—Ventilator assembly. 3—Window regulator. 4—Ventilator division channel. 5—Door lock remote control. 6—Window down stop support. 7—Inner panel cam. 8—Door lock. 9—Lower sash channel cam. 10—Ventilator attaching screws.*

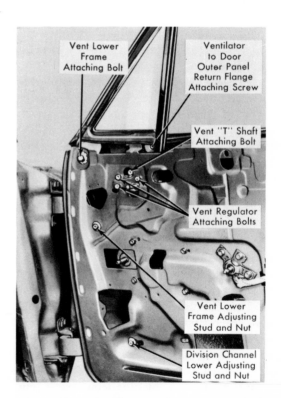

*Fig. 19-2. Vent window hardware. Typical of Fisher bodies. Location of adjustments varies with different type bodies.*

dow to full down position and remove bolt securing ventilator lower frame to door outer panel. Remove division channel lower adjusting stud nut, Fig. 19-3. Remove ventilator to door upper frame attaching screws. Disengage upper front end of glass run channel from door upper frame to permit rearward movement and removal of vent from door upper frame. Tilt vent assembly rearward and remove vent inboard of door upper frame.

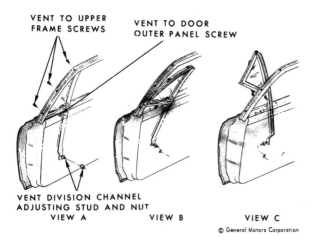

VENT TO UPPER FRAME SCREWS

VENT TO DOOR OUTER PANEL SCREW

VENT DIVISION CHANNEL ADJUSTING STUD AND NUT

VIEW A      VIEW B      VIEW C

© General Motors Corporation

*Fig. 19-3. Front door ventilator removal procedure (Fisher).*

Installation is accomplished by reversing the procedure.

Front Door Window: The front door window on Fisher body A and X closed styles consists of a frameless piece of glass pressed into a thin section lower sash channel. When cycled, the glass operates within the ventilator division channel and window glass run channel.

To remove the front door window assembly, first remove the front door ventilator as previously described. Slide window lower sash channel cam off window regulator lift and balance arm rollers on two door styles and off lift arm roller on four door styles. Remove window inboard of door upper frame.

To install, reverse the procedure.

To adjust lower portion of ventilator division channel to proper alignment with door window assembly, lower door window and loosen ventilator adjusting nut. Turn adjusting nut in or out, or position lower end of channel fore or aft as required; then tighten adjusting nut. On two door styles, the door

window inner panel is adjustable at the front and can correct a rotated (cocked) front door window.

## REAR WINDOW ASSEMBLY (FISHER BODY A STYLE)

To remove rear door window assembly on late model Fisher A closed style, Fig. 19-4, first remove door trim assembly and inner panel water deflector. With window in a three-quarter closed position, remove window lower sash channel cam attaching screws. Loosen rear glass run channel upper and lower attaching screws. Rotate rear edge of glass downward and remove window by lifting front edge of glass upward outboard of door upper frame.

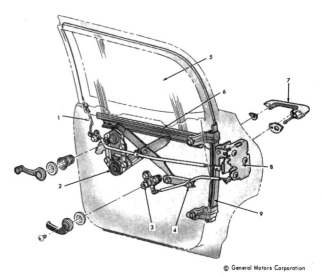

© General Motors Corporation

*Fig. 19-4. Rear door hardware Fisher A closed style bodies. 1—Inside locking rod. 2—Window regulator, manual. 3—Door lock remote control. 4—Inner panel cam. 5—Rear door window. 6—Lower sash channel cam. 7—Door outside handle. 8—Door lock. 9—Glass run channel.*

To install, reverse the procedure. Adjust window for proper operation and alignment. Adjustments are provided to relieve a binding door glass due to misalignment of glass run channel, Fig. 19-4. In addition, the door window inner panel cam is adjustable which can correct a rotated (cocked) rear door window.

Older type rear doors, Fig. 19-5, are provided with wedge plates which are used to adjust the windows.

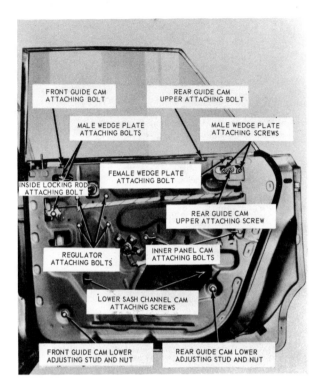

*Fig. 19-5. Rear door window hardware as installed on many recent model Fisher bodies.*

To remove the rear door window illustrated in Fig. 19-5, manual and electric and on four and six window sedans, first raise the door window. Remove door trim assembly and detach inner panel water deflector. Through access holes in door inner panel, remove screws fastening rear door window front and rear male wedge plates to window lower sash channel and remove wedge plates, Fig. 19-5.

Lower door window and remove lower sash channel cam attaching screws. On styles equipped with electric window regulators, disconnect harness electric feed plug from regulator motor at connector.

Carefully raise window and remove from door.

## VENT WING AND DOOR GLASS REPLACEMENT (PLYMOUTH)

While the following instructions apply particularly to Plymouth Fury models they will also act as a general guide to other Chrysler built cars.

The procedure for removing the vent wing and door glass is as follows: Lower door glass fully and remove approximately 4 in. of glass run at forward end, Fig. 19-6. Remove screws attaching vent wing to end facing of door and to belt line. Move glass forward and disengage regulator arm from lift bracket and guide assembly. Remove screw attaching vent wing swivel to vent wing regu-

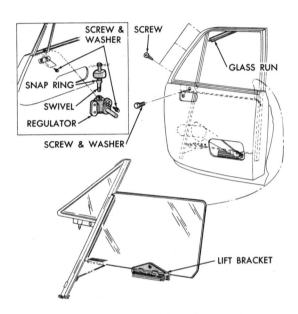

*Fig. 19-6. Vent wing and door glass attachment (Chrysler-Plymouth).*

lator. Remove glass and vent wing assembly from door. Remove cotter pin from lower end of division channel, Fig. 19-7, and separate door glass and vent wing assembly. Remove plastic rivet attaching lift bracket and

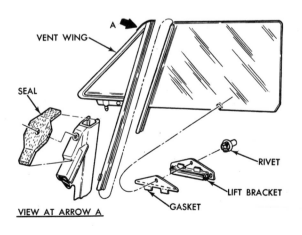

*Fig. 19-7. Details of Plymouth glass lift bracket.*

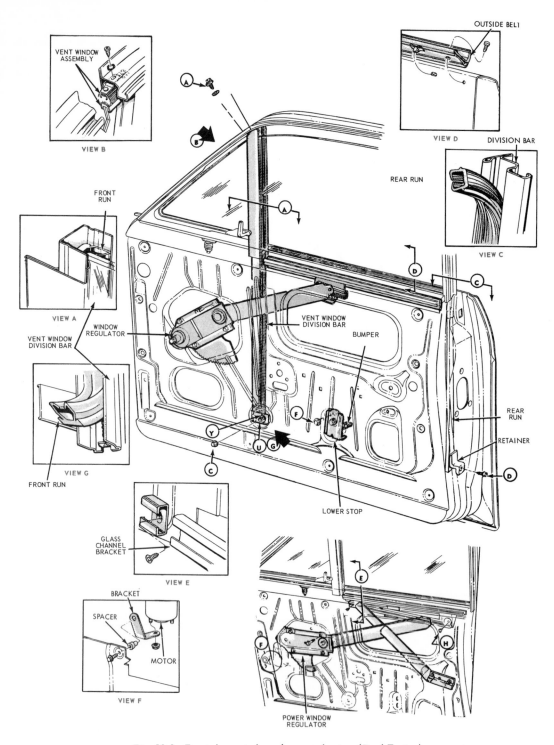

Fig. 19-8. Front door window glass mechanism (Ford Torino).

guide assembly to glass and remove assembly, Fig. 19-7.

When installing the vent wing and door glass, reverse the procedure. In addition, lubricate the sliding surfaces of the lift bracket.

## FRONT DOOR GLASS (CHRYSLER)

The procedure for removal of front door glass varies slightly in different Chrysler built bodies; however, the following procedure which applies particularly to recent model

## Glass Service

Plymouth four-door sedans, is typical.

Remove the door inside handles, arm rest, remote lock knob, trim panel and water shield. With glass in the down position, insert a screwdriver under the retainer ring and pry the retainer from regulator stud ends.

Remove the leather washers from the regulator arm studs. Then pull the regulator arm studs from the glass lower channel. Loosen the division bar in the front run channel mounting bolts. Move the division bar downward and disengage from glass. Move the glass forward between the division bar and inner door panel, and remove the glass up and out of the door glass opening.

### FRONT DOOR GLASS REMOVAL (FORD)

To remove the front door glass from late model Ford cars, remove the door trim panel and water shield. Support the glass and push the button from the center of the retainer at the front of the drive arm bracket, Fig. 17-14. Then pry the retainer from the glass and bracket.

Remove two nuts retaining the glass bracket to the glass. Separate the glass bracket and the channel bracket from the glass. Remove the glass support and remove the glass from the door.

Installation: Position the glass in the door with the front edge of the glass in the front run. Position the glass bracket and glass channel bracket, Fig. 17-14, to the glass and install the retaining nuts. Tighten the nuts to 40 - 80 in. lb. torque.

Install the retainer at the front of the glass channel bracket. Then tighten the two glass bracket retaining nuts to 40 - 80 in. lb. torque. Check the operation of the window and install the water shield and door trim panel.

To remove the front door glass from recent model Torino models, first remove the trim panel and the water shield from the door. Remove the lower stop. Lower the window and unsnap the belt inside weatherstrip from the door. Remove the vent window division bar, lower adjusting screw and nut, Fig. 19-8. Pull the front run and retainer from the vent window division bar.

Rotate the glass and channel assembly 90 deg. and remove the glass and channel assembly from the door. Remove the glass channel from the glass, using special tool if available.

### REAR DOOR GLASS REMOVAL (FORD)

To remove the rear door glass on recent model Ford cars, first remove the door trim

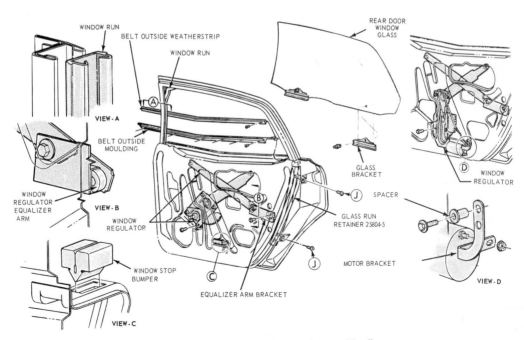

*Fig. 19-9. Rear door window mechanism (Ford).*

panel and water shield. Remove two rear run retainer attaching screws. Pull the rear run from the retainer and remove the retainer. Push the center pin from the retainers attaching the glass brackets to the glass, Fig. 19-9, with a small drift punch or screwdriver. Support the glass and pry the retainer from each glass bracket by inserting a screwdriver behind the retainer flange. Then remove the glass brackets from the glass. Tilt the forward edge of the glass up and remove the glass from the door.

To install the glass in a rear door of a recent model Ford, position the glass in the door. Position the glass brackets to the glass and install the retainers. Then install the center pin in each retainer until it is flush with the retainer flange. Install the rear run retainer, and install the run in the retainer. Replace the water shield and trim.

To remove the glass from the rear door of a recent model Ford Torino, first remove the trim panel and water shield from the door. Lower the glass and remove one screw attaching the top of the division bar to the door frame. Remove one screw attaching the bottom of the rear run to the bracket, Fig.

19-10. Remove the screw attaching the bracket to the inner panel and remove the bracket. Remove the rear run from the retainer and remove the division bar from the door. Raise and support the glass and remove three screws attaching the channel bracket to the glass channel. Remove the glass from the door.

## QUARTER GLASS REPLACEMENT (FORD)

To remove the quarter window glass from Ford Mustang models, first remove the quarter trim panel and water shield. Remove the upper front and upper rear stops, Fig. 19-11. Remove five screws attaching the belt weatherstrip to the bottom of the glass opening and remove the weatherstrip. Support the glass and remove the spring retainer and washer from the glass bracket stud. Then remove the regulator arm and washer from the glass bracket stud, Fig. 19-11.

Remove three screws attaching the glass bracket to the rollers and lift the glass and bracket from the quarter panel. Remove one screw attaching the bracket to the glass and separate the glass from the bracket.

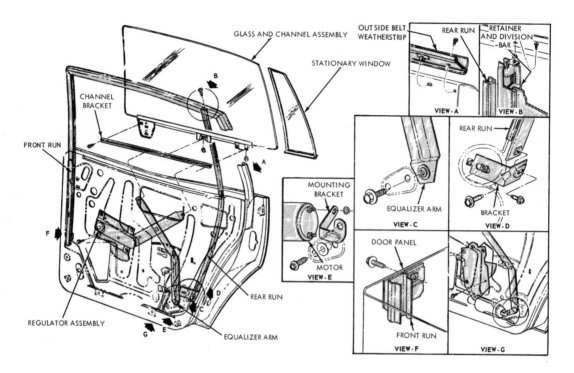

*Fig. 19-10. Rear door window mechanism (Ford Torino).*

# Glass Service

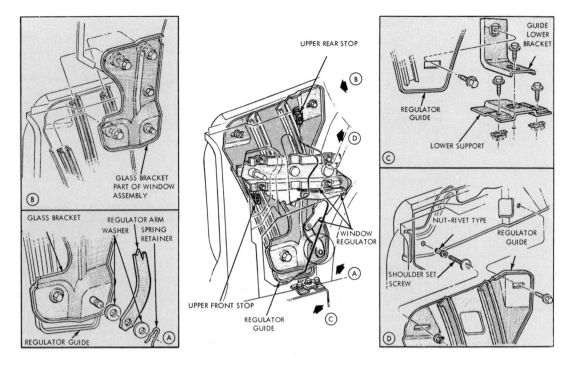

*Fig. 19-11. Quarter window mechanism (Ford Mustang).*

## QUIZ – Chapter 19

1. What usually causes windows to stick so they cannot be raised or lowered?
    Lack of lubrication.
    Wrong type weatherstrip.
    Wrong type windlace.
    Misalignment.
2. On cars equipped with electric window regulators should the motor be disconnected from the circuit before removing window assemblies?
    Yes.
    No.
3. To remove the front door ventilator assembly on recent model Fisher bodies, it is not necessary to first remove the door trim assembly.
    True.
    False.
4. Is it necessary to remove the arm rests from front door on Plymouth cars before removing front door window glass?
    Yes.
    No.
5. Is it necessary to remove the rear seat cushion on late model Ford cars when replacing quarter glass?
    Yes.
    No.

# Chapter 20
# WINDSHIELD, REAR WINDOW REMOVAL, INSTALLATION

Windshields are frequently broken as a result of collision, flying gravel, and also as a result of strain from twisting of the car body. It is therefore, important for body repair men to be familiar with the different methods of removal and installation.

In general, modern windshields are held in position primarily with caulking compound and to a degree with garnish moldings and reveal moldings. The terms garnish and reveal are loosely used by manufacturers to identify the metal strips (chrome plated or painted) placed around the outer and inner edges of the windshield. Most General Motors' manuals refer to the molding used along the outer edge of the windshield as reveal moldings, Fig. 20-1, and that used on the inside edge as the garnish molding. Some other companies reverse this, while still others refer to both inner and outer moldings as garnish moldings, or simply molding.

## REMOVING AND REPLACING MOLDINGS (FISHER)

Before removing the windshield glass or rear window glass from recent model Fisher bodies, it is necessary to remove all trim and hardware immediately adjacent to the glass being removed. This in the case of windshields would include reveal moldings, garnish moldings and windshield wiper arms.

The reveal molding, Fig. 20-1, around the windshield (and other stationary glass) is retained by clips which are attached to the body opening by welded-on studs or screws. A projection on the clip engages the reveal molding flange, retaining the molding between the clip and body metal, Fig. 20-2. To disengage a molding from the retaining clips, use a tool such as shown in Fig. 20-3.

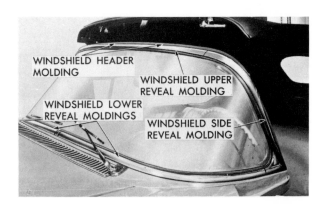

Fig. 20-1. Typical windshield reveal molding on Fisher body.

Another method of attaching the reveal moldings is shown in Fig. 20-4. This method is used on Fisher bodies of recent manufacture on the Fisher B, C, D, E and F hardtop moldings. In this method the molding is retained by barbed clips. A thin flat bladed tool such as a putty knife must be inserted from the windshield side of molding to disengage barbed clips while lifting the molding.

In most cases, the garnish molding used on the inner face of the windshield consists

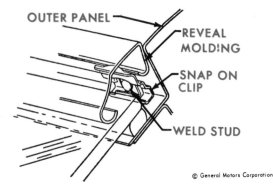

Fig. 20-2. A clip engages the reveal molding flange, on some Fisher bodies.

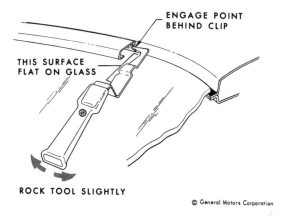

*Fig. 20-3. Type of tool used to disengage retaining clips (Fisher).*

of several pieces and is held in position by means of screws. The windshield reveal molding consists of several pieces as shown in Fig. 20-1. On some bodies the upper reveal moldings are held in position by clips and in others by screws as previously mentioned. The lower reveal molding on many bodies are secured to the upper shroud assembly by molding clip tabs.

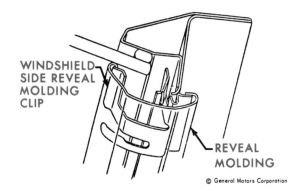

*Fig. 20-4. Barbed clips are used to retain the molding in some Fisher bodies of recent manufacture.*

## REMOVING AND REPLACING WINDSHIELD GLASS

The windshield and back window on all styles of recent model Fisher bodies are bonded to the body opening with a synthetic, self-curing, rubber adhesive caulking compound.

To replace a windshield or back window installed with this material requires either partial or complete replacement of the caulk-ing compound. Partial replacement is referred to as the "short method." Complete replacement is known as the "extended method."

The short method can be used in those situations where original adhesive caulk material remaining on window opening pinch weld flanges after glass removal can serve as a base for the new glass. This method would be applicable in cases of cracked windshields or removal of windows that are still intact. In these situations, the amount of adhesive that is left in the window opening can be controlled during glass removal.

The extended method is required when the original caulking compound remaining in the window opening after glass removal cannot serve as a base for the replacement glass. Examples of this latter situation would be cases requiring metal work or paint refinishing in the opening, or where there is a considerable loss of adhesion between original caulk and body metal. In these cases, original caulk is removed and replaced with fresh material during window installation.

The window removal procedure is the same for both the short and extended installation methods, with one exception. If the short method installation is to be used, more care must be taken during removal to make certain that an even, uniform bead of adhesive caulk material remains on the window opening to serve as a base for the replacement glass. Also make certain that glass lower spacers are not disturbed.

The removal procedure is as follows: First place protective coverings around area where glass is being removed. Remove all trim and hardware immediately adjacent to glass being removed.

On styles equipped with optional rear window electric defogger, disconnect wire harness connectors from glass. If same glass is to be reinstalled, tape electric leads to inside surface of glass to protect them during handling.

On styles equipped with radio antenna built into the windshield glass, disconnect antenna lead at lower center of windshield. If same windshield is to be reinstalled, fold and tape wire back onto outer surface of windshield to protect it during removal and reinstallation.

Secure one end of steel music wire to a piece of wood that can serve as a handle. Using long nose pliers, insert one end of wire through caulking compound at edge of glass; then secure that end of wire to another wood handle, Fig. 20-5.

Fig. 20-5. Cutting the adhesive caulk material with the aid of a piece of steel music wire.

With the aid of a helper, carefully cut (pull wire) through caulking material around entire perimeter of windshield (or rear window as the case may be). If short method will be used to install new glass, hold wire close to inside plane of glass to prevent cutting an excessive amount of adhesive caulking from window opening. Keep tension on wire throughout cutting operation to prevent wire from kinking and breaking, Fig. 20-5. After the cutting of the caulking material has been completed, the glass can be lifted from the opening.

An optional method which can be performed by one man is illustrated in Fig. 20-6. In this method the cutting wire is pulled through upper and lower edges of glass at the same time. When using this method, insert one end of wire through caulking material at inner upper edge of glass and other end of wire through caulking material at inner lower edge. Attach handles to both wire ends outside of body.

If glass being removed is to be reinstalled, place it on a protected bench or holding fixture. Remove old caulking compound using a razor blade. Any remaining traces of caulk-

Fig. 20-6. One man method of cutting caulking material.

ing compound can be removed with toluene or thinner dampened cloth.

When cleaning laminated glass, avoid contacting edge of plastic laminate material (on edge of glass) with volatile cleaner. Contact may cause discoloration and deterioration of plastic laminate by "wicking" action. It is important that petroleum base solvent such as kerosene or gasoline NOT be used as the presence of oil will prevent adhesion of the caulking compound.

## SHORT METHOD OF INSTALLING ADHESION CAULKED GLASS

The short method of glass installation can be used if original adhesion caulk material remaining on window opening flanges after glass removal can serve as a base for the replacement glass. If there is a substantial loss of adhesion between caulk material and body metal, opening must be reworked or refinished and the extended replacement method will be required.

Short Method Installation: Inspect reveal molding retaining clips. Replace or reshape clips which are bent away from body metal 1/32 in. or more.

Position glass in opening. If new glass is being installed, check relationship of glass to adhesive caulk material on pinch weld flange. Gaps in excess of 1/8 in. must be corrected by shimming or by applying more adhesive caulk material. If more caulk is needed, apply a smooth continuous bead around entire inside edge of glass. Material should be 1/16 to 3/16 in. in diameter, Fig. 20-7.

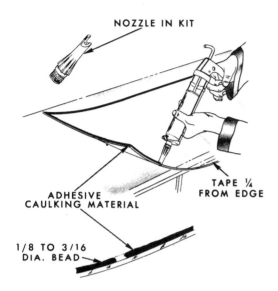

Fig. 20-7. Short method of applying adhesive material.

When glass is in proper position in opening, apply a piece of masking tape over each side edge of glass and adjacent to body pillar. Slit tape vertically at edge of glass. During installation, type on glass can be aligned with tape on body to guide window into desired position.

Using clean lint-free cloth, liberally dampened with adhesive caulking primer, briskly rub primer over original adhesive material remaining on pinch weld flange.

While allowing primer to dry for 5 to 10 min. apply 1 in. wide masking tape to inside of windshield glass 1/4 in. inboard from edge of glass, across top and down each side, to facilitate cleaning after installation. Wipe surface of glass to which adhesive caulking compound will be applied (around edge of inside surface) with a clean water dampened cloth. Dry glass with a clean cloth. Apply continuous bead of adhesive caulking material around entire inside edge of glass. Material should be 1/8 to 3/16 in. in diameter, Fig. 20-7.

Due to fast curing characteristics of adhesive caulking material, glass installation should be completed within 15 min. from start of application of material to glass.

With the aid of a helper, lift the glass into the opening. On back window installations it will be necessary to use suction cups to position glass in opening. Windshield glass can be positioned without the aid of carrying devices. As shown in Fig. 20-8, carry glass with one hand on inside of glass and one hand on outside. At opening, put glass in horizontal position. While one man holds glass in this position, second man can reach one arm around body pillar and support glass while other man assumes same position. Quarter window glass can be installed in the same manner.

Using tape guides previously installed, carefully position glass in opening. Guide outer lower surface of glass along rear edge of front fenders, making certain glass is properly centered and positioned on lower metal supports.

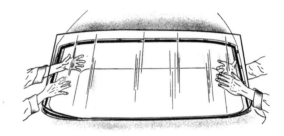

Fig. 20-8. Installation of windshield glass. Fisher method.

Press glass firmly to "wet-out" and "set" caulking material. Use care to avoid excessive squeeze out which would cause an appearance problem.

Water test car immediately, using cold water spray. Do not direct strong stream of water at fresh adhesive material. If any leaks are found, paddle-in extra adhesive material at leak point using a flat bladed tool.

Complete job by replacing reveal molding and other trim. Also remove masking tape from inner surface of glass.

## EXTENDED METHOD OF INSTALLING ADHESIVE CAULKED GLASS

If adhesive caulked material remaining in windshield or rear window opening after removal of glass is damaged, or must be removed to permit refinishing of glass opening, or has insufficient adhesion to body material to serve as a base for replacement glass, it will be necessary to use the extended installation method. The procedure is as follows:

Remove screw retained lower glass supports on windshield. Using a sharp scraper or chisel, remove major portion of old caulking material from opening flanges around entire opening. It is not necessary that all traces of material be removed, but there should not be any mounds or loose pieces left.

Inspect reveal molding clips. If upper end of clip is bent away from the body metal more than 1/32 in., replace or reform clip.

Using black weatherstrip adhesive, or adhesive caulking material, cement rubber spacers to window opening pinch weld flanges, Fig. 20-9, location B. Spacers should be positioned to provide equal support around entire perimeter of glass.

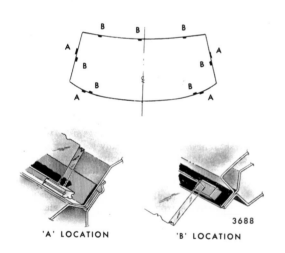

'A' LOCATION     'B' LOCATION

*Fig. 20-9. Showing location of spacers on window pinch weld flange (Fisher).*

If weatherstrip adhesive is used, apply sufficient material to obtain a watertight seal beneath spacer, however, DO NOT allow excessive squeeze out. Weatherstrip adhesive is not compatible with replacement adhesive caulking compound and water leaks may develop at locations where these two materials are used together to form a seal.

Fig. 20-9, location A, illustrates rectangu-

lar spacers positioned in typical back window installations. Reinstall metal supports at lower edge of windshield glass (in lieu of two lower A spacers indicated in back window installation).

With aid of a helper, lift glass into position. On back window installations it will be necessary to use suction cups to position glass in opening. With one hand on each side of glass, put window in vertical position and support it on lower glass support spacers. While one man holds glass in this position, second man can reach one arm around body pillar and support glass while other man assumes same position. With glass positioned in opening, check relationship of glass to pinch weld flange around entire perimeter. Overlap of pinch weld flange should be equal with a minimum overlap of 3/16 in. Overlap across top of windshield may be corrected by repositioning lower metal support spacers. Overlap across top of back window may be varied by shimming or shaving lower glass support spacers.

Check relationship of glass contour to body opening. Gap space between glass and pinch weld flange should be no less that 1/8 in., nor more than 1/4 in. Correction can be made by repositioning flat spacers, or by applying more caulking material, by reworking pinch weld flange or by selecting another glass.

After final adjustments have been made and glass is in correct position, apply pieces of masking tape over edges of glass and body, depending on glass being installed. Tape on glass can be aligned with tape on body to guide glass into opening during final installation.

Remove glass from opening and apply one inch masking tape around inner surface of glass 1/4 in. inboard from outer edge. On windshield installations, apply tape to top and sides only. Do not use tape across bottom. Remove tape after glass installation to aid in cleanup and give a smooth even edge to adhesive material.

Using clean lint-free cloth liberally dampened with adhesive caulking primer, briskly rub primer over original adhesive remaining on pinch weld flange.

While primer is drying (five to ten minutes), notch caulking gun as indicated in Fig. 20-10, carefully apply caulking material 3/8 in. high and 3/16 in. wide at base, Fig. 20-10. As caulking material begins to cure within 15 min. of exposure to air, glass must be installed as quickly as possible. Using tape guides previously applied carefully position glass in opening. Guide lower outer surface of glass along rear edge of front fenders to avoid smearing fresh adhesive caulk material on instrument panel, Fig. 20-8. Make sure glass is properly aligned to tape guides on pillars, and positioned on lower metal supports. Apply light hand pressure to "wet-out" adhesive material and obtain bond to body opening.

*Fig. 20-11. Removing windshield lower molding (Chrysler-Plymouth).*

fiber wedge, Fig. 20-11. Remove the windshield upper molding using fiber wedge. Unlock the windshield weatherstrip by prying the lip of the weatherstrip apart, by inserting a fiber wedge and with a slight twist of the wedge, block the weatherstrip by moving the tool around the weatherstrip.

Carefully loosen the weatherstrip from the windshield inner and outer sides. Then with an assistant supporting one end of the windshield, exert pressure to force the windshield out of the weatherstrip and carefully remove the windshield from the vehicle.

When installing a windshield in Plymouth and most other Chrysler built vehicles, first remove old sealer and cement from original weatherstrip. Then apply sealer in fence and glass groove portions of weatherstrip. On Valiant models install filler strip in lower part of weatherstrip. Apply a 3/8 in. bead of sealer cement completely across cowl top panel lower windshield frame area, Fig. 20-12A. Position weatherstrip lower section to tab area, starting at corners install over

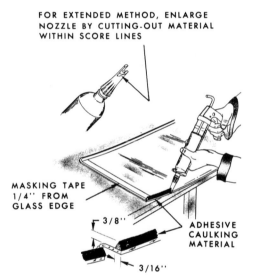

FOR EXTENDED METHOD, ENLARGE NOZZLE BY CUTTING-OUT MATERIAL WITHIN SCORE LINES

MASKING TAPE 1/4" FROM GLASS EDGE

3/8"

ADHESIVE CAULKING MATERIAL

3/16"

*Fig. 20-10. Application of adhesive material by Fisher extended method.*

Water test installation as previously described, allowing water to spill over edges of glass. If water leak is encountered, work-in additional caulking material at leak point. Complete job by installation of reveal moldings.

## WINDSHIELD SERVICE (CHRYSLER)

The first step in removal of the windshield as used on Chrysler built cars starts with the removal of the chrome moldings from the windshield. Remove the windshield lower moldings and molding center cap using a

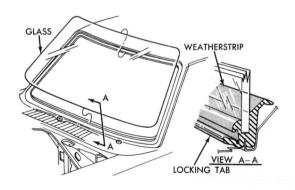

GLASS

WEATHERSTRIP

A

A

VIEW A-A

LOCKING TAB

*Fig. 20-12A. Details of windshield installation on Plymouth. Other cars are similar.*

tabs and work toward center. Install weather-strip on fence at sides and upper opening. With hand pressure, seat weatherstrip fully on fence. With assistance, slide upper edge of glass into channel of weatherstrip. Use a fiber tool to force weatherstrip over glass, Fig. 20-12A. Seat glass in weatherstrip, pounding glass with palm of hand, using an upward movement. Insert a fiber tool between weatherstrip and glass, at either corner, slide tool across top and completely around windshield to seat glass in place.

Using a fiber tool and working across top, down sides and over bottom, force weather-strip locking tab into locked position, Fig. 20-12B.

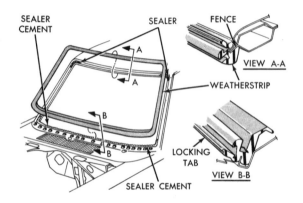

Fig. 20-12B. Showing details of sealer and cement on wind-shield weatherstrip on Plymouth.

After sealing the weatherstrip, align and install the chrome moldings and other parts which were removed prior to the removal of the windshield.

This description, while applying particu-larly to the Plymouth, also applies in general to other Chrysler built vehicles.

## WINDSHIELD SERVICE (FORD)

To remove a Ford windshield with a butyl seal, first remove the windshield wiper arms and then the windshield moldings. Using a special tool insert the blade under the edge of the glass, Fig. 20-13. Cut the butyl seal as close to the inside surface of the glass as possible. To cut the butyl at the lower cor-ners of the windshield, move the handle of the tool as close to the corner as possible.

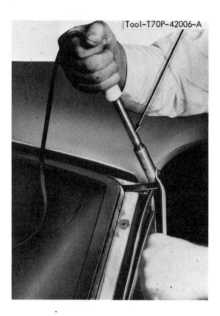

Fig. 20-13. Using a special tool to tape butyl seal from re-cent model Ford windshield.

Then rotate the blade downward to cut the corner butyl seal, Fig. 20-14. Remove the windshield from the vehicle, using the glass holding tool, Fig. 20-14.

To install a windshield in a recent model Ford with a butyl seal, first position the new windshield in the glass opening. Use the spacers provided with the special tool to prevent the glass from sticking to the butyl. Adjust the glass until it is properly seated. Mark the location of the glass.

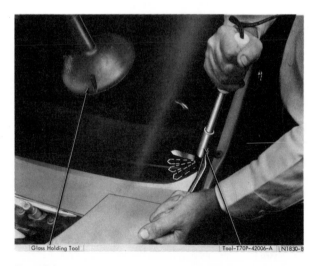

Fig. 20-14. Cutting corner seal with special tool on recent model Ford windshields.

Remove the glass and thoroughly clean the inside edge. Apply the butyl bead on top and in the center of the existing butyl all around the glass opening. Start at the side opposite the original butyl splice. Do not stretch the butyl. Apply primer to the inside edge of the glass where it will contact the butyl, Fig. 20-15. Allow the primer to dry for 10 min.

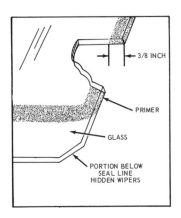

*Fig. 20-15. Installation of primer on Ford windshields using butyl type seal.*

Position the windshield in the body opening. With an assistant applying hand pressure from the outside, pull the draw cord to pull the lip of the weatherstrip over the windshield opening flange. Draw the weatherstrip lip over the lower flange, each side flange, and then the upper flange. Install the windshield interior garnish moldings.

To remove a Ford windshield with a weatherstrip type seal, first remove the glass outside moldings, Fig. 20-16. Note: If the moldings are retained with retainers set in the glass opening, the molding should be released from the retainers as shown in Fig. 20-16. On some models, it will be necessary to remove the cowl top grille and/or the roof rail weatherstrip at the A windshield pillar to gain access to the windshield molding retainers and/or retaining screws.

Remove the windshield interior garnish moldings. With an assistant, push the glass and weatherstrip from the windshield opening.

Clean all the sealer from the glass and/or weatherstrip if either is to be used again. Also clean all the sealer from the windshield opening.

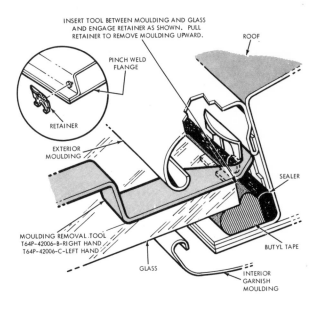

*Fig. 20-16. On Ford windshields with weatherstrip type seal the moldings are removed with a tool as shown.*

To install a windshield with weatherstrip type seal: Check all the molding retainers. Repair or replace damaged retainers to insure adequate molding retention. Replace any missing or damaged weld studs with screws. Apply sealer in the glass groove of the weatherstrip. Position the weatherstrip on the windshield.

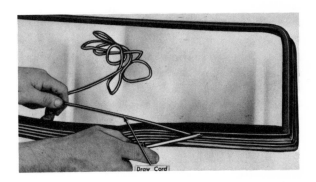

*Fig. 20-17. Installing a draw cord, prior to installation of Ford windshield with weatherstrip type seal.*

Insert a draw cord in the pinch weld opening of the weatherstrip all around the weatherstrip, Fig. 20-17, and overlap the cord about 18 in. at the lower center of the glass. Tape the ends of the cord to the glass as shown in Fig. 20-18.

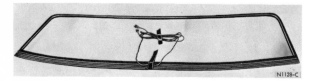

Fig. 20-18. Draw cord installed.

Position the glass in the glass opening and align the markings previously made. Press the glass firmly into seal, using only hand pressure. Inspect the appearance of the glass. A dull spot indicates an area where the glass is not contacting the butyl seal. Use additional pressure to seal these areas. When installing a windshield, no more than 0.20 in. clearance should exist between the surface of the glass and the pinch weld flange.

From the outside of the vehicle, apply liquid butyl sealer around the outer edge of the glass. Allow the liquid butyl sealer to form a skin, then water test the glass seal for leaks. Remove the excess primer from the inside of the glass with a razor blade. Wipe the glass with a cloth dampened with naptha. Install the windshield moldings and windshield wiper arms.

## GLASS POLISHING

Minor scratches on glass can be removed by polishing. A low speed polisher (600 to 1300 rpm) is used together with a wool felt polishing pad about 3 in. in diameter and 2 in. thick. Commercial polishes are available or cerium oxide can be used.

Fig. 20-19. Method of removing minor scratches from windshield glass.

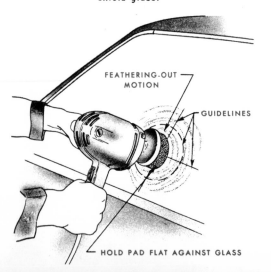

Mix a small quantity of polish with water to obtain a creamy consistency. Draw a circle on opposite side of glass from scratches to act as a guide when polishing. Dip the polishing pad in the polish and use a moderate but steady pressure against the scratched area of the glass. Use less pressure on outer edges of scratched area.

Do not hold tool in one spot. Also less polishing can be done on windshield as drivers vision may be affected.

## QUIZ - Chapter 20

1. Before removing the windshield glass or rear window glass from recent model Fisher bodies, it is necessary to remove all trim and hardware immediately adjacent to the glass being removed.
　　True.
　　False.
2. Windshields and back windows of recent model Fisher bodies are bonded to the body with an acrylic caulking compound.
　　True.
　　False.
3. How is the caulking compound cut on the windshields in Fisher bodies?
　　Sharp chisel.
　　Razor blade.
　　Steel music wire.
　　Knife blade.
4. How are the lower moldings on Chrysler and Plymouth windshields loosened?
　　Removal of clips.
　　Fiber wedge.
　　Removal of screws.
5. On Ford windshield of recent production cut the butyl seal as close to the inside of the glass as possible.
　　True.
　　False.
6. When installing a windshield on a Ford car, what is the purpose of the cord?
　　To cut through the synthetic compound.
　　To pull the lip of the weatherstrip over the body opening flange.
7. When polishing glass to remove small scratches, should a slow speed or fast speed polisher be used?
　　Slow.
　　Fast.

# Chapter 21
# POWER SEATS, WINDOWS, TOPS, TAIL GATES

Power operated seats, windows and tops are electrically operated, and it is, therefore, important that the storage battery be in a fully charged condition in order to have satisfactory operation of the units. Equally important is the condition of the wiring and connections. Insulation must be in good condition, and all electrical connections must be tight.

The electrical motors used to operate these accessories are either the series or multiple wound units. The series type motor should never be operated without a load, otherwise the high rotational speed which it develops will damage the motor.

Unless otherwise specified, frictional surfaces of the transmissions used should be lubricated with "Lubriplate" or some similar lubricant. Such frictional surfaces include: Gears, thrust washers, dog washers, gear shaft, solenoid plungers, etc.

There are power operated seats adjustable in two ways, four ways, and six ways. Four-way seats will be discussed, as they are the most typical.

## FOUR-WAY TILT SEAT (FISHER)

The four-way tilt front seat assembly as used on many General Motors cars is shown in Fig. 21-1. The seat adjusters are actuated by a 12 V reversible shunt wound motor with a built-in circuit breaker. The motor is installed at the left side of the seat assembly,

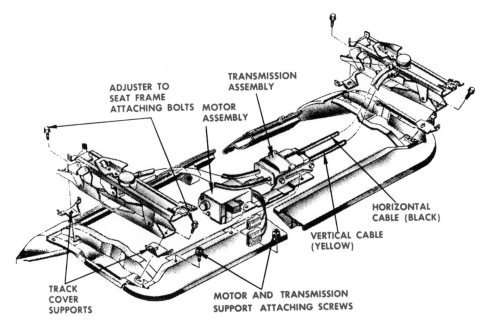

*Fig. 21-1. Four-way tilt seat assembly.*

139

Fig. 21-1, and is controlled by a toggle type control switch installed in the left seat side panel.

The seat adjuster operating mechanism incorporates a transmission assembly which includes two solenoids and four drive cables leading to the seat adjusters. One solenoid controls the vertical movement of the seat, while the other solenoid controls the horizontal movement. When the control switch is actuated, the motor and one of the solenoids are energized simultaneously. Then the solenoid plunger engages with the driving geardog. When the adjusters reach their limit of travel, the drive cables stop their rotating action and torque is absorbed by the rubber coupler connecting the motor and transmission. When the switch contacts are opened, a return spring returns the solenoid plunger to its original position, disengaging it from the driving geardog.

## FOUR-WAY SEAT (FORD)

The power seat (four-way type) as installed on Fords is controlled by a single toggle switch which can be operated in four directions. The switch, mounted on the front seat cushion left side shield and independent of the ignition switch, controls a single electric motor.

When the switch is operated for vertical seat motion, the left solenoid actuates the clutch and transmits power to the vertical screw. The seat is raised or lowered by two pivot arms at each side of the seat. The vertical motion is transmitted to the right seat track by a vertical equalizer bar. When the switch is operated fore-or-aft movement of the seat, the right solenoid actuates the clutch and couples the motor to the horizontal screw. The fore-and-aft motion is transmitted to the right seat track by the horizontal equalizer bar.

Fig. 21-2, shows the wiring diagram of the power seat used on recent model Ford cars. The following symptoms are sometimes found in power seat failures: (The battery must be in a fully charged condition before any tests are made). If the seat does not operate in any direction, the cause is most likely to be an open circuit or power failure due to defective wiring, 20 amp. circuit breaker, switch, or motor.

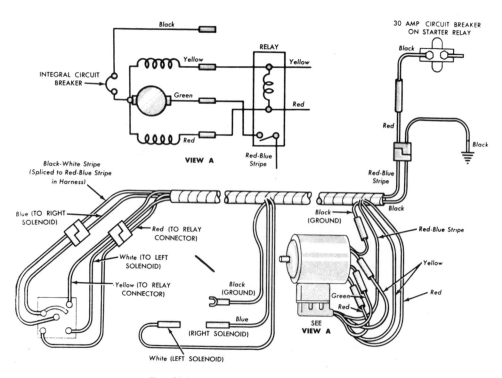

*Fig. 21-2. Four-way power seat wiring.*

If the seat moves in one plane only, the cause is most likely to be a defective solenoid, switch, or wires from the switch solenoid.

## POWER WINDOWS (FISHER)

The wiring harness for electrically operated windows on recent model Fisher bodies consists of four major sections, and in the 1971 models five sections. The crossover harness is installed beneath the instrument panel. The impact bar and reinforcements incorporated into some door construction reduces the accessibility for power wiring harness. Therefore if replacement of wiring harness should be necessary, attach a leader to the end of the harness before removal from the door. This will permit drawing the new harness into position.

## TROUBLE SHOOTING

The following typical failures and corrections are provided as an aid in locating the cause of troubles.

If none of the windows operate, the trouble may be caused by a short or open circuit in the power feed circuit. When that occurs check operation of the circuit breaker. Also operation of ignition relay. Also check feed connection to power harness beneath instrument panel. Also check feed circuit wires for possible short or open circuit. On Cadillac styles only check window black-out switch.

If right rear window does not operate from master control switch on left door or from control switch on right rear door and left door window operates, there are four possible causes: (1) Short or open circuit between right rear door harness and power window front harness. (2) Short or open circuit in affected window control switch or window motor circuit. (3) Possible mechanical failure or bind in window channels. (4) Defective window motor. To correct these conditions, first check harness connectors beneath outer end of instrument panel for proper installation. Also check wires in power window front harness for possible open or short circuit. Also check operation of rear door window control switch. Also check cir-

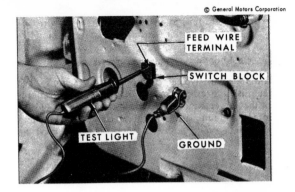

*Fig. 21-3. Checking feed circuit of Fisher power window.*

cuit from window control switch to window motor for open or short circuit. Also check window regulator and channels for possible mechanical failure or bind. Also check operation or motor.

If right door windows will operate from left door master control switch but will not operate from right door control switch and left doors will operate, check for short circuit or open circuit in front harness feed wire circuit. Follow up feed wire in front harness for possible short or open circuit.

To check feed circuit continuity at circuit breaker: (1) Connect one test light lead to battery side of circuit breaker and ground other lead. If tester does not light, there is an open circuit or short circuit in feed circuit to breaker. (2) To check circuit breaker, disconnect the output feed wire (the wire opposite the power source feed to the breaker) from the breaker and with test light, check terminal from which wire was disconnected. If tester does not light, the circuit breaker is inoperative.

To check ignition relay assembly; with test light, check relay feed (orange/black wire). If tester does not light, there is an open or short circuit between relay and circuit breaker. Turn ignition switch on and with test light check output terminal of relay (red/white wire). If tester does not light; put test light on ignition relay terminal (pink or tan wire). If tester lights replace ignition relay. If tester does not light, locate short or open circuit along pink or tan wire. Also check fuse at dash panel.

To check for current at Master Control Switch, place ignition switch in "on" position. Connect one test lead to master window control switch feed terminal (red-white

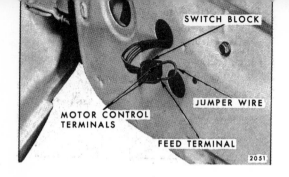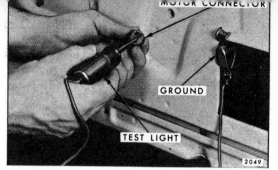

© General Motors Corporation

*Fig. 21-4. Left. Checking window control switch (Fisher). Fig. 21-4A. Right. Checking circuit between switch and motor of power window (Fisher Body).*

stripe) of switch block and ground other test lead. If tester does not light, there is an open or short circuit between relay and master control switch.

To check feed circuit continuity at window control switch connect one test lead to feed terminal of switch block and ground other test lead to body metal, Fig. 21-3. If tester does not light there is an open or short circuit between switch and power source.

To check window control switch: Insert one end of a No. 12 gauge jumper wire to switch feed terminal and the other end to one of the motor leads terminal in the switch block. Repeat this check on the remaining motor lead terminal, Fig. 21-4. If window operates with jumper wire, but does not operate with switch, the switch is defective.

To check wires between door window switch and door window motor, disengage harness connector from window motor. The thumb release on the harness connector must be depressed before it can be disengaged from the motor. Insert one end of No. 12 gauge jumper wire to switch feed terminal and the other end to one of the motor lead terminals in the switch block, Fig. 21-4. With test light, check for current at motor harness connector terminal being tested. If tester does not light there is an open or a short circuit in the harness between the control switch and the motor connector, Fig. 21-4A. Also check other terminal.

## POWER WINDOWS (FORD)

A wiring diagram of recent model Ford power windows is given in Fig. 21-5. Before making any of the following trouble checks, make sure battery is fully charged and turn ignition switch to accessory position:

The power window, power seat and convertible top electrical systems are connected through the same 20 amp. circuit breaker. If failure occurs in all systems at same time, 20 amp. circuit breaker is probably defective.

If all the windows do not operate, check to make sure that current is reaching the circuit breaker and if no voltage is available repair or replace the circuit breaker or wires leading to it.

If one window does not operate, operate the switch and listen for the noise of the motor running free. If the motor is running, it is loose and has pulled away from its coupling. Short out the ground circuit breaker of the inoperative window and operate the switch. If the motor runs, replace the circuit breaker.

If the window operates in one direction only, check the window operation with both switches. If window operates properly with one switch but not the other, check the switch and the red and yellow wires for voltage. Replace switch or wires as necessary.

If the window operates sluggishly check the regulator and window runs for excessive friction. Adjust the runs, repair and lubricate the regulator. Lubricate runs with silicone lubricant. Be sure to check for frayed insulation where wires may partially ground.

## POWER TOP OPERATION (FISHER)

On recent model General Motors cars equipped with power operated tops, the hydraulic-electric unit consists of a 12 volt reversible type motor, a rotor-type pump, two hydraulic lift cylinders and upper and lower hydraulic hose assembly. The unit is installed in the body directly behind rear seat back, Fig. 21-6.

Fig. 21-7 illustrates and identifies the individual parts of the motor and pump assembly.

When servicing the motor assembly or pump end plate assembly, it is important that the small motor shaft "O" ring seal is properly installed over the motor armature shaft and into the pump and plate assembly prior to installing the pump rotor or the rotor shaft drive ball.

When the control switch is actuated to the up position, the battery feed wire is connected to the red motor lead and the motor and pump assembly operate to force the hydraulic fluid through the hoses to the lower ends of the double acting cylinders. The fluid presses piston rods upward, thus raising the

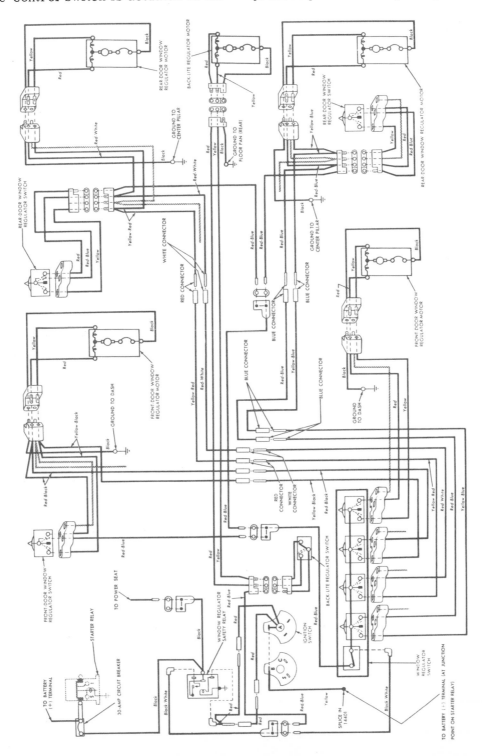

*Fig. 21-5. Power window wiring diagram as used on some Ford cars.*

top. The fluid in the top of the cylinders returns to the pump for recirculation to the bottom of the cylinders. When the control switch knob is actuated to the down position,

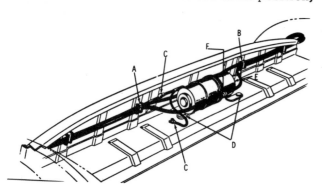

Fig. 21-6. Hydraulic-electric motor and pump assembly.

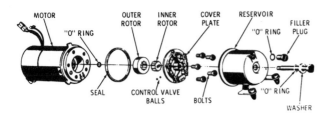

Fig. 21-7. Motor and pump disassembled.

the feed wire is connected to the dark green motor lead, and the motor and pump assembly operates in a reverse direction to force the hydraulic fluid through the hoses to the top of the cylinders. This forces the piston rod and the cylinders downward, thus lowering the top. The fluid in the bottom of the cylinders returns to the pump for recirculation to the top of the cylinder.

If there is a failure in the hydraulic electric system and the cause is not evident, the mechanical operation of the top should first be checked. If the folding top assembly appears to have a binding action, disconnect the top lift cylinder piston rods from the top linkage, and then manually raise and lower the top. The top should travel through its up-and-down cycle without any evidence of a binding action. If a binding action is noted when the top is being locked at the header, check the alignment of the door windows, ventilators and rear quarter windows with relation to the side roof rail weatherstrips.

Make adjustments necessary for correct top operation. If a failure continues to exist after a check for mechanical failure has been completed, the hydraulic-electric system should then be checked for electrical or hydraulic failures.

If a failure in the hydraulic-electric system continues to exist after the mechanical operation has been checked, the electrical system should be checked. A failure in the electrical system may be caused by a low battery, breaks in the wiring, faulty connections, mechanical failure of an electrical component, or wires or components shorting to one another or to body metal. Before beginning checking procedure, make sure the battery is in a fully charged condition.

To fill the hydraulic-electric reservoir, a filler plug adapter should be made as follows: Drill a quarter inch diameter hole through center of a spare reservoir filler plug. Install two inch length of metal tubing (1/4 in. OD by 3/16 in. ID) into center of filler plug and solder tubing on both sides of filler plug to form airtight connections.

Then to fill and bleed the reservoir, place the top in a raised position and remove folding top compartment bag material from rear seat back panel. Remove pump and water shield.

Place absorbent rags below reservoir at filler plug. Using a straight-blade screwdriver, slowly remove filler plug from reservoir.

When installing new or overhauled motor and pump assembly, as a bench operation, fill reservoir to specified level with hydraulic fluid. This operation is necessary as pump must be primed prior to operation to avoid drawing excessive amounts of air into hydraulic system.

Install filler plug adapter to reservoir and attach 4 or 5 in. length of 3/16-in. ID rubber tubing or hose to filler plug tubing.

Install opposite end of hose into a container of hydraulic brake fluid, Fig. 21-8. Note: Container should be placed in rear compartment area of body, below level of fluid in the reservoir. In addition, sufficient fluid must be available in container to avoid drawing air into hydraulic system.

Operate top to down or stacked position.

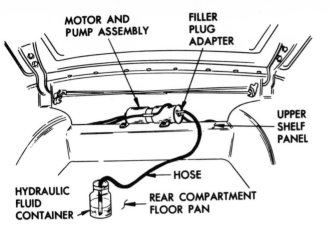

Fig. 21-8. Bleeding hydraulic system.

After top is fully lowered, continue to operate motor and pump assembly for approximately 20 seconds or until noise level of pump is noticeably reduced. Reduction in pump noise level indicates that hydraulic system is filling with fluid.

Operate top several times or until operation of top is consistently smooth in both up-and-down cycles.

With top in down position, remove filler plug tubing and remove filler plug adapter

the trouble is not readily apparent, it is advisable to make the following mechanical electrical and hydraulic tests to find the cause of the trouble:

First, check the battery.

If the action of the top is slow, raise and lower it slowly and look for bent or misaligned linkage. If binding is noted when clamping the top at the header, check the alignment of the door and quarter windows with the side rail weatherstrips. Also check the top sag adjustment and toggle clamp adjustment.

To check the current in the operating circuit, disconnect the black wire at the circuit breaker (located on the starter relay) and connect an ammeter in series in the circuit. Operate the top control switch and note the ammeter readings. The current draw should be 35 amp. maximum operating and 40-50 amp. stalled, with a voltage reading of 9-10 volts. Current in excess of 75 amp. indicates a frozen pump or cylinder, or a mechanical

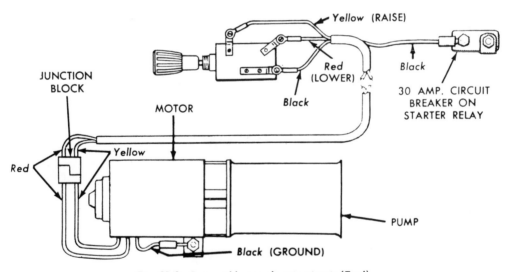

Fig. 21-9. Convertible top electric circuit (Ford).

from reservoir. Check level of fluid in reservoir and reinstall original filler plug hole. The fluid level should be within 1/4 in. of lower edge of filler plug hole.

## POWER TOP OPERATION (FORD)

If the power top as installed on Ford automobiles cannot be lowered or raised satisfactorily, or if it fails to operate at all, and

obstruction. Low amperage with the motor running and no top movement, indicates a defective pump or low fluid metal in the reservoir.

The convertible top electrical circuit is shown in Fig. 21-9.

If the top is misaligned, correction should be made after a check has been made for bent linkage. Before aligning the top, visually determine if the trouble results from top

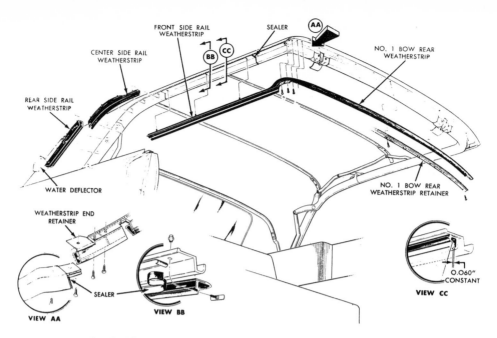

Fig. 21-10. Convertible top weatherstrip and adjustment (Ford).

misalignment or window misalignment. It may be necessary to align both the top and the windows, because of the relationship between the two. Adjustments of the door and quarter windows must be checked and any necessary changes made before making top adjustment. These windows must be fully closed to insure proper adjustment.

The side rail weatherstrips can be adjusted laterally and also fore-and-aft, Fig. 21-10. Adjust the weatherstrips laterally so that the sealing lips make full contact with the door and window frames. Adjust the weatherstrips fore-or-aft to butt the ends of the weatherstrips together for a watertight seal.

The striker plates must be aligned with

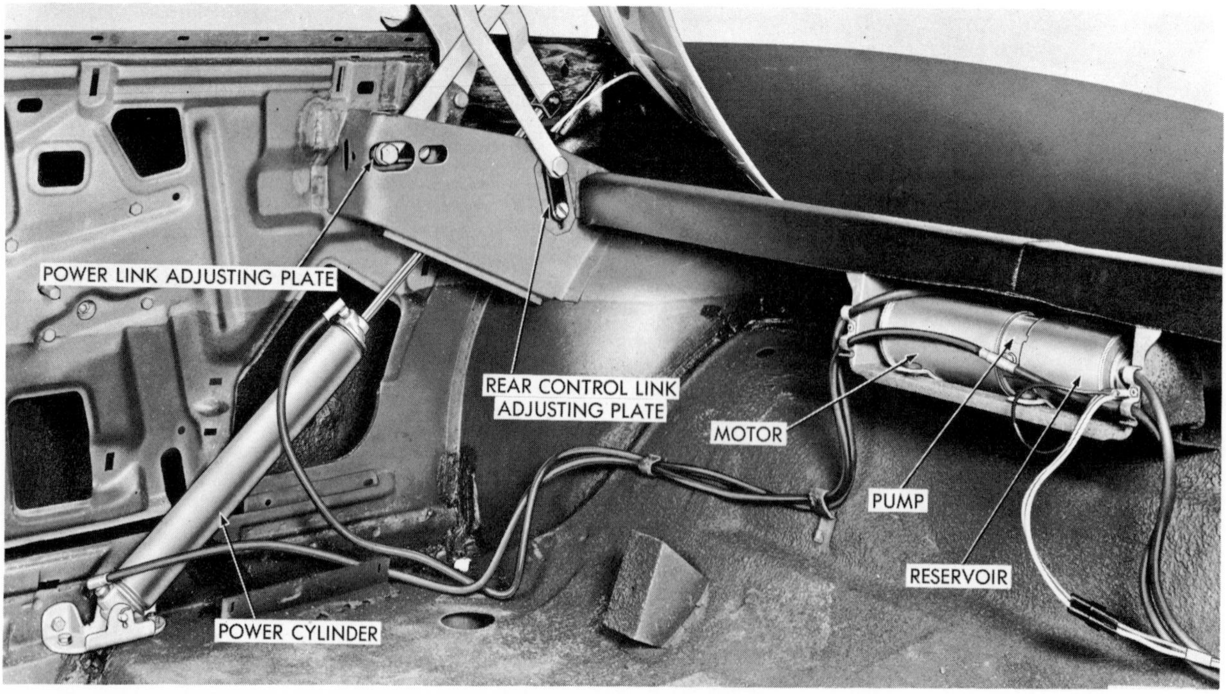

Fig. 21-11. Power top equipment as installed on Plymouth (typical).

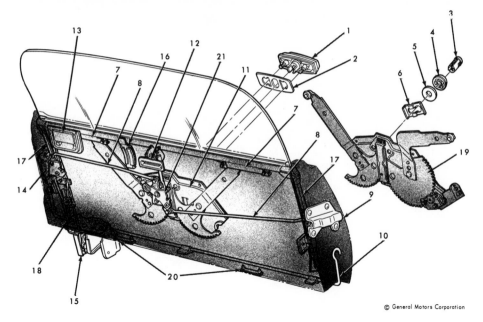

© General Motors Corporation

*Fig. 21-12. Dual acting tail gate hardware.*  (Fisher Body)

1. Outside handle
2. Gasket
3. Lock cylinder
4. Elec. feed block
5. Gasket
6. Lock cylinder retainer
7. Sash channel cam

8. Remote control con. rod
9. Left upper lock and hinge
10. Torque rod
11. Regulator, manual
12. Inside remote gate handle
13. Inside door handle and cable
14. Right upper lock

15. Right lower lock
16. Glass stabilizer
17. Lower glass run channels
18. Glass block-out rod
19. Regulator, electrical
20. Sealing strip
21. Remote control assembly
    (Gate operation)

the dowel pins prior to making other top adjustments. The dowel pins are not adjustable. A slight lateral movement of the striker plate is provided by loosening the striker plate retaining screws.

The toggle clamps that hold the header bow against the header can be adjusted to provide a good seal. To determine which side is not sealing, check the weatherstrip between the heading bow and the header. Refer to Fig. 21-10, for side rail weatherstrip installation. Both toggle clamps need not be adjusted unless necessary. Release the toggle clamps and thread the toggle hook in or out until adequate sealing pressure is applied at the header weatherstrip. Excessive tightening of the toggle hooks will distort the number one bow and cause poor weatherstrip sealing.

## POWER TOP OPERATION (CHRYSLER)

Principles of operation of the power top unit as installed on Chrysler built vehicles are similar to that used on General Motors cars. A typical installation is shown in Fig. 21-11.

## DUAL ACTING TAIL GATE (FISHER)

The dual acting tail gate incorporates a unique hinge and locking arrangement that permits the tail gate to be operated in the conventional manner and, in addition, as a door. All wagons so equipped utilize either a manually or electrically operated window that can be lowered into the gate or raised into the back body opening. The manual window is operated by a regulator control handle located in the tail gate outer panel. The power window can be operated by any one of three control switches; one on the instrument panel, one at the lock cylinder on tail gate outer panel (key operated) and one on the wheelhouse cover panel. The tail gate is unlocked to "gate position" by means of a remote control inside handle located in the top center of gate inner panel. Unlocking to "do or position" is accomplished with an inside handle located at top right side of inner panel. The tail gate cannot be opened in either direction, however, until the window has been fully lowered.

Following any replacement or realignment of the tail gate, or component hardware, all

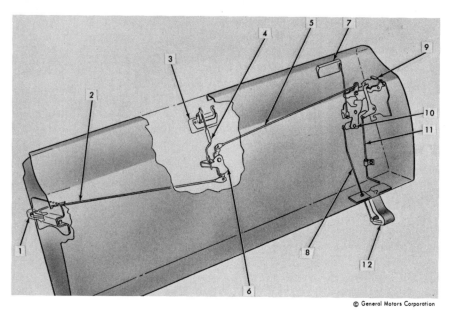

© General Motors Corporation

*Fig. 21-13. Dual acting tail gate lock and remote control linkage.   (Fisher Body)*

locks must be checked for synchronization.

Details of the dual acting tail gate hardware are shown in Fig. 21-12, and the lock and remote control linkage in Fig. 21-13.

## SYNCHRONIZATION CHECK AND PROCEDURE

The lock system on the dual acting tail gate is designed to perform the following two "block out" functions:

1. Allow the tail gate to be opened as a door and at the same time prevent accidental operation of the upper left lock (which allows the gate to be opened as a gate).

2. Allow the gate to be opened and closed as a tail gate and at the same time prevent accidental operation of the lower right lock (which allows the gate to be opened as a door).

The above "block out" functions are accomplished by levers in the upper right lock, Fig. 21-14. That illustration shows the upper right lock (in closed door position) and identifies the levers which perform block out functions.

To assure that the upper right lock levers perform the block out functions properly, the upper right lock and gate remote control must be synchronized with the rest of the tail gate system (lower right lock and upper left lock). This synchronization is required to prevent accidental operation of the upper left lock when the gate is opened as a door and to prevent accidental operation of the lower right lock when the gate is opened as a gate.

IMPORTANT: When locking system components inside the tail gate are serviced, the locking system MUST be synchronized.

## LOCK SYNCHRONIZATION CHECKS

1. Synchronization check for lower right lock.
   A. Open tail gate as a gate (horizontal position). Take precautions to prevent damage if tail gate should become disengaged from the lower right lock by placing a protective support beneath the gate. Then grasp right inside lock release handle and pull upward until the gate is in the vertical position and close gate. Open gate as a door and close gate.
   B. Repeat above procedure (Step 1-A) five times. If tail gate lower right lock does not become disengaged, synchronization of lower right lock is correct. If tail gate becomes disengaged at lower right lock, reinstall gate on lower right lock and proceed with "synchronization" as described and illustrated.

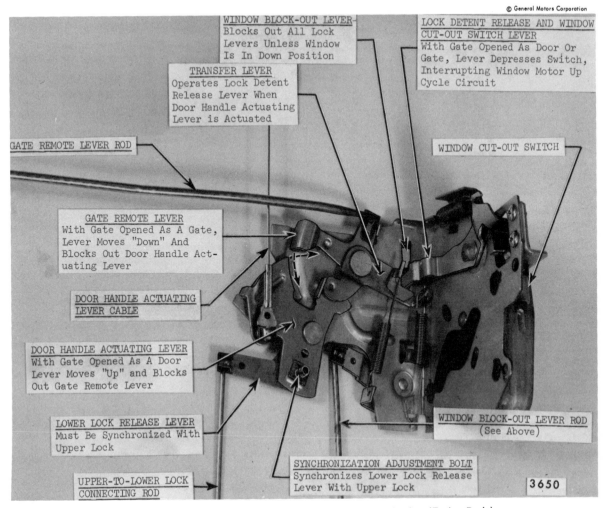

© General Motors Corporation

WINDOW BLOCK-OUT LEVER
Blocks Out All Lock
Levers Unless Window
Is In Down Position

LOCK DETENT RELEASE AND WINDOW
CUT-OUT SWITCH LEVER
With Gate Opened As Door Or
Gate, Lever Depresses Switch,
Interrupting Window Motor Up
Cycle Circuit

TRANSFER LEVER
Operates Lock Detent
Release Lever When
Door Handle Actuating
Lever is Actuated

GATE REMOTE LEVER ROD

WINDOW CUT-OUT SWITCH

GATE REMOTE LEVER
With Gate Opened As A Gate,
Lever Moves "Down" And
Blocks Out Door Handle Act-
uating Lever

DOOR HANDLE ACTUATING
LEVER CABLE

DOOR HANDLE ACTUATING LEVER
With Gate Opened As A Door
Lever Moves "Up" and Blocks
Out Gate Remote Lever

LOWER LOCK RELEASE LEVER
Must Be Synchronized With
Upper Lock

WINDOW BLOCK-OUT LEVER ROD
(See Above)

UPPER-TO-LOWER LOCK
CONNECTING ROD

SYNCHRONIZATION ADJUSTMENT BOLT
Synchronizes Lower Lock Release
Lever With Upper Lock

3650

*Fig. 21-14. Dual acting tail gate lock synchronization check. (Fisher Body)*

2. Synchronization check for upper right and left locks.
   A. Open tail gate as door.
      Important: Place a protective support under right side of gate in the event gate becomes disengaged from upper left lock.
   B. Operate center remote control handle (gate operation) with a moderately heavy pressure, then operate right inside lock release lever (door operation) in the same manner. Operate both handles at the same time.
   C. Close tail gate and repeat above operation (Step 2-A and B) five times. If tail gate upper left lock does not become disengaged, the upper locks are in synchronization. If tail gate becomes disengaged at the upper left lock, re-

install gate at upper left lock and proceed with "synchronization procedure" which follows.

## LOCK SYNCHRONIZATION PROCEDURE

1. Open gate as a door then close securely. Open to "gate" (horizontal position).
2. Remove tail gate inner cover panel; carefully remove inner panel water deflector or detach water deflector sufficiently to gain access to gate remote control and door lock synchronization bolts. Remove right inner panel access hole cover.
3. Place tape over door lock handle to prevent accidental operation of lower right lock after upper locks have been manually locked as outlined below.

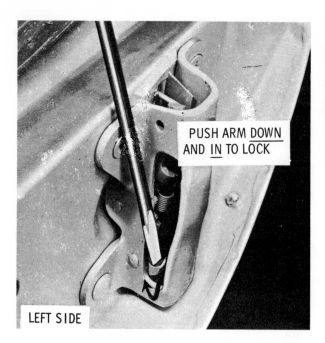

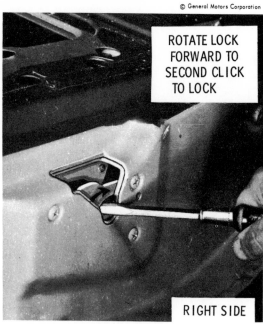

*Fig. 21-15. Dual acting tail gate right and left upper lock manual locking. (Fisher Body).*

4. Manually lock both upper right and upper left locks as shown in Fig. 21-15.

5. With all locks in locked position, visually check gate remote synchronization holes in gate remote control levers (center of gate as shown in Fig. 21-16). If holes line up, proceed with step 7. If the holes do not line up, loosen (turn to right approximately three turns) gate remote control synchronization bolt (this bolt has left hand threads). With synchronization bolt loose, check that there is no bind in remote levers. Align holes by inserting a cotter pin through alignment hole in both levers (Fig. 21-16). Then tighten synchronization bolt to 57-87 in. lb. Remove cotter pin.

6. With all locks in locked position and with the right lower lock securely engaged with the striker, loosen by approximately three turns, the door lock remote synchronization bolt at upper right lock, Fig. 21-16.

This adjustment is "self seeking" and and should automatically synchronize the right upper and lower locks when the synchronizing bolt is loosened. However, to assure that the levers automatically assume their proper position, reach in through the access hole and hold lower-to-upper lock connecting rod FORWARD Fig. 21-16, while tightening door lock synchronization bolt to 76-116 in. lb. Make sure tab on door lock remote synchronization lever is properly engaged in hole.

Note: The action of loosening the lock synchronization bolt can readily unlock the right lower lock causing the right side of the gate to disengage from the striker. To help prevent this from occurring, reach through access hole and hold the upper-to-lower lock connecting rod, Fig. 21-16, FORWARD while loosening synchronization bolts.

If lower right lock should unlock and become disengaged from striker, lift right side of tail gate up and forward to reengage lock with striker.

7. Unlock upper locks by actuating tail gate handle at center of gate.

8. Remove tape from door handle and close gate.

9. Perform lock synchronization checks, check window operation.

10. Reseal tail gate inner panel water deflector and install tail gate inner cover panel.

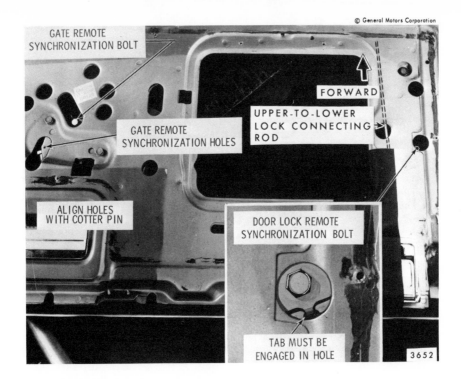

GATE REMOTE SYNCHRONIZATION BOLT

GATE REMOTE SYNCHRONIZATION HOLES

FORWARD

UPPER-TO-LOWER LOCK CONNECTING ROD

ALIGN HOLES WITH COTTER PIN

DOOR LOCK REMOTE SYNCHRONIZATION BOLT

TAB MUST BE ENGAGED IN HOLE

© General Motors Corporation

3652

*Fig. 21-16. Dual acting tail gate lock synchronization check. (Fisher Body)*

## QUIZ - Chapter 21

1. What is the first check to be made when trouble shooting power operated seats?
    Electric motor.
    Condition of the starting battery.
    Wiring circuit.

2. What type of motor is used to operate the four-way tilt seat on General Motors cars?
    Series wound.
    Compound wound.
    Shunt wound.

3. On the four-way seat installed on Ford cars, vertical motion is transmitted to the right seat track by a vertical equalizer bar.
    True.
    False.

4. The wiring harness on 1971 electrically operated windows on Fisher bodies consists of how many major sections?
    Four.
    Five.
    Three.
    Six.

5. To check feed circuit continuity at window control switch on recent model Fisher bodies, connect one lead to feed terminal of switch block and ground the other lead.
    True.
    False.

6. The power window, power seat and convertible top electrical systems are connected through the same 20 amp. circuit breaker on Ford cars.
    True.
    False.

7. If the action of a power operated top is slow and the battery is in good condition, the next point to check is bent or misaligned linkage.
    True.
    False.

8. Toggle clamps that hold the header bow against the header cannot be adjusted on Ford installations of the power operated top.
    True.
    False.

9. How many control switches are provided with the dual acting tail gate on Fisher bodies.
    One.
    Two.
    Three.
    Four.

10. Is it necessary to check all locks for synchronization on Fisher dual acting tail gates.
    Yes.
    No.

# Chapter 22
# RECOVERING CONVERTIBLE TOPS
# FABRIC ROOFS, WOODGRAIN OVERLAY

While the following description applies particularly to the method of removing and installing the fabric top on Ford convertible cars, it can also be used in general for other vehicles.

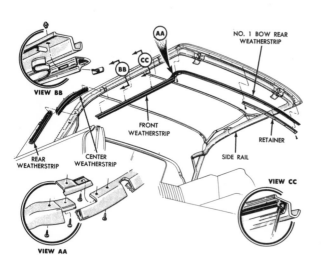

*Fig. 22-1. Weatherstrip installation on convertible.*

In the case of Ford cars the convertible top consists of the deck and two side quarters, bonded into one piece of material. The bonded seams eliminate the possibility of leaks, and also separation, due to thread deterioration. In most cases, it will be advantageous to replace the back curtain when replacing the top fabric.

To remove the top fabric, first place a protective cover across the deck, cowl and hood to prevent scratching the finish when replac-ing the top.

Remove the rear seat cushion and seat back. Raise the top to gain access to the underside of the front bow. Remove the front weatherstrip retainer, Fig. 22-1, and the weatherstrip.

Remove the two front side rail weatherstrip retainers and the weatherstrips.

Remove the two center side rail and the two rear side rail weatherstrips. Remove the metal screw and washer that secures each end of the folding top compartment weld to the pivot bracket supports.

Starting at one end of the compartment, carefully pull the trim retainer out of the channel. Fold the trim over the seat area and quarter panel trim.

Remove the tip from each end of the molding on the rear bow. Carefully pull the molding out of the retainer. Pry the molding retainer off the bow.

Remove the bolts that attach the top and back curtain tacking strips to the body.

Remove the staples that secure the top material to the rear bow.

Carefully pull the top material free from the underside of each side rail. Remove the staples that secure the top material to the underside of the front bow. Carefully separate the top from the listings on number two and number three bows.

To install the new top fabric, first remove the tacking strips from the old top.

Staple them to the new top in the same location as they were on the old top. Fit the new top on the roof bows.

Working from the center outward, staple the top deck to the rear bow. Make sure that the rear sections of the slits are stapled to the bow before drawing and stapling the front portion of the slits.

Secure, and tighten the quarterdeck tacking strips to the body as required to align the listings with number two and number three bows.

Center the top material and pull it forward over the front bow to remove the wrinkles from the top deck and quarters. While the material is pulled over the front bow, make a reference mark on the material at the leading edge of the bow with a piece of chalk. The mark should extend the entire length of the bow.

Raise the top high enough to gain access to the underside of the front bow. Align the reference mark to the leading edge of the bow and staple the material in place.

Install the weatherstrip and the three retainers on the number one bow.

Secure the flaps to the underside of the side rail with trim cement. Trim the excess material from the flaps.

Install the rear, center and the front weatherstrips on the side rails so that the ends of the weatherstrip are in alignment of the side rail joints.

Tighten the quarterdeck packing strips as required to remove wrinkles from material and obtain a tight seal at the moldings. Install a piece of tape across the rear bow to cover the staples.

Install the molding retainer, molding and the two tips on the rear bow.

Secure the back curtain to the upper part of the zipper. Secure the back curtain packing strip in place with the attaching bolts. Tighten the bolts as required, working from the center outward.

Starting at one end of the folding top compartment, insert the trim retainer into the channel. Secure each end of the trim to the pivot bracket supports with a metal screw and washer.

Install the rear seat back and cushion. Cement the top material to the listings on number two and number three bows. Remove the protective covers from the deck and the hood and clean all chalk reference marks from the top material.

## FABRIC ROOF COVER REPAIR

The fabric roof cover material used on recent model bodies is a vinyl coated fabric which exhibits a grain pattern in the exterior vinyl surface. In the event the vinyl surface becomes damaged, (cut, scuffed, gouged or torn) it is possible in most cases to make repairs without removing the cover assembly from the roof panel.

One method of making repairs to such roof material utilizes a teflon coated metal graining tool, heating iron and variable heat control unit, Fig. 22-2. The procedure for making repairs is as follows:

The additional equipment required is shown in Fig. 22-3. The pallet knife is used to apply vinyl repair patching compound and the razor knife is used to remove frayed edges from damaged area prior to application of the vinyl patching compound. The vinyl cleaner (detergent type) is an all purpose cleaner for removing dirt, grease and dust from the area to be repaired. The solvent type vinyl cleaner is used for removing wax, silicone, or oil from the repair area.

Preheat the graining tool at the 60 setting plus or minus 2 on variable heat control for a minimum of 15 min. or until the temperature has reached 300 deg. F.

While the graining tool is being heated, prepare the surface as follows: If the cover has an overall soilage, clean repair area with detergent type all purpose vinyl cleaner. Mask off areas adjacent to repair area (body panels, moldings, glass, etc.). Using the razor knife, trim the damaged area to remove all frayed or damaged edges.

It is important that the trimming of vinyl at damaged area be kept to a minimum. On cuts, scuffs or gouges with clean unfrayed

*Fig. 22-2. Fabric roof cover repair equipment.*

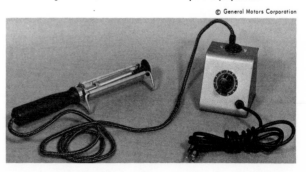

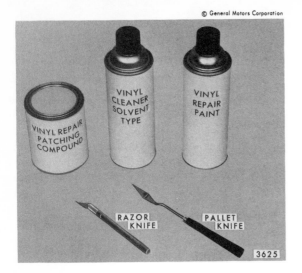

*Fig. 22-3. Fabric roof cover repair materials and tool.*

edges, no trimming is necessary.

On damaged areas where no trimming is necessary, apply vinyl patching compound to the edges of the area. Where trimming is required, apply compound to area being repaired and trowel flush with adjacent area. Remove any excess material (compound) with a clean cloth.

The next step is graining the repaired area. This is performed by exerting light hand pressure and applying preheated graining iron over damaged compounded filled area for approximately one and one half minutes, Fig. 22-4. Curing and graining time can be increased slightly depending on size of repair.

During graining operation, it is important that the iron be held in a stable, perpendicular position. The use of the tool must be compatible to the repair area surface (round edge in drip rail areas; tapered edge adjacent to reveal moldings; crown surface for flat areas). For large repairs, repeat curing and graining using an overlapping technique.

After the graining operation is completed, clean the graining tool with solvent type vinyl cleaner and apply a small amount of silicone to prevent adhesion of vinyl paint during future use of the tool.

Apply vinyl paint (solid colors) as follows: Using a soft lint-free cloth, wipe the repair area with solvent type vinyl cleaner to remove any wax, silicone, oil, etc. that may be present.

Thoroughly mix the vinyl color according to instructions on the container. If an aerosol

type container is used, pretest spray pattern on a sheet of paper; then apply vinyl color to repaired area with two or three light passes. Use a "fanning" motion to create a feathering condition around the perimeter of the repair area. Heavy, wet coats of paint must be avoided.

## WOOD GRAIN TRANSFER REPLACEMENT

The body surface to which wood grain overlay is to be applied must be free from grease, oil and other foreign material. Sand all areas to be covered with the overlay, using No. 360 paper soaked in water or mineral spirits. The area to be sanded should be approximately 1/4 in. larger in all dimen-

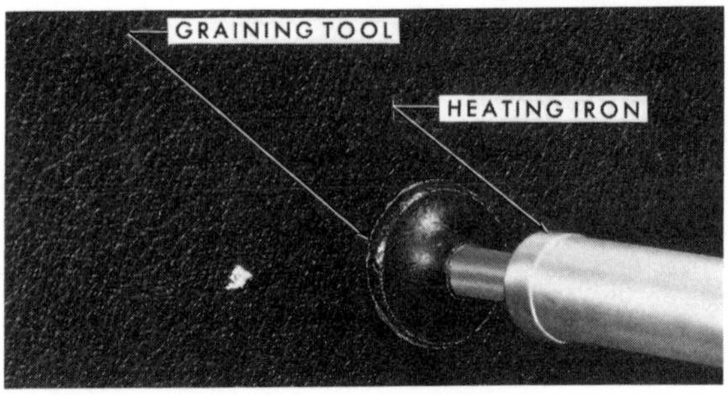

*Fig. 22-4. Graining is accomplished by applying heating iron for approximately 1 1/2 minutes.*

sions than the overlay, except when the overlay is turned at the door or other comparable areas, Fig. 22-5. All metal and/or paint nibs must be removed prior to the application of the overlay. Tack off all dust and dirt particles from the sanded areas.

Temperature: The overlay is most easily handled when the air and application surface temperatures are between 70 and 90 deg. For application below 70 deg. use heat lamps to warm the surfaces.

Wetting Surface: Thoroughly mix two or three level teaspoons of mild powdered household detergent per gallon of clean warm (80 to 90 deg.) water in a non-rusting container.

Application: It is mandatory to remove the paper backing from the overlay and not the overlay from the backing as possible stretching or tearing will result.

Cut overlay 1/2 in. larger than the area to be covered and lay on a clean flat surface

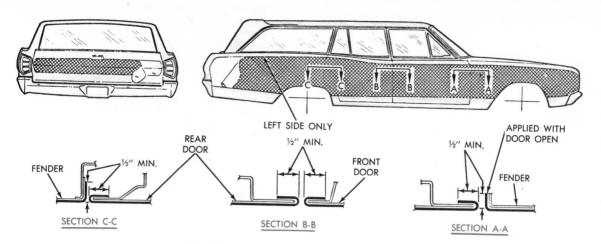

Fig. 22-5. Application of wood grain overlay.

with the paper backing surface up. Hold over-lay firmly and remove backing paper in a smooth 180 deg. motion. Under hot, humid conditions, a slight jerking motion will aid in the paper backing removal.

Thoroughly wet application surfaces of body and the adhesive surface of the overlay with the wetting solution and immediately apply overlay, grain side out, to the body. Adjust overlay so 1/2 in. of material shows beyond all edges and apply wetting solution to outer surface of overlay.

Follow details of application, Fig. 22-5. Flat Surfaces: Use a plastic squeegee with cloth sleeve, or Teflon coating, and pres-surize all flat surfaces with firm, over-lapping strokes to remove air bubbles, water wrinkles and to insure good adhesive contact. On vertical surfaces, pressurize and level off entire top edge first with a 3 x 4 in. squeegee, then work from top to bottom.

On horizontal surfaces, start at the center and work toward the edges using a 3 x 4 in. squeegee. Do not apply pressure to edges that will be wrapped around doors, fenders, gas cap areas or to compound curve areas.

Flange Areas: After being sure all metal and/or paint nibs and sanding residue have been removed, hand brush 3M Vinyl Adhesive 8064, or equivalent, to entire flange area with a smooth even coverage.

Warm the unapplied overlay with a heat lamp. Avoid trapping air when turning the edge and wrap overlay around flange area. Press firmly with the fingers, making sure overlay overlaps the flange.

Using a single-edge razor blade, trim off all material extending beyond the flange.

Pressurize the flange area with a 2 in. rub-ber roller to be sure the overlay is well ad-hered to the metal surface.

Contoured Areas: Warm the unapplied overlay with a heat lamp, working on an area no more than 1/2 in. larger than the squeegee.

Using 3 x 4 in. plastic squeegee, pres-surize and level off the small warmed area. Repeat warming and pressurizing until entire contoured surface is completely adhered and free of air, water and wrinkles.

Inspection: Upon completion of an area, inspect for blisters due to trapped air or water. All blisters should be worked out with squeegee, or punctured with a sharp needle and then pressurized until film adheres to the body surface. All edges must be adhered to the body surface.

## QUIZ - Chapter 22

1. In the case of Ford convertible tops, the top consists of the deck and two side quarters, bonded into one piece of material.
   True.          False.
2. When removing an old top is it necessary to remove the front weatherstrip retainer?
   Yes.          No.
3. How are ends of folding top compartment attached to the pivot bracket supports?
   Special clip.
   Metal screw and washer.
   Special garnish molding.
4. When repairing a damaged vinyl coated fabric roof material how is the patching com-pound applied?
   Trowel.     Brush.     Pallet knife.

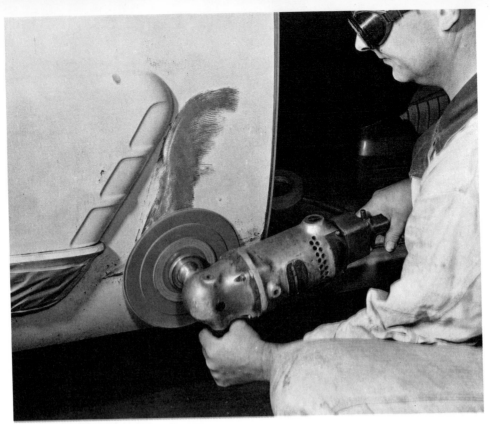

*Fig. 23-1. Using disk grinder to remove paint.*

# Chapter 23

# PAINT REMOVAL

On most cases it is necessary to remove all the paint from a vehicle before repainting only when the original paint is in poor condition. This is because the original paint has poor adhesion and tends to flake off.

There are several different methods used to remove paints including:

1. Sandblasting.
2. Hot caustic solution with pressure equipment.
3. Paint remover.
4. Power sanding equipment.

The method used depends largely on the quantity of work and personal preference. When there are a large number of vehicles to be completely refinished, and the supply of such work is steady, either sandblasting or hot caustic is usually selected.

Sandblasting, as the name applies, uses air pressure to direct a stream of sand against the painted surface. The force is such that the sand chips or blasts off the paint from the surface, leaving the bare metal exposed. The sand also makes tiny indentations in the surface of the metal, and in that way provides good adherence for the new paint.

Sandblasting leaves the raw metal exposed and unless the metal is painted promptly rusting soon takes place.

Sandblasting should be performed in an area where the dust does not get out to the rest of the shop. Particular care should be taken that such work is not done close to a painting area, and the mechanics doing the sandblasting should use respirators and goggles.

The hot caustic process is also a popular means of removing all paint from vehicles. This is also known as the flow on, or steam spray method. This process of paint removal uses steam under pressure to spray a hot caustic solution of a special paint removing compound on the surface of the auto body. Chrome and other decorative parts should be removed before the caustic spray is used. Parts which are not removed should be carefully masked so they are protected from the action of the caustic.

In operation, the hot chemical solution is first sprayed on the painted surfaces. After it has remained on the vehicle a sufficient time to loosen the paint, the paint is flushed off by hot steam. Every care must be taken to remove all traces of the chemical. If any remains, the newly applied paint will not adhere to the surface.

After the chemical remover and old paint have been flushed off, and all crevices blown out with compressed air, the surface is then treated with a metal conditioner to prevent rusting.

Paint removing compounds, because of cost, are not used extensively in removing paint from auto bodies. Detailed instructions vary with the make of remover, and the instructions of the manufacturer should be carefully followed. In general, the liquid paint remover is applied with a brush, and after it has remained on the surface a sufficient length of time, the paint will have been loosened and is scraped off with a putty knife. All traces of the remover must be removed from the surface before the car is painted.

## REMOVING PAINT WITH A DISK GRINDER

The use of a disk grinder, Fig. 23-1, for removing old paint is probably the most popular method and is used extensively by auto body shops. It is used not only when the paint from the entire vehicle is to be removed, but is also used when only small areas and single panels are to be repainted.

If the original paint is in good condition, without cracks, blisters, or other blemishes,

it is not necessary to remove all the paint before refinishing. When the original paint is smooth, all that is necessary is a light sanding.

The old finish can be removed with No. 16 open-coat disk on a conventional rotary grinder. The exposed metal should be finished with No. 50, and then No. 220 grit paper. If only a portion of the panel is being refinished all edges of the paint film should be feathered, that is, tapered back, Fig. 23-2. This tapering

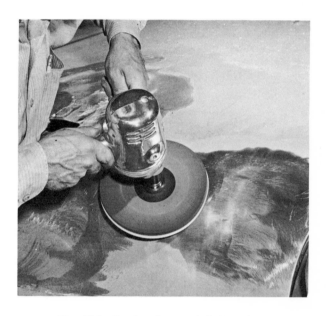

Fig. 23-2. Featheredging with disk sander.

back of the original paint is known as featheredging, and simply means that the finish adjoining the surface to be sprayed is sanded so as to eliminate any sharp edge. To do this, first use No. 320 grit paper and finish with No. 400 grit paper.

If the original finish is lacquer, a minimum of sanding should be done. Either lacquer or enamel may be applied over it.

If the original finish is acrylic, little sanding is required, and new acrylic can, in most cases, be sprayed directly on the original acrylic. If enamel is to be used as a finish coat, most painters advise spraying the acrylic with a special sealer and then spraying the enamel.

The super enamels used since 1958 as original finishes are very hard and require a thorough sanding to get good adhesion of a new coating. Putting enamel over old enamel will cover sand scratches provided that No. 360 or finer paper was used for the finish sanding. Because of the difficulty of blending the edge of an enamel spot, it is advisable to refinish the entire panel.

Lacquer will tend to show sand scratches

Greatly enlarged scratch in an old finish showing insoluble outer-layer.

The solvents in the fresh coat of lacquer cause swelling in the freshly exposed parts of the scratch.

The swelling recedes after all of the solvents have evaporated and the new finish shrinks leaving furrows similar to the old scratches.

*Fig. 23-3. As lacquer dries, it shrinks into cracks as shown in these illustrations.*

in enamel unless the surface is very carefully finished with No. 320 grit paper, or finer.

It is essential that a smooth surface be provided for the primer surfacer. Modern primer surfaces and glazing putties will fill almost any rough surface, but much time and material can be saved, if the metal is quite smooth before the material is applied.

A good practice is to use three or four grades of paper from coarse to fine and to take off most of the ridges left by the coarser papers. In otherwords, start with a No. 16 paper and follow through with a No. 50 close-coated disk and finally sand with No. 220

paper. Featheredge the area with No. 320 and final finish with No. 400 grit paper.

It must be remembered, particularly when spraying lacquer, that as the thinner in the lacquer evaporates, the lacquer shrinks into the cracks and depressions left by sanding, then the cracks become quite visible, Fig. 23-3.

## QUIZ - Chapter 23

1. Sandblasting is used to remove the paint from what areas of an automobile body?
    Rear deck, top and hood.
    Doors and quarter panels.
    Entire vehicle.
2. What is the method used most for removing paint from an auto body in auto body shops?
    Sandblasting.
    Hot caustic solution.
    Chemical paint remover.
    Disk grinder.
3. If the original paint is in good condition is it ordinarily necessary to remove all the paint before refinishing?
    Yes.
    No.
4. If the original finish is acrylic lacquer a great deal of sanding is needed before refinishing.
    True.
    False.
5. The super enamels used in recent years are very soft.
    True.
    False.
6. The super enamel used in recent years requires a great deal of sanding before refinishing.
    True.
    False.

# Chapter 24
# STEPS IN MASKING

When painting an automobile it is important to cover and protect certain areas from paint overspray while adjacent areas are being painted. Areas to be protected are covered with masking paper, which is attached to the auto body by means of masking tape.

*Fig. 24-1. Stand designed to speed dispensing of masking paper.*

Manufacturers of masking tape and paper have devoted much time and expense to improve their products and their research has produced products which materially reduce the time and costs required to mask a vehicle.

Good quality masking paper will not permit any paint to penetrate or seep through to the panel it is protecting. The paper should be capable of withstanding rough handling. It must also have a slight amount of stretch which is needed when masking along curved edges. At the same time there must be no possibility of the paper scratching newly painted surfaces.

Tape must adhere easily to painted and unpainted surfaces, chrome, stainless steel, aluminum and other materials. Equally important, none of the tape adhesives must remain on the surface after the tape is removed. Quality tape must also retain its adherent qualities when it is drenched during wet sanding operations.

Special dispensers are available which speed up the preparation of the masking paper and tape for application. See Figs. 24-1, and 24-5. As the paper is pulled from the roll, the tape is automatically applied to the edge of the paper, one-half of the width of the tape is applied to the edge of the paper, while the remaining half is free so it can be applied to the car body to hold the paper in position.

## PRECAUTIONS WHILE MASKING

Masking tape should be applied only to clean, dry surfaces. Such surfaces must be free from silicone polish, rubber lubricants, dust, rust, etc.

Unless masking curved surfaces, tape should not be stretched. Simply lay it on the surface and press down, making sure that the edges of the tape are adhering to the surface, not just the center. Unless the edges of the tape are adhering to the panel, water from sanding operations, or paint spray will seep under the tape and free it from the panel.

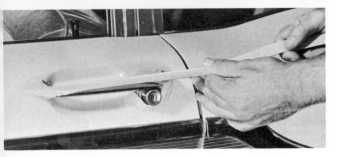

Fig. 24-2. Method of masking door handles.

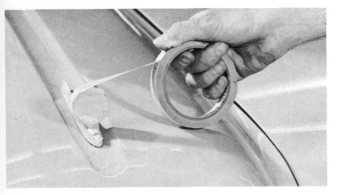

Fig. 24-3. Masking decorative emblem.

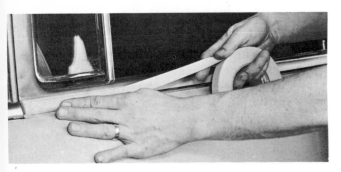

Fig. 24-4. Chrome trim strips are easily masked.

Tape manufacturers caution against applying or removing tape at temperatures below 50 deg. F. Masking paper and tape should not be removed until the newly applied paint is dry (no longer sticky). When removing tape it should be pulled directly outward at an angle of 90 deg.

Masking tape should be stored in a cool place and never placed on a hot radiator or other hot surface.

## MASKING TRIM AND HARDWARE

When masking chrome trim, door handles and similar ornamentation, no paper is required, only masking tape. Select a tape of sufficient width to cover the parts as completely as possible. In Fig. 24-2, tape of

1 in. width is being applied to the door handle. In this instance, the tape is applied to the upper area of the handle. The second piece will be used to cover the lower side and at the same time slightly overlap the tape which was first applied.

A small ornamental light is being masked in Fig. 24-3. In this case, the base of the light is first covered with tape, then the front and back faces. Finally, as shown, tape is wound around the outer circumference, which also helps seal the edges of the tape on front and rear faces.

## MASKING MOLDING AND BEADING

Chrome beading, molding and similar trim can be quickly and effectively masked by using masking tape of the correct width. By having tape of the correct width, the entire surface can be masked with a single strip of tape. Fig. 24-4, shows the operation being performed on front door molding strip, this is typical of the procedure to be used on other moldings.

## MASKING WINDSHIELD

Two or three sheets of masking paper are needed to successfully mask a windshield on a modern car. The number of sheets is dependent on the height of the windshield and also on the width of paper that is available.

Fig. 24-5. Pulling off a sheet of masking paper to mask the windshield.

Figs. 24-5 and 24-6, show the step-by-step procedure. It will be noted that the lower portion of the windshield is covered first. In that way any water will run down over the masking paper and will not reach the covered

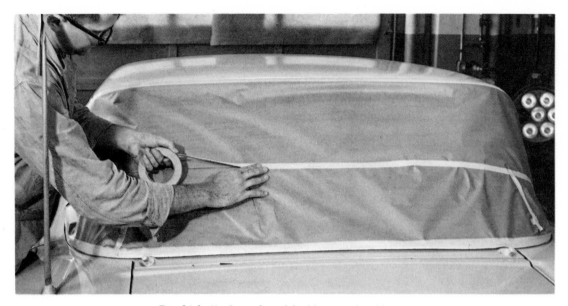

*Fig. 24-6. Masking of windshield is completed by covering the lapped edges of the masking paper with tape.*

area. Other large areas can be masked by using the same method. After the windshield is completely covered, apply tape so that each edge of the paper is taped down.

## MASKING A PANEL

When masking a panel for a two-tone paint job, as in Fig. 24-7, select paper which is slightly wider than the panel to be masked.

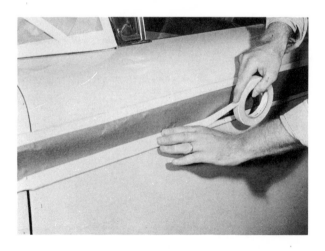

*Fig. 24-7. Masking a panel with paper and tape.*

Attach tape to one edge, and apply upper edge to car body. Then crease paper to needed width and tape into position.

## MASKING WINDOWS

The procedure for masking a window is shown in Fig. 24-8. First apply paper to lower area, and then to the upper. When two sheets are in position, run a length of tape on the overlapping edge to completely seal it.

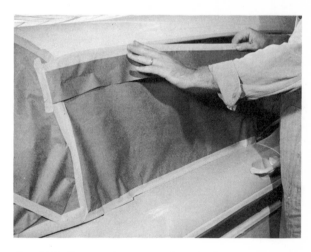

*Fig. 24-8. When masking a window, the lower area is first covered and then the upper.*

## MASKING UPHOLSTERY

When painting the inside of a door jamb it is necessary to protect the upholstery from overspray. Use a narrow strip of masking

Fig. 24-9. Method of masking door and door frame.

paper approximately 10 ft. long. Starting at the outside lower corner, continue around the door in a single operation. Follow the same procedure on the door frame, Fig. 24-9. Place a piece of masking paper over the seat, seat edge, and seat back.

## MASKING HEADLIGHTS

To mask a headlight use 6 in. wide paper and cut a piece that will go approximately three-quarters the distance around the light. Place the tape along one edge of the paper so

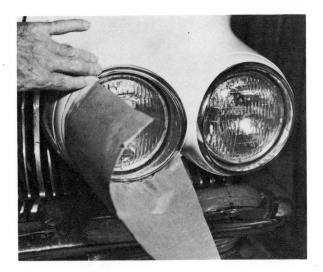

*Fig. 24-10. First step in masking a head lamp.*

*Fig. 24-11. Second step in masking a head lamp.*

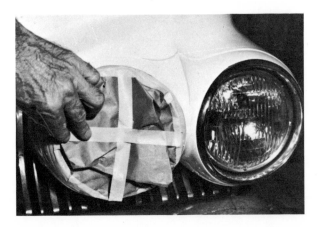

*Fig. 24-12. Final step in masking a head lamp.*

that one-half of the tape is exposed. Place the paper and tape at the desired point along the edge of the lamp rim, Fig. 24-10, leading with the right hand and adjusting the position of the tape with the left. Then apply a second piece of paper in a similar manner to close exposed gap, Fig. 24-11. When paper and tape have been applied all around the lamp rim, the masking paper should be slightly cone shaped, Fig. 24-11. Twist and fold the cone against the front of the lamp. Take two short pieces of tape and place them so that the paper will be held flat against the front of the lamp, Fig. 24-12.

## MASKING WHEELS

When it is necessary to mask a circular surface, it is advisable to first pleat an apron. This will make it easier to follow the curved contour and will prevent the apron from bunching and wrinkling. This is the way it is done: First cut a piece of masking paper the desired length. Next make a pleat about 1/4 in. deep by crimping both edges. The pleat should extend the full width of the apron. Continue pleating the full length of the apron, making a pleat every 2 to 4 in. Apply the apron to the surface. Then after pleated apron is

*Fig. 24-13. Masking a tire prior to painting the wheel.*

securely in place, fold the untaped edge so it will catch the overspray. This pleating method can be used to good advantage on wheels as shown in Fig. 24-13.

## FRONT END MASKING

Masking a car with large areas of chrome on the front end can be most quickly accomplished by using wide paper. Each car re-

*Fig. 24-14. Large sheets of masking paper are used to mask the front end.*

quires different treatment. The masking procedure for one modern car is shown in Figs. 24-14, and 24-15. The operation is started at one side of the vehicle, and the tape on the edge of the masking paper is applied to the edge of the chrome area. At the inner edge of the head lamp, the paper is folded as shown in Fig. 24-14. The masking is then carried straight over to the other head lamp as shown. The car completely masked and ready for the spray booth is shown in Fig. 24-15.

## MASKING ANTENNAS

Radio antennas can be most quickly masked by using a length of carbdoard tubing which is slipped over the antenna and then taped around the bottom. If such tubing is not available, make a long sleeve of masking paper, taping the edges together. Then slip them over the antenna and tape the bottom as shown in Fig. 24-16.

*Fig. 24-15. Front of car, wheels and windshield after masking.*

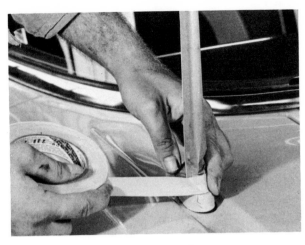

*Fig. 24-16. Masking a radio antenna.*

## QUIZ - Chapter 24

1. Good quality masking paper will permit paint to seep through to the panel beneath.
    True.
    False.
2. A masking paper dispenser will automatically apply masking tape to the edge of the paper.
    True.
    False.

3. Should masking paper be applied to damp surfaces?
    Yes.
    No.
4. Tape manufacturers caution against applying masking tape below what temperature?
    75 deg. F.
    50 deg. F.
    32 deg. F.
    20 deg. F.
5. Where should masking paper be stored?
    In refrigerator.
    In a cool place.
    On heated radiator.
6. When masking a windshield with two pieces of masking paper, which sheet of paper should be installed first?
    Upper sheet.
    Lower sheet.
7. When masking a wheel, or similar circular area, what procedure should be followed?
    Cut the paper in a circular form to fit the area.
    Pleat the paper into an apron.
8. How should a radio antenna be masked?
    Make a sleeve of masking paper.
    Wind the masking paper in a spiral manner around the antenna.

# Chapter 25

# PAINTING MATERIALS

In addition to nitrocellulose lacquers, synthetic enamels, acrylic lacquers and acrylic enamels which are used as finish coats when painting automobiles, there are several other materials which are equally important. These include: thinners, primers, surfacers, reducers, solvents, sealers, metal conditioners and putties.

First of all, paints as used for painting automotive vehicles are composed of two basic ingredients: One, the volatiles; two, film forming material.

The volatile is that portion of the paint which evaporates, while the film forming material is that part which remains in the dried film and is not volatile.

The main purpose or function of the volatile, which is also known as the thinner, is to make it possible to properly apply the material. It must be of sufficient solvent power to dissolve the binder portion of the film.

The nonvolatile, or film forming materials, are made up of binders in pigment. The binder is that portion which acts as a carrying medium for the pigment and carries body, toughness and gloss to the film.

The pigment is the coloring portion and serves to produce opacity or hiding quality, as well as protection to the binder.

Conventional lacquers, that is, nitrocellulose lacquers and acrylic lacquers, dry by evaporation of the thinner or volatile material. They remain more or less soluble so that when recoated with the same material, the new coat bonds or unites with the old.

Acrylic lacquers have been in use on General Motors cars since 1959. On Chrysler and American Motors cars acrylic enamels were first used on the 1965 models.

Desirable qualities of acrylic lacquer and acrylic enamel are durability, gloss, gloss retention and hardness.

Synthetic enamels dry by evaporation of the solvents in the first stage, and by oxidation or polymerization of the binder in the second stage. Oxidation is a change in the binder as a result of combining with the oxygen of the air. Heat makes the actions more rapid. Thoroughly dry synthetics are not readily soluble in ordinary solvents. The longer the drying period, the more insoluble and tougher they become. A thorough sanding before repainting is therefore necessary. Because of the slower drying time, dust in the working area is more of a problem with enamel than with lacquer. Enamel dries to a full gloss and does not require polishing, but lacquer usually requires polishing to attain fullest gloss. Broadly speaking, lacquers are said to dry from the outside in, and enamels from the inside out.

Thoroughly dry synthetic enamels are not soluble in ordinary solvents. This knowledge is used frequently by painters in determining what type of material was last used to refinish the vehicle. The procedure is to rub a small area of the vehicle with a cloth dampened with thinner. If no color comes off on the cloth, the refinish material is synthetic enamel. If color does come off, then the refinishing material is lacquer. To distinguish between nitrocellulose lacquer and acrylic lacquer, rub a small area with silicone polish remover. Acrylic lacquer will be rubbed off with this method, while conventional nitrocellulose lacquer will not be affected.

## PRIMER SURFACERS

The color or finish coat is also known as the top coat, Fig. 25-1, and before that is sprayed on the vehicle a coat known as the primer surfacer is first applied. Primer surfacers are intended to provide adhesion to the metal and fill slight imperfections in the metal surface. The primer surfacer coats are then sanded down to a smooth flat surface. They must be thoroughly dry before sanding. If not dry, shrinking of the primer over cracks will produce an uneven surface.

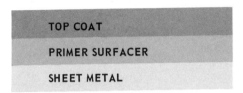

*Fig. 25-1. The primer surfacer is a primer and is also designed to fill small depressions and cracks in the sheet metal of the body.*

There are two general types of primer surfacers, one a lacquer-base product with fast drying characteristics, and the other a synthetic-base product of slower drying properties. It is generally not advisable to use a synthetic base primer surfacer under a lacquer finish for refinishing work. However, the instructions provided by the manufacturer should be followed. Be sure to use a primer surfacer that will provide good adhesion to the surface and also good adhesion for the color coat to follow.

## PRIMERS

For adhesion to special surfaces, manufacturers provide materials generally known as primers, to distinguish them from the primer surfacers, Fig. 25-2. For example when painting aluminum, a zinc chromate primer is used. If the surface to be painted is galvanized, a zinc dust primer is usually recommended.

Primers are intended for adhesion, and do only a small amount of filling imperfections in the metal. Where the metal requires filling, a primer surfacer should be used, applying it directly on the metal under normal conditions, but over a primer if a special primer is required.

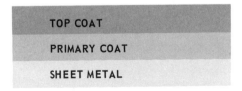

*Fig. 25-2. The primer forms a bond between the sheet metal of the body and the top coat.*

## SEALERS

Sealers are used for sealing down sand scratches when recoating a lacquer or acrylic surface. Bleeder sealer is used for sealing reds, maroons, etc., so that they will not "bleed" or show through the new coat. Sealers are formulated from resins, and when dry are not easily soluble in the common solvents. They act as a shield for material over which they are sprayed by preventing the penetration of the solvents that are used in the final coats.

## METALLICS

Both lacquers and enamels come in all colors of the rainbow and appear to have the same color value regardless of the angle from which they are viewed. However, to give the paint a "luminous" quality, small metallic flakes (usually aluminum) are mixed with the paint. These flakes are often of different sizes and such paint is known as metallic paint. When viewed from different angles, the color shade seems to vary. The reason for the apparent variation in shade is that the metallic flakes are all at different angles in the paint and consequently reflect the light differently.

These metallic paints are very popular, but present a problem to the painter when attempting to get the same shade and reflective quality.

## THINNERS AND REDUCERS

Thinners and reducers are solvents used to thin or reduce paints to the correct viscosity for spraying. Thinners are used for lacquer and acrylic products, while reducers are used for synthetic base resins. In general, they are not interchangeable.

The best results are obtained with the refinish material when it is thinned with a reducer or thinner designed specifically for the material being sprayed.

Some manufacturers provide special thinner for use under conditions of different spraying temperatures.

## PUTTY

For deep nicks or scratches there are materials known as putties. Such material is used when the nicks or scratches are too deep to be filled by the primer surfacer. Putty, while of the same general consistency as the familiar glazer's putty, has an entirely different composition, usually being made of the same basic materials as the primer surfacer, but heavier in solids. Some manufacturers provide one type of putty for lacquers and another for enamels.

## WAX, POLISH AND GREASE REMOVERS

Before spraying any primer surfacer or color coats, it is essential that all wax and grease be removed from the area to be sprayed. This is important, as the adhesion of any paint film to the surface depends first on whether or not the surface is absolutely clean. By clean, we mean not only physically clean, but chemically clean as well. The slightest film of oil, grease, wax, rust, or moisture will prevent paint from adhering to the surface. Wax and grease removers are solvent type materials that will dissolve partly oxidized waxes and greases that are imbedded in the old finish. A final wipe off with a clean rag saturated with wax and grease remover will insure against the new coat peeling.

Most polishes and waxes used today contain silicone resin. This is more difficult to remove than conventional polishes. When paint is applied to a surface on which silicone is present, the paint will tend to crawl and leave craters or "fish eyes." In addition, there will be poor adhesion of the new paint to the surface.

Special preparations have been prepared for removing waxes and polishes containing silicone products.

## METAL CONDITIONER

When auto bodies are stripped to the bare metal before repainting, rust will form quickly. In order to prevent the formation of such rust, make sure that the metal is chemically clean and also etch the surface so there will be better adhesion of the new paint. Manufacturers have prepared metal conditioner and rust inhibitors. Such materials also prevent the formation of rust.

## TACK RAG

A tack rag is a special piece of cheesecloth that has been dipped in a thin nondrying varnish and then wrung out. It is kept in a container so that the varnish will not harden, but will remain tacky. The tack rag is used to wipe a surface to remove all dust just before spraying the color coat.

## RUBBING COMPOUNDS

Rubbing compounds or pastes, are mild abrasives and are used to polish lacquer and acrylic lacquer surfaces. Rubbing compounds will impart a higher than normal lustre to finished surfaces. Rubbing compounds are available for hand rubbing and machine polishing.

## LACQUER? ENAMEL? ACRYLIC?

When refinishing a car, the question arises as to what type of refinishing material should be used. In general, less trouble is experienced if the same type of material is used for refinishing as was used originally.

Prior to 1955 all Ford, Chrysler, Studebaker and American Motors cars used standard baked enamel. During 1956 through 1958 those same cars, in some instances, used

Fig. 25-3. Some of the painting materials used in a typical auto paint shop.

super-enamel and in 1959 - 1964 those cars were finished at the factory in super-enamel. In 1965 acrylic enamel was adopted for Chrysler built cars and those of American Motors.

In the case of General Motors cars, nitro-cellulose lacquer was used exclusively prior to 1955. From 1956 through 1958 some cars were finished in nitrocellulose lacquer and some in acrylic lacquer. Since 1959 all General Motors cars have been finished in acrylic lacquer.

Today most cars are refinished in either synthetic enamel, acrylic enamel or acrylic lacquer. In only a few cases is nitrocellulose lacquer used and then only when there is little drying time. Nitrocellulose lacquer is also used often for retouching small scratches and nicks such as occur on the edges of door panels and fenders. In such cases a small striping brush is used to apply the lacquer. But the spots must be small enough that no sanding or priming is needed. It should also be understood the color match to the original finish will not be perfect under such conditions.

Acrylic lacquer is recommended for use

in all cars which were originally finished in lacquer. If acrylic lacquer is used over enamel, a sealer should be applied over the enamel. Further in that connection, complete panels, never a portion of a panel should be sprayed.

When spraying acrylic lacquer, old nitrocellulose lacquer and acrylic lacquer, a surface in good condition need not be sanded before applying the finish coat, but the surface should be thoroughly cleaned. If acrylic lacquer is applied over a synthetic enamel surface, the surface must be cleaned and sanded to achieve the necessary adhesion.

When repairing or refinishing over acrylic enamels, the surface must be thoroughly cleaned and sanded to provide the necessary adhesion and resist peeling and chipping.

Synthetic enamels are recommended for use on all cars which were originally painted with enamel. Complete panels should be refinished when enamel is used for repair because of the difficulty of spotting in with enamel without leaving a ring around the spot. Enamel can also be used over lacquer finished cars.

The choice of top coat whether synthetic

enamel, nitrocellulose lacquer, acrylic lacquer or acrylic enamel depends mostly on whether the car is being completely refinished or partly painted and on personal preference.

Some painters prefer nitrocellulose lacquer because it dries quickly and their shop is too dusty for spraying enamels. In addition, they are used to the lacquer and are familiar with its application. Other painters dislike the polishing operation that is associated with nitrocellulose lacquer. Most painters finish with the same material with which the car was originally painted.

## DETERMINING TYPE OF OLD FINISH

Before applying any paint to an old finish it is important to determine whether the old finish is acrylic lacquer, lacquer, alkyd enamel or acrylic enamel. There are several ways of making such a determination and the easiest method, provided the vehicle has not been repainted is to consult a paint manufacturer's production book which will list the type of paint used by each manufacturer.

Another method which is used particularly when the type of finish material is not known is to use one of the special compounds which the larger paint manufacturers have for that purpose. The procedure is rub a small area with the special compound. The compound will dissolve lacquer very quickly and acrylic lacquer with considerable rubbing. Alkyd enamel and acrylic enamel will not be dissolved.

## QUIZ - Chapter 25

1. What characterizes the volatile material in automotive paint?
    Coloring material.
    It evaporates quickly.

2. Acrylic lacquers have been in use on General Motors cars since what year?
    1957.
    1958.
    1959.
    1960.
3. Synthetic enamels dry in what manner?
    Evaporation only.
    Evaporation and polymerization.
    Polymerization only.
4. The major advantage of acrylic lacquer over nitrocellulose lacquer is superior gloss retention.
    True.
    False.
5. Lacquers are said to dry from the outside in.
    True.
    False.
6. To tell whether a car is finished with nitrocellulose lacquer or with acrylic lacquer, what procedure should be used?
    Rub surface with thinner.
    Rub surface with silicone polish remover.
    Rub surface with rubbing compound.
7. Primer surfacers are used to provide adhesion.
    True.
    False.
8. What is the purpose of a bleeder sealer?
    To prevent reds and maroons from bleeding through following coats.
    To seal off scratches.
    Provide adhesion on rusted surfaces.
9. What is the purpose of a tack rag?
    It is used to wipe off dust from the surface immediately before spraying.
    Special rag used for holding upholstery tacks.
    Special cloth used to wipe off spray gun.
10. Is acrylic recommended for use on cars originally finished in lacquer?
    Yes.
    No.

# Chapter 26
# PREPARING SURFACE FOR PAINT

Before any paint is applied to an automobile it is important that the surface be prepared correctly. It must be smooth, clean and dry.

In many cases it is not necessary to remove the original finish, but it must be determined that the old finish has good adhesion, and that rust has not developed under the paint. A method of checking the adhesion is to sand through the finish and featheredge a small spot, Fig. 26-1. If the thin edge of the paint does not crumble or break, it is reasonable to assume there is no rust under that particular area. However, it is important to make such a check at several critical points of the vehicle: Along the lower edge of the doors, the rocker panels, and the area below the lower edge of the deck lid. Developing rust can usually be detected by a roughness and pitting of the surface. The paint over such areas must be removed down to the bare metal.

## REMOVE WAX AND POLISH

All traces of wax, polish and grease must be removed. A specially blended wax and grease remover should be used to remove all traces of such foreign matter. Gasoline should not be used, as this often contains materials which will prevent good adhesion of the new paint. Reducers should never be used to clean up the surface, particularly when the car has been finished with acrylic lacquer, as acrylic will absorb reducer into the paint film and blistering and lifting will result.

When applying and removing the wax and grease remover, always use new, clean wiping cloths. Cloths that have been laundered often still contain a certain amount of grease or other materials that would be harmful and prevent good paint adherence.

The paint is usually removed by grinding, Fig. 26-2. First a No. 16 open-coat disk is used. This is followed by a No. 50 and then a No. 220 disk. All edges are then feathered with No. 320 and then No. 400 grit paper.

If the original finish is nitrocellulose lacquer only a minimum of sanding is needed. Either nitrocellulose lacquer or synthetic enamel may be applied over it. If the original finish is acrylic lacquer, sanding can be held to a minimum. In the case of acrylic enamel, the surface must be thoroughly sanded using No. 400 grit paper. Some manufacturers state their particular type of acrylic lacquer may be applied directly over the original acrylic lacquer; others state a sealer should be applied first.

If synthetic or acrylic enamel is applied over acrylic lacquer, a special sealer should be applied. The super-enamels used as original equipment on some makes of vehicles since 1958 are extremely hard and require thorough sanding to provide good adhesion

*Fig. 26-1. Featheredging to check adherence of paint.*

for the new paint. Putting enamel over old enamel will cover small sand scratches provided the final sanding has been done with No. 360 or finer grit abrasive.

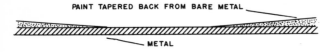

PAINT TAPERED BACK FROM BARE METAL

— METAL

*Fig. 26-2. Illustrating how edge of paint is tapered back or featheredged.*

Nitrocellulose lacquer will tend to show sand scratches in enamel unless the final sanding has been done with No. 400 grit abrasive. To reduce the sand scratches and reduce compounding of the new lacquer finish, a sealer is used, but it is necessary to refinish the entire panel.

Primer coats should not be applied until the bare metal has been treated with special metal conditioner to prevent future rusting. The etching action of metal conditioners produces maximum paint adherence.

Modern primer surfacers and glazing putties will fill almost any rough surface, but much time and material will be saved if the metal is quite smooth before such materials are applied.

After the surface has been cleaned and prepared for painting care must be exercised that the surface is not touched with hands, gloves or in any other manner. Checking the surface for smoothness by rubbing your hands over it should not be done before the final cleaning. Your hands always have a certain amount of oil on them, even after washing, and this is sufficient to destroy the durability, adherence and appearance of the new finish.

## ACRYLIC ENAMEL

Instructions covering the use of acrylic enamel have been included in the previous paragraphs together with those for other refinishing materials. However, because of the newness of this material, refinishing and repair procedures applying specifically to acrylic enamel are given in more detail as follows:

Because of the hardness of acrylic enamel, the surface must be thoroughly sanded to en-

able repair materials to adhere and resist peeling and chipping.

For panel and section repair, first remove surface contamination by thoroughly cleaning the section with wax and grease remover. Sand and featheredge any broken areas and completely remove evidence of gloss with No. 400 grit paper or finer. Blow off area with compressed air and treat the bare metal with metal conditioner and rust inhibitor. Then apply primer surfacer and sand with No. 400 grit paper. Reclean the surface and follow with a tack rag. Spray on one even coat of sealer for acrylics and allow to dry a minimum of thirty minutes.

Because of variations of application procedures in different factories, the same metallic color can appear to vary in richness. Special care must therefore be taken in matching the color and also when spraying the color coat. After the finish coat has dried overnight, the surface should be compounded with fine polishing compound.

## QUIZ - Chapter 26

1. Gasoline may be used to remove traces of wax and grease from the surface.
    True.
    False.
2. Is a cloth that has been laundered satisfactory for removing wax and grease from the surface to be painted?
    Yes.
    No.
3. What grit abrasive should be used for featheredging?
    16.
    24.
    80.
    320 - 400.
4. If the original finish on a vehicle is lacquer, a maximum amount of sanding is required?
    True.
    False.
5. Does a car finished with acrylic lacquer require more sanding than one finished in nitrocellulose lacquer?
    More.
    Less.
    The same.

# Chapter 27

# PREPARING PAINT, MATCHING COLORS

Fig. 27-1. Color of original paint is indicated on tag on dash panel or on door frame.

A very important part of painting an automobile is the selection and preparation of the paint. Selecting the correct color is particularly important when only a panel or portion of a panel is being repainted. In addition to selecting the correct color so that it will match the color of the rest of the vehicle and meet the desires of the car owner, it is also important that the paint be thoroughly mixed and thinned to the proper consistency for spraying.

## COLOR IDENTIFICATION

To aid the automobile body painter each color is given a code number. This is placed on a tag which is usually mounted on the fire wall under the hood, Figs. 27-1, and 27-2. In some instances, it is mounted on the door frame. Information on these colors with identifying names and numbers is published by the paint manufacturer, and is supplied to auto body refinishers and paint suppliers in what are generally known as paint chip books. Fig. 27-3, shows a page from one of those books. As a result, the body refinisher has

only to note the paint number on the tag on the vehicle and use this number to order identical colors, when refinishing the vehicle.

## PREPARING THE PAINT

Many paint failures are caused as the result of not properly mixing and stirring the paint before it is sprayed.

Pigments which give color, opacity and specific performance properties to the paint vary greatly in weight. Some of the commonly used pigments will weigh seven to eight times as much as the liquid part of the paint.

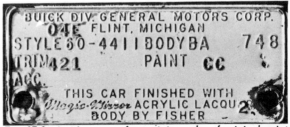

Fig. 27-2. Another type of tag giving color of original paint.

Because of this weight, they will settle to the bottom of the container. This is particularly true of whites, chrome yellow, chrome orange, chrome green, red and yellow iron oxides. Most other pigments are light and fluffy and have little or no tendency to settle.

The consistency or viscosity of the liquid part of the paint has a great deal to do with the rate of settling. If its viscosity is high (a heavy consistency) the rate of settling will be slower. Heavy pigments will settle out of straight thinners in a few minutes. Careful judgment in thinning only sufficient material to do the job and discarding the small amount that is not used is a practice followed by many experienced painters.

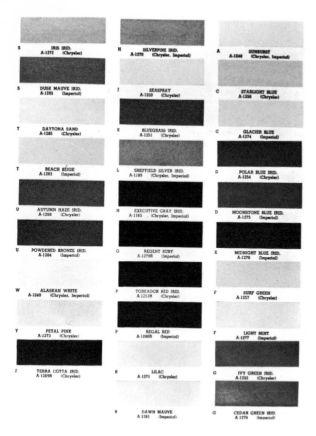

| | | |
|---|---|---|
| S IRIS IRID. A-1272 (Chrysler) | H SILVERPINE IRID. A-1270 (Chrysler, Imperial) | A SUNBURST A-1248 (Chrysler, Imperial) |
| S DUSK MAUVE IRID. A-1282 (Imperial) | J SEASPRAY A-1250 (Chrysler) | C STARLIGHT BLUE A-1256 (Chrysler) |
| T DAYTONA SAND A-1285 (Chrysler) | K BLUEGRASS IRID. A-1251 (Chrysler) | C GLACIER BLUE A-1274 (Imperial) |
| T BEACH BEIGE A-1283 (Imperial) | L SHEFFIELD SILVER IRID. A-1189 (Chrysler, Imperial) | D POLAR BLUE IRID. A-1254 (Chrysler) |
| U AUTUMN HAZE IRID. A-1288 (Chrysler) | N EXECUTIVE GRAY IRID. A-1183 (Chrysler, Imperial) | D MOONSTONE BLUE IRID. A-1275 (Imperial) |
| U POWDERED BRONZE IRID. A-1284 (Imperial) | O REGENT RUBY A-1279R (Imperial) | E MIDNIGHT BLUE IRID. A-1276 (Imperial) |
| W ALASKAN WHITE A-1249 (Chrysler, Imperial) | P TOREADOR RED IRID. A-1253R (Chrysler) | F SURF GREEN A-1257 (Chrysler) |
| Y PETAL PINK A-1273 (Chrysler) | P REGAL RED A-1280R (Imperial) | F LIGHT MINT A-1277 (Imperial) |
| Z TERRA COTTA IRID. A-1269R (Chrysler) | R LILAC A-1271 (Chrysler) | G IVY GREEN IRID. A-1252 (Chrysler) |
| | R DAWN MAUVE A-1281 (Imperial) | G CEDAR GREEN IRID. A-1278 (Imperial) |

*Fig. 27-3. Typical page from color code book showing colors used on one make of vehicle in one year.*

If a color which contains one or more of the heavy pigments is thinned to spraying consistency, and is allowed to stand 10 to 15 minutes without being stirred, it will settle enough in that time to be off-color when sprayed.

Factory-mixed lacquers and enamels are carefully proportioned at the factory to give the desired color, but it is important that they be carefully stirred before using. A good practice is, after a can of paint has been thoroughly stirred, is to empty it into the gun cup, wash the can clean with a little thinner and add this to the gun cup. In that way it will be sure that all of the pigment and solid matters will have been thoroughly mixed.

If the paint has been in inventory for an extended period and has settled out hard, the liquid part should be poured off and the solid part thoroughly broken up. Then pour back the liquid part and stir vigorously.

A clean spatula or a one inch wide clean wooden stirring paddle, Fig. 27-4, should be used for stirring. Above all, the implement must be clean and free from dirt, grease and other paint. Do not use a screwdriver or other tool for stirring.

Commercially mixed automotive paints are usually shipped at a high rate of viscosity as practical to aid in slowing down the rate of settling. It is, therefore, necessary to add thinners or reducer in order to obtain a viscosity that can be properly sprayed. A power driven shaker for mixing the paint should be used whenever possible.

When adding thinner or reducer, it should always be added slowly and stirred in at the same time. Adding thinner quickly may result in "seedy" looking paint jobs.

Each paint manufacturer has specific recommendations covering the amount of thinner, or reducer, to be added to lacquer, enamel, or acrylic. The amount to be added in some cases varies with the individual color. For example: One paint manufacturer recommends 1-1/2 parts thinner to one part of lacquer color. For enamel the same manufacturer recommends 4 parts of color to one of reducer. All manufacturers have particular recommendations for their products.

There are many different types of thinners available. Some are slower drying than others, some prevent moisture blush, and are designed for use on excessively damp, humid days. Others are for normal conditions. Whatever type is selected, the manufacturer's instructions should be carefully and accurately

*Fig. 27-4. Paint must be thoroughly mixed and stirred before use.*

followed. It must be remembered that, adding thinner is a precision job; too much or too little can easily spoil an otherwise good job.

## COLOR MATCHING

Color matching is one of the most difficult jobs a painter has to do. If the entire vehicle has to be repainted, there is relatively no problem, as the color prepared by the paint manufacturer closely matches the paint chips in the paint catalog. But in many cases only small areas of the car are to be painted. Then matching the color of the rest of the vehicle becomes a major problem if the original color has faded as the result of weather conditions. Some colors fade lighter, others become darker as they weather. Yellow, for example, fades quite rapidly. If the yellow fades from a cream, it usually becomes lighter. If the yellow fades from a green component of blue and yellow, the color usually becomes darker. To those who are not experienced in colors, and tones of colors, it comes as a surprise to learn that there are many different shades of black and also of white.

Every color weathers a little differently than any other color, depending upon its pigment composition. It has been found on occasion that if cars are parked always in the same position and location, the finish will fade more on one side of the vehicle than on the other. In general, the color on cars that are stored in a garage will change less than those that are always parked outside. Those cars operated in hot climates will fade more than those in colder areas. Also those cars which are rubbed and polished a lot generally fade more than those which are not polished.

Weathering and coloring change is most rapid during the first few months after the car has been painted, and then the rate of change slows considerably.

In order to provide customer satisfaction, many paint shops tint colors to match the weathered color on the car.

Although the ability to match colors is mostly a matter of experience, it must be emphasized that anyone with poor color perception cannot do such work successfully. Statisticians tell us that one man in 12 is partly or totally color blind. Men with normal color perception will find that with patience, observation and experience, they can do a good job of color matching.

For tinting work a number of single pigment colors are needed. Such colors must be uniform in tinting strength, and should be in lacquers, acrylic and enamel, as these three types will not mix satisfactorily.

Paint manufacturers supply such basic single pigment colors designed especially for auto painters as an aid in matching colors. Some thirty basic colors are available in each type of material, but for most work the following nine single pigment colors are sufficient:

White
Black Weak
Blue
Black Strong
Rich Brown
Green
Oxide Yellow
Oxide Red
Burnt Sienna

The art of knowing how tinting colors will behave in hundreds of different combinations is a matter of practice and experience. Each color has what is known as mass tone and tint tone. The mass tone can be judged from the color as it appears in the can, or as it is indicated on the painted panel. The tint tone of a color is a shade resulting from mixing a small amount of color with a large amount of white. A dark green mass tone, for example, will often give a blue tint tone. Some maroons have a violet or purple tint tone. Usually adding white to dark green does not give light green, or adding white to maroon does not produce light red. Small additions of tinting color will tint according to their tint tone, while large additions influence color according to their mass tone.

Polychromatic (multicolored) colors are particularly difficult to tint because they often have what is known as flop. That is the color looks different from an angle than it does straight on. When looking directly into the color, the tint tones have the greatest effect, while at an angle the mass tones show the most.

Paint manufacturers provide equipment designed to aid and simplify matching colors. One type of equipment is shown in Fig. 27-5.

When tinting a color some device must always be used for measuring the quantities being used, and a list of colors and amount used on each paint job should be kept. A lot of paint will be saved, if only a small amount is tinted initially. Remember that color tone will change as it dries, and in general the tint should be kept in the light side until a final dried match is determined. And color should always be checked in the daylight as well as artificial light. When a refinished color matches in one light, but not in another, it usually indicates that the same pigments were not used in the refinish material as in the original material.

## MATCHING COLORS WITH SPRAY GUN

It is important to remember that the strength or tone of a color is affected by the manner in which it is sprayed. Spraying technique can change the color considerably. This is particularly true when high polychromatic colors (that is colors with high metallic content are sprayed).

Too great a distance between the gun and the surface of the work will produce a dry spray and tend to lighten the color, Fig. 27-6. A wet spray, produced by holding the gun too close to the work will darken the color. Insufficient air pressure will also darken the color. The type of thinner may affect the color tone.

The number of coats applied will also affect the color or shade. Most colors, particularly pastel colors, will produce a lighter shade by spraying an excessive number of coats, and darker shades will be the result if a lesser number of coats are applied. As a general rule the thickness of automotive finishes is .004 in. The undercoat will be .002 in. thick, and the color coat .002 in. thick. To obtain a good color match, the film thickness of the refinish paint should be the same as the original.

The following method may be used to check for difference in color. First use a rubbing compound to clean an area of the original finish. Select an area that can be viewed from several different angles to observe the

Fig. 27-5. Supplies and equipment used to accurately match colors and mix paint.

light reflection. A good spot is a lower corner of the trunk lid, as it can be raised or lowered to permit easier viewing for light reflection. Rubbing compound should be used because it has enough abrasive action to cut through wax

Normal spray 6" to 8"
Air pressure 40 to 45 lbs.
at the gun.

Dry spray.
Too far away 10" to 12"
Too much air pressure.

Fig. 27-6. Note how excess air pressure and holding the spray gun too far from the surface affects color of paint.

and oxidized finish, and brings out the true shade of the existing color. Then clean the area with a wax and grease remover, to remove any traces of oil left by the rubbing compound. Do not let the cleaner dry, but wipe it dry with clean (not laundered) cloth. With the area clean, take a piece of masking paper about 18 in. square and cut a 2 in. hole in the center. Place this hole over the cleaned area and hold the masking paper in position with masking tape, Fig. 27-7. Now with the correct color correctly reduced and with the right air pressure, spray the 2 in. hole in the normal manner. Remove the masking paper and allow the sprayed area to dry. The newly finished area can be accurately compared with the original finish.

*Fig. 27-7. Spraying a restricted area helps determine accuracy of paint match.*

Because there can be a difference in gloss between the compounded area and the newly sprayed test patch, it may be desirable to wet the area with cleaner's naphtha. If there is a color shade difference between the original finish and the test patch, it then becomes necessary to determine which way the color is off, and how much.

First decide which way the color is off. If still in doubt as to which way the tinting should progress, take a small amount of the reduced color and start by adding a darker or lighter shade, and note the result. After the lighter or darker problem has been solved, the proper tinting color can be chosen to further the tinting process.

It is always a good idea to start by taking a small amount of reduced color in case you over-tint. Any time any one color is added to excess, it throws the entire color formula out of balance. To compensate for it, a corresponding amount of each of the colors that it takes to make up the original, should be added to bring the color back to its original shade.

This is impractical, however, and the easiest thing to do is to use some of the original material that was held back. Only a drop or two of base color should be added at a time. Also it should be remembered that contrasting colors change the shade more quickly than colors of a close hue.

The chart, Fig. 27-8, can be used as a guide when tinting.

Now by deciding which way the color should go, and by use of the tinting chart, the tinting color is selected and added to a small amount of the reduced color. This in turn is sprayed just to one side and overlapping over the first test patch. This process is repeated until an exact match is obtained.

In general, metallic colors can be tinted in the same manner as solid colors, with the exception of dealing with the metallic effect. These colors must definitely be viewed from different angles when checking the test patches to insure getting the same light reflection quality from the metallic particles disbursed through the paint film. In viewing a comparison patch against the original finish, with the light at your back, look directly into the test patch color. If it appears too dark, it needs more metallic tinting material. If the patch is too light, it has too much metallic and needs some of all the other colors used in formulating the shade.

Now look at the patch from an oblique angle. In that way you get away from the distraction of the reflection of the metallic particles and allow the eye to see the basic shade. This color may be tinted using the same procedure as described for a solid color. Keep in mind it should not be attempted to make a large amount of color change in a metallic shade, particularly in the so-called "high glamour" colors. They are formulated with a high content of clear material in order to make the material more transparent and thereby allow more of the reflecting metallic particles to be seen.

So with a high percentage of clear, it stands to reason there is very little color pigment in this type of material. Therefore, just a small amount of tinting color is needed to make a decided change in shade. Also in these "high glamour" colors, there are usually not less than two kinds or sizes of metallic particles. This makes it difficult to know what kind or how much to add to a given color when more metallic is needed to change the effect for a better match. Medium metallic tends to lighten a color "face on," but has little effect on the angle view. Fine metallic lightens a color from the angle view. Coarse metallic lightens a color "face on," but less than medium or fine metallic. Coarse metallic is used mainly in high glamour colors.

Some custom colors are very difficult to duplicate. One is a metallic color in which the metallic particles are not aluminum flakes. In some cases gilt or bronze powder is used.

Another type of finish that is difficult to

| COLOR | IF COLOR TOO STRONG ADD | IF COLOR TOO LIGHT ADD | IF COLOR TOO GREEN ADD | IF COLOR TOO RED ADD | IF COLOR TOO YELLOW ADD | IF COLOR TOO BLUE ADD | IF COLOR TOO "DIRTY" ADD |
|---|---|---|---|---|---|---|---|
| Gray | White | Black | Mix White and Oxide Red | Medium Green | Mix White and touch of Indo Blue | Mix Med. Yellow and either Cadmium Red or Oxide Red | Mix White and either Blue Toner or Indo Blue |
| Blue | White | Blue or Blue Toner or Indo Blue | Deep Maroon | Medium Green | Deep Maroon | Mix Med. Yellow and either Cadmium Red or Oxide Red | Mix White and Blue Toner |
| Green | White or Yellow | Medium Green or Blue or Blue Toner | | Mix Blue Toner and Med. Yellow and Medium Green | Blue Toner | Mix Med. Yellow and either Cadmium Red or Oxide Red | Mix Med. Yellow and Blue Toner |
| Red | Mix White and Cadmium Red | Oxide Red or Light Maroon | | | Light Maroon | Oxide Red | Mix Light Maroon and Touch of White |
| Maroon | Light Maroon or Cadmium Red | Deep Maroon | | | Deep Maroon | Light Maroon or Oxide Red or Medium Yellow | Mix Deep Maroon and touch of White |
| Yellow | White or Medium Yellow | Ferrite Yellow or Medium Yellow | Mix White and touch of Cadmium Red | Mix White and Light Green | White | | Mix White and Medium Yellow |
| Orange | Medium Yellow | Cadmium Red or Orange | Mix Cadmium Red and Medium Yellow | Medium Yellow | Cadmium Red or Toluidine Red | | Mix Med. Yellow and either Cadmium Red or Toluidine Red |
| Ivory | White | Ferrite Yellow or Medium Yellow | Orange or touch of Cadmium Red | Mix White and Light Green | White | | Mix White and touch of either Ferrite Yellow or Medium Yellow |
| Brown | Mix White and either Orange or Burnt Sienna | Mix Black and Medium Yellow and Oxide Red | Oxide Red or Burnt Sienna | Mix Light Green and Burnt Sienna (Add White if Necessary) | Mix Oxide Red and Black | | Mix Ferrite Yellow and Oxide Red and touch of either Orange or Burnt Sienna |
| Cream | White | Ferrite Yellow or Medium Yellow | Mix White and either Orange or Cadmium Red | Mix Medium Yellow and White (Add Light Green if necessary) | White | | Mix White and touch of either Ferrite Yellow or Medium Yellow |
| Tan | White | Burnt Sienna or Mix Ferrite Yellow and Black | Cadmium Red or Toluidine Red (Add White if necessary) | Mix White and Touch of Light Green | Mix White and either Cadmium Red or Toluidine Red | | Mix White and either Oxide Red or Ferrite Yellow |

| GLAMOUR COLOR | IF COLOR TOO GREEN ADD | IF COLOR TOO BLUE ADD | IF COLOR TOO "DIRTY" ADD |
|---|---|---|---|
| Blue | Indo Blue or Deep Maroon | Green Toner | Blue Toner and touch of White |
| Green | Blue Toner | Old Gold | Touch of White |
| Brown | Burnt Sienna and Light Maroon | Old Gold or Burnt Sienna | Burnt Sienna or Old Gold |
| Maroon | | Burnt Sienna or Light Maroon | Cadmium Red |

CAUTION: A few drops of shading color may be enough, especially when the fresh color is too yellow, blue, green or red. Occasionally, two shading steps are needed for an accurate match. Glamour colors are very sensitive. Be very careful toning colors with these bases: Old Gold Toner, Blue Toner, Green Toner, Indo Blue.

If the color contains not more than 20 parts of the glamour color base, use the regular tinting instructions. If the color contains more than 20 parts of the glamour color base, follow the instructions in the small chart.

If necessary, add polychrome base, a very small amount at a time, to maintain brilliance.

Fig. 27-8. Chart which may be used as a guide when tinting.

match is the "candy apple" finish. This attractive colorful finish has an amazing appearance of depth as obtained by spraying many coats of tinted clear material (usually a rich maroon or lime green) over a metallic base coat. The base coat often used resembles burnished brass. The clear material has just enough color to give a definite cast or shade and as much as twenty-five coats of it may have been sprayed over the base coat to give an illusion of depth.

Acrylic and conventional lacquer are tinted to the desired shade in the same manner as just described. However, because acrylic has greater durability and does not fade as readily as lacquer, matching colors is not so great a problem. Colors in enamel are more difficult to match because it takes so long for the enamel to dry in order to compare the new color with the original.

## QUIZ - Chapter 27

1. How can you determine the color used to finish the vehicle originally?
   Comparing with color code books.
   Noting color code number placed on tag
      on vehicle.
   Read owner's manual.

2. It is not necessary to thoroughly stir the paint before using.
   True.
   False.
3. When adding thinner or reducer, it should be added as quickly as possible.
   True.
   False.
4. All colors fade lighter.
   True.
   False.
5. When is color change most rapid?
   First few months after painting.
   After car is a year old.
6. Polychromatic colors are easy to tint.
   True.
   False.
7. Can spraying technique affect the tone of the color being sprayed?
   Yes.
   No.
8. Will the number of coats being sprayed affect the color or shade?
   Yes.
   No.
9. What is the approximate thickness of automotive finishes?
   .010 in.
   .002 in.
   .004 in.
   .005 in.

# Chapter 28

# SPRAY PAINTING
# EQUIPMENT

Fig. 28-1. Using spray gun to paint a car.

Automotive vehicles, both passenger car and commercial, are painted with a spray gun, Fig. 28-1. By using such equipment, the paint is applied evenly and without any brush strokes to mar the appearance and smoothness of the finished surface. However, skill and care are required in the operation of the spray gun, in order to obtain good results.

Fig. 28-2. Spray gun used for painting cars.

## THE SPRAY GUN

The paint spray gun, Fig. 28-2, is a device which uses air pressure to atomize sprayable material and apply it to a surface. Air and paint enter the gun through separate passages and are mixed and ejected at the air cap in a controlled pattern, Fig. 28-3. Adjustments are provided to control the air pressure and the amount of paint being sprayed.

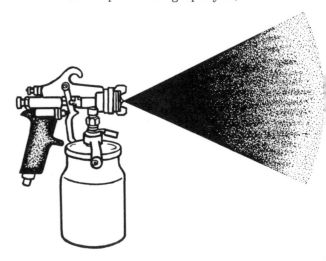

Fig. 28-3. Shape of spray from spray gun.

There are two basic types of paint spraying equipment. One type, Figs. 28-1 and 28-4, has the gun and paint container forming a single unit, while the other type has the paint container separate from the spray gun, Fig. 28-5.

These two basic types can be further divided into bleeder and nonbleeder, external and internal mix, and pressure, gravity or suction feed guns.

The spray gun designed without an air valve is known as a bleeder type gun. Air passes through the gun at all times, preventing pres-

Fig. 28-4. Using spray gun with paint cup attached.

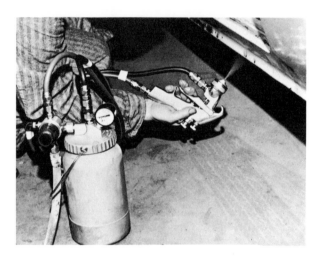

Fig. 28-5. Spray gun with paint in separate container.

sure build-up in the air line, and is used with small air compressors of limited capacity and pressure. No pressure controlling device such as an unloader, or pressure switch, is provided. The trigger controls only the flow of paint in this type gun.

A nonbleeder type gun is equipped with an air valve which shuts off the air when the trigger is released. In this type gun, the trigger controls both the air and the flow of paint.

A spray gun that mixes and atomizes air and paint outside the air cap is known as an external mix gun, Fig. 28-6. This type of gun can be used for spraying all types of fluid materials, and is the type best suited for spraying fast drying materials, such as lacquers.

An internal mix gun mixes air and material inside the cap before expelling them, Fig. 28-7. This type of gun is used for spraying slow drying materials, not containing any abrasive. It is frequently used for spraying flat wall paint or outside house paint.

A suction feed gun utilizes a stream of compressed air to create a vacuum so that paint is forced from an attaching container. This type gun is usually limited to containers of one quart capacity, and is easily identified by the fluid tip extending slightly beyond the air cap, Fig. 28-8. Such guns are used primarily when there are many color changes and small amounts of paint, such as is the case when refinishing an automobile.

A spray gun with an air cap is not necessarily designed to create a vacuum. In the case of a pressure feed gun, Fig. 28-9, the fluid tip is generally flush with the air cap

Fig. 28-6. External mix gun.

Fig. 28-7. Internal mix gun mixes air and material inside the cap.

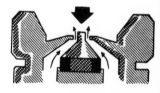

Fig. 28-8. Suction feed gun.

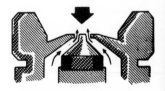

Fig. 28-9. Pressure feed gun.

and material is forced to the gun by air pressure from a tank, cup or pump. This type of gun is used extensively when large amounts of the same color are to be sprayed such as production finishing of automobiles.

Other types of spray guns are available for production finishing of various types and are usually adaptations of some of the previously described guns. Such guns are usually automatic in their operation and are mounted on special fixtures and movable conveyors.

## DETAILS OF SPRAY GUNS

A typical spray gun such as is used in the refinishing of automobiles is shown in Fig. 28-10. The principal parts of this DeVilbiss Spray Gun are: Air Cap A, Fluid Tip B, Fluid Needle C, Trigger D, Fluid Adjustment Screw E, Air Valve F, Spreader Adjustment G, Gun Body H.

As shown in Fig. 28-10, the air cap is located at the front of the gun and directs the compressed air into the material stream to atomize it and form it into a spray. The cross section of this spray is called the spray pattern, Fig. 28-3. There are various style caps producing different sizes and shapes of patterns for all types of applications. Air caps are either of the external or internal mix types.

## SELECTING THE AIR CAP

There are two types of air caps: External and Internal Mix Types. The external mix caps, Fig. 28-6, are used with either suction or pressure feed and eject air through one or more holes to atomize the paint. External mix caps may have from one to as many as four orifices for production spraying.

The internal mix caps, Fig. 28-7, mix air and material inside the gun before ejecting them through a single slot or round orifice and are used only with pressure feed, and consequently are used primarily for spraying heavy viscous (sticky) materials.

Multiple jet caps have the advantage of providing better atomization for such materials and synthetics and heavy body lacquers. Also higher pressures can be used on more viscous materials with less danger of

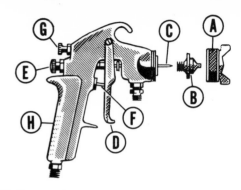

Fig. 28-10. Details of typical spray gun as used in auto paint shop, A—Air cap, B—Fluid tip, C—Fluid needle, D—Trigger, E—Fluid adjustment screw, F—Air valve, G—Spreader adjustment valve.

distorting the spray pattern. For materials that can be sprayed at lower pressures, multiple jet caps provide better atomization with less air.

## FLUID TIP

The nozzle directly behind the air cap is known as the fluid tip. It meters and directs the paint into the air streams. The fluid tip forms a seat for the fluid needle which shuts off the flow of material. Fluid tips are available in a variety of nozzle sizes and the larger the nozzle, the greater the amount of material that can be sprayed. Sizes range from .086 in. to .110 in. The size can be identified by a letter or dimension stamped on the fluid tip and needle. Sizes ranging from .070 in. to .041 in. are most frequently used for automobile spray painting. To obtain a given rate of fluid flow, pressure feed setups operate with smaller tips than suction feed. Tips and needles must always be the same size. For suction feed guns, such as are usually used when repainting automobiles, a nozzle size of .041 in. is often used.

## SPREADER ADJUSTMENT VALVE

To control the air to the air horn, a spreader adjustment valve, Fig. 28-10, is provided. By this means the size of the spray pattern is controlled.

## FLUID NEEDLE ADJUSTMENT

The fluid needle adjustment controls the travel of the fluid needle, and in that way permits more or less material to pass through the fluid tip.

## CARE OF PAINT SPRAY GUN

Paint spray guns should be cleaned immediately after use. If this is not done, the paint will dry in the nozzles making cleaning exceedingly difficult.

To clean a suction feed gun and cup, first loosen the cup from the gun and while the paint tube is still in the cup, unscrew the air cap about two or three turns. Hold a cloth over the air cap and pull the trigger. Air diverted into the fluid passageways forces material back into the container, Fig. 28-11.

Fig. 28-11. Material is forced back into container, when cloth is held over air cap and trigger is pulled.

Fig. 28-12. Solvent is being sprayed through gun to flush out fluid passages.

Next empty cup of material and replace with a small quantity of clean solvent. Spray solvent through the gun to flush out fluid passages, Fig. 28-12. Wipe off the gun with a solvent soaked rag or, if necessary, use a fibre bristle brush moistened with thinner and scrub the gun. Then remove the air cap and clean as follows: The air cap should be removed from the gun and cleaned by simply immersing in clean solvent and then drying by blowing it off with compressed air. If small holes become clogged, soak the cap in solvent. If reaming out the hole is still necessary, use a wooden match stick, a broom straw, or other similar material. A wire or nail should not be used as this may permanently damage the cap.

A pressure feed system is cleaned by following this procedure: Back up the air pressure regulator adjusting screw on the tank, release pressure from the tank by means of a relief valve, or safety valve. Loosen spray gun air cap ring three turns. Hold a cloth over air cap and pull trigger to force material back into tank, Fig. 28-13. Remove fluid hose from gun and attach it to a hose cleaner, A, Fig. 28-13. Run air and solvent through the hose and fluid tube on the tank. Dry hose with compressed air. Clean air cap and tip as described in connection with suction type guns. Clean out tank and reassemble for future use.

A hose cleaner is a device which forces

Fig. 28-13. Holding cloth over cap and pulling trigger, forces material back into tank.

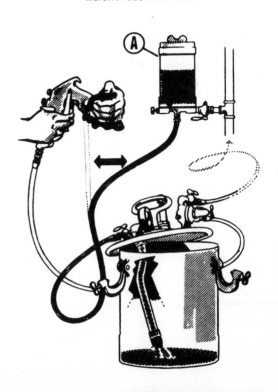

air and solvent through fluid hose and guns, cleaning them of paint residue.

Spray guns should never be immersed in solvent. Such a practice allows sludge and dirt to collect in the air passages of the gun. Such accumulations will then be blown on the surface being sprayed the next time the gun is used. Solvents also remove lubricants and dry out the packings of the spray gun.

Caustic alkaline solutions should never be used to clean spray guns, because they will corrode the aluminum and die cast parts of which spray guns are made.

Spray guns require occasional lubrication. The fluid needle packing A, Fig. 28-14, air valve packing B, and the trigger bearing screw C, require a drop or two of light oil occasionally. The fluid needle D should be coated with petrolatum.

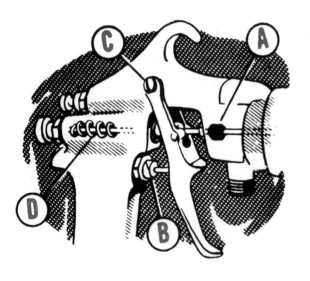

Fig. 28-14. *Points requiring lubrication, A—Fluid needle packing, B—Air valve packing, C—Trigger bearing screw.*

## PRESSURE AND SUCTION FEED GUN

Most auto paint shops are equipped with the suction feed type spray guns in which the spray gun is attached directly to the cup, Fig. 28-4. However, when painting any surface except a vertical surface, it is necessary to hold the gun at an angle with the result the applied thickness of paint will be uneven. The suction feed gun employs a partial vacuum created by the air stream just outside the fluid tip of the spray gun. Paint in

the attached cup is therefore under atmospheric pressure via a vent hole in the top of the cup cover. This pressure forces the paint

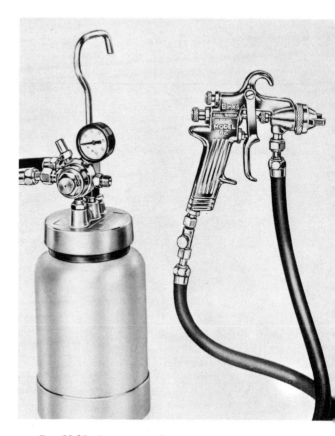

Fig. 28-15. *Spray gun and separate paint container.*

up the fluid tube into the path of the air jets, and in that way becomes atomized.

However, if the gun and its container are tilted (as would be necessary when painting the top or the hood) paint would flow over the vent hole and air pressure will no longer reach the paint to force it up the fluid tube. Another disadvantage is the same air flow that atomizes and sprays the paint is used to operate the syphon. In many cases the amount of air pressure required to operate the syphon is greater than that needed to atomize the paint. This is particularly true when painting large areas. With the fluid adjustment wide open for maximum pattern size, the atomization pressure could be 25 to 35 lbs. higher than needed.

In addition, the amount of paint that can be sprayed is limited to about 12 oz. per minute.

To overcome these disadvantages, many

paint shops are turning to pressure feed systems, such as shown in Fig. 28-5. In this type system, paint is fed from a pressurized tank that is separate from the gun, Fig. 28-15. Atomization here is fed through the gun in the same manner as suction feed. The advantage of this system is that the gun is not dependent

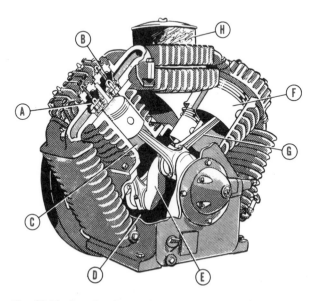

Fig. 28-16. Details of typical compressor. A—Air compressor, B—Motor for driving compressor, C—Air receiver or storage tank, D—Check valve, E—Pressure switch which automatically controls pressure, F—Centrifugal pressure relieves motor of starting against load. G—Safety valve to protect lines and equipment.

upon atomization air pressure, and consequently the air pressure can be set at its proper level without affecting the flow of paint. Paint flow can be adjusted independently with the fluid adjusting screw without changing atomization air pressure. In other words, two separate controls are provided, one for air and the other for fluid. The paint is in a container separate from the gun, which leaves the gun free of the weight and restricting size of the cup. Most important, it leaves the gun free so that it can be used at any angle. Also more paint can be applied in the same amount of time.

However, more skill is required to use a pressure feed system than a suction or syphon system. The reason is that the greater paint flow requires faster and fewer passes of the gun to prevent flooding and consequent sagging of the paint.

## TYPES OF COMPRESSORS

The compressors used for spray painting are of two basic types known as single-stage and two-stage compressors.

A single-stage compressor has only a single cylinder and provides pressures up to 100 psi (pounds per square inch). A two-stage compressor, Figs. 28-16, and 28-17, has two cylinders of unequal size with an intercooler between the two cylinders. It is

Fig. 28-17. Complete air compressor and storage tank.

used for pressures of over 100 psi. In the two-stage compressor, air is compressed first in the larger of the two cylinders, this is the low-pressure cylinder, and as a result of being compressed the temperature of the air is increased. From the low-pressure cylinder the air passes into an intercooler where its temperature is reduced. Then it passes to the smaller cylinder where it is further compressed and then forced into the storage tank.

## COMPRESSOR SIZE

Compressors must be of adequate size to supply all the requirements of the shop. If the air compressor is for the paint department only, the air requirements would include air for the spray guns, pneumatic lifts, pneumatic fender hammers, vacuum cleaner. If the same compressor is to be used to supply the air for the entire shop, then all of the tools and equipment must be included. The amount of air needed to operate the various types of shop tools and equipment is as follows:

For example, from Chart No. 1, determine the average free air consumption required to operate all the tools in the department, or a shop. Spray guns require 8.5 cu. ft. per minute. If three guns are being used, the total

CHART NO. 1

| Quantity | Type Device | Air Pres. Range | Avg. Free Air Cons. | Total Avg. Air |
|---|---|---|---|---|
| | Air Filter Cleaner | 70-100 | 3.0 | |
| | Air Hammer | 70-100 | 16.5 | |
| | Body Polisher | 70-100 | 2.0 | |
| | Body Sander | 70-100 | 5.0 | |
| | Brake Tester | 70-100 | 3.5 | |
| | Carbon Remover | 70-100 | 3.0 | |
| | Car Rocker | 120-150 | 5.75 | |
| | Car Washer | 70-100 | 8.5 | |
| | Dusting Gun (Blow gun) | 70-100 | 2.5 | |
| | Engine Cleaner | 70-100 | 5.0 | |
| | Fender Hammer | 70-100 | 8.75 | |
| | Grease Gun (high pressure) | 120-150 | 3.0 | |
| | Hoist (one ton) | 70-100 | 1.0 | |
| | *Hydraulic Lift | 145-175 | 5.25 | |
| | Paint Spray Gun (production) | 70-100 | 8.5 | |
| | Paint Spray Gun (touch-up) | 70-100 | 2.25 | |
| | Pneu. Garage Door | 120-150 | 2.0 | |
| | Radiator Tester | 70-100 | 1.0 | |
| | Rim Stripper | 120-150 | 6.0 | |
| | Spark Plug Cleaner | 70-100 | 5.0 | |
| | Spark Plug Tester | 70-100 | .5 | |
| | Spray Gun (Undercoating) | 70-100 | 19.0 | |
| | Spring Oiler | 70-100 | 3.75 | |
| | Tire Changer | 120-150 | 1.0 | |
| | Tire Inflation Line | 120-150 | 1.5 | |
| | Tire Spreader | 120-150 | 1.0 | |
| | Trans. & Diff. Flusher | 70-100 | 3.0 | |
| | Vacuum Cleaner | 120-150 | 6.5 | |

*For 8000 lbs. capacity. Add .65 cfm for each additional 1000 lbs. cap.

CHART NO. 2

| Compressor Pressures per Square inch | | COLUMN A Average Service Station or Garage Use Free Air Consumption in Cubic Feet per Minute of Total Equipment | COLUMN B Continuous Operation Free Air Consumption Cubic Feet per Minute of Total Equipment | COM-PRESSOR Horse-power |
|---|---|---|---|---|
| Cut-in | Cut-out | | | |
| | | 10.6- 13.6 | 3.1- 3.9 | 1 |
| 80 | 100 | 13.7- 20.3 | 4.0- 5.8 | 1-1/2 |
| | | 20.4- 26.6 | 5.9- 7.6 | 2 |
| | | 30.5- 46.2 | 8.8-13.2 | 3 |
| | | 46.3- 60.0 | 13.3-20.0 | 5 |
| | | 60.1- 73.0 | 20.1-29.2 | 7-1/2 |
| 100 | 125 | 73.1-100.0 | 29.3-40.0 | 10 |
| | | 100.0-125.0 | 40.1-50.0 | 15 |
| | | up to - 3.8 | up to - 1.1 | 1/2 |
| | | 3.9- 7.3 | 1.2- 2.1 | 3/4 |
| 120 | 150 | 7.4- 10.1 | 2.2- 2.9 | 1 |
| | | 10.2- 15.0 | 3.0- 4.3 | 1-1/2 |
| | | 15.1- 20.00 | 4.4- 5.7 | 2 |
| | | up to - 11.9 | up to - 3.4 | 1 |
| | | 12.0- 18.5 | 3.5- 5.3 | 1-1/2 |
| | | 18.6- 24.2 | 5.4- 6.9 | 2 |
| | | 24.3- 36.4 | 7.0-10.4 | 3 |
| 140 | 175 | 36.5- 51.0 | 10.5-17.0 | 5 |
| | | 51.1- 66.0 | 17.1-26.4 | 7-1/2 |
| | | 66.1- 88.2 | 26.5-35.3 | 10 |
| | | 88.3-120.0 | 35.4-48.0 | 15 |

will be three times 8.5, or 25.5 cfm. After all the needs of the shop have been totaled, note the highest pressure required for any of the tools or equipment. Then using Chart No. 2, select the pressure range capable of meeting the maximum pressure requirements. Within that range, locate the line indicating the air consumption adequate for the shop requirement. On the same line, in the next column, is the size of the compressor needed.

For suction feed guns, the compressor should deliver a minimum of 11.5 cfm and for pressure feed guns it should deliver 14 cfm. A compressor of the preceding size is adequate in shops where the gun is used intermittently, as the unit will have time to cool off during periods when the gun is not being used. When the spraying operation is continuous, a compressor of one-third higher capacity is required.

## CARE OF COMPRESSORS

The crankcase of the air compressor should be filled to the proper level with a good grade of motor oil. Most manufacturers specify S.A.E. 10 for most conditions, and S.A.E. 20

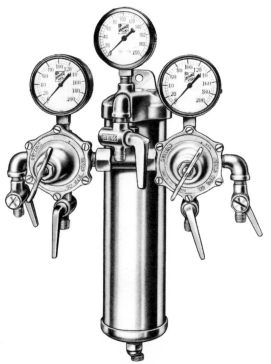

*Fig. 28-18. Type of transformer or regulator.*

for temperatures above 100 deg. F. Oil level should be checked at least once each week and the oil changed every three months. Electric motor bearings should be oiled monthly unless they are of the grease-packed type.

Belt tension should be maintained so that there is no slippage. Cooling fins on compressor and intercooler should be kept clean and free of dust. The air cleaner on the air intake should be cleaned weekly, or oftener, if the compressor is located in a dusty area. The drain cock on the air storage tank should be opened monthly to drain any condensed moisture that may be present. To insure the operation of the safety valve, it should be operated by hand once each week.

## AIR FOR PAINTING

In order for the finished painted surface to be smooth and without defects, it is essential that the compressed air supplied to the spray gun be cleaned and free from all dirt, moisture and oil. Also air pressure must be maintained between 80 and 100 lb.

In order to supply such clean air, and maintain the desired pressure, many paint shops provide a separate compressor used for painting only, Fig. 28-17. Another compressor being provided to supply other needs of the shop. The compressor used for painting should always be maintained in top-notch condition. In addition to using a special compressor for spraying paint, the system is provided with an air transformer and/or oil and moisture separators.

## AIR TRANSFORMER

The air transformer, Fig. 28-18, as designed for use with spray painting equipment, is able to maintain the pressure of air supply to the spray gun within narrow limits and also prevent oil, dirt and water from entering the air lines, which would spoil the paint job.

A high quality air transformer will maintain air pressure within three-quarter pound variation for each ten pound fluctuation in the main line, and will also extract oil, water, and other foreign materials.

Various types of filter elements are used to filter out all foreign matter from the line.

In addition to having the filter elements of the replaceable type, drain cocks are provided, so that oil and moisture can be easily drained from the system.

Air transformers without cleaners are also available. When transformers of that type are used, it is necessary to use individual oil, dirt, and moisture separators.

In operation the air transformer catches dirt, oil and moisture. It does this by means of baffles, centrifugal force, expansion chambers, impingement plates, and filters. The transformers allow only clean, dry air to emerge from the outlets. The air regulating valves provide positive control, insuring uniform regulated pressure. Gauges indicate air pressure, and valves provide outlets for hose lines to the spray guns and other equipment. The drain valve provides for elimination for accumulated sludge, dirt and moisture.

## LOCATING COMPRESSORS AND TRANSFORMER

It is advisable to place the air compressor and air transformer as close to the paint spray booth as possible. In that way the air lines are kept short. This will reduce the amount of moisture condensing in the pipes.

The transformer should be installed in the paint booth for convenience in reading gauges and operating the valves. In addition, it should be installed at least 25 ft. from the compressor.

Piping should be as direct as possible. If a large number of fittings are used, large size pipe should be installed to help overcome the excessive pressure drop. The takeoff for the transformer should be from the top of the line as shown at C, Fig. 28-19. Piping should slope toward the compressor, or a drain leg D, Fig. 28-19, should be installed at the end of the air line, or at the end of each branch, to provide for drainage of moisture from the air line. Valves at the lower end of the drain leg should be opened each morning to drain any accumulated condensation, and the drain cock on the transformer should also be opened daily in order to drain the unit.

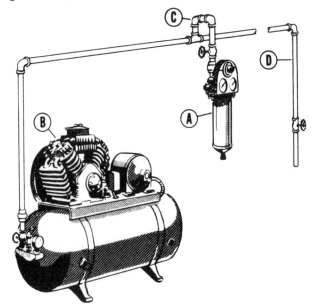

Fig. 28-19. Air piping should be direct and takeoffs should be made from the top of the line.

Piping from compressor to transformer must be of sufficient size for the volume of air passed. Pipe size recommendations being as follows:

MINIMUM PIPE SIZE RECOMMENDATIONS

| COMPRESSING OUTFIT | | MAIN AIR LINE | |
|---|---|---|---|
| SIZE | CAPACITY | LENGTH | SIZE |
| 1-1/2 & 2 H.P. | 6 to 9 C.F.M. | Over 50 ft. | 3/4" |
| 3 & 5 H.P. | 12 to 20 C.F.M. | Up to 200 ft. Over 200 ft. | 3/4" 1" |
| 5 to 10 H.P. | 20 to 40 C.F.M. | Up to 100 ft. Over 100 to 200 ft. Over 200 ft. | 3/4" 1" 1-1/4" |
| 10 to 15 H.P. | 40 to 60 C.F.M. | Up to 100 ft. Over 100 to 200 ft. Over 200 ft. | 1" 1-1/4" 1-1/2" |

## HOSE SIZE

It is important to use hose of adequate size when connecting the spray gun to the air transformer. Resistance to the flow of air or paint, as the case may be, increases rapidly as the diameter of the hose decreases.

For maintenance refinishing of automobiles, two types of hose are used: Air hose and paint hose. Air hose usually has a red rubber cover, although on small low pressure systems the hose may be black and orange braid covered. The paint or fluid hose is black or brown.

For automotive refinishing the fluid hose used for large guns is usually 1/2 in. or 3/8 in. inside diameter. For small guns, such as are used with 1/4 and 1/3 HP compressor outfit, 5/16 in. inside diameter hose is generally used. For spraying underbody coatings, 3/4 in. inside diameter hose is specified.

The air hose from compressor or transformer to the spray gun is usually 5/16 in. ID hose. Hose of 1/4 in. inside diameter may be used for small guns provided the hose length does not exceed 12 ft.

If a pressure feed tank is used, 7/16 in. inside diameter air hose is used from the compressor to the pressure feed tank on large units, and 5/16 in. inside diameter on small units.

## PRESSURE DROP

Pressure drop is the loss of air pressure due to friction between the source of air and point of usage. This loss can become quite serious particularly on long distances and when small diameter hose is used. The following table should be consulted to determine pressure drop when locating compressor and transformer, and when purchasing hose.

tion, built to confine an exhaust overspray and fumes resulting from spray painting or similar operations.

There are two major reasons for placing vehicles in a spray booth while they are being painted.

1. Dust is excluded and in that way will not settle on the vehicle while the paint is being applied, nor while it is drying.

2. Paint booths are provided with exhaust fans which force out the paint odors and thereby reduce fire hazards, and also greatly improve working conditions for the painter, which in turn results in less sickness and lost time.

Painting materials and fumes are highly flammable, and when spraying is done on the open shop floor, where sparks from welding are common, fire may result.

If a commercial booth is not available, a room approximately 9 ft. high, 14 ft. wide and 25 ft. long may be used. Adequate lighting to eliminate all shadows should be provided. an exhaust fan capable of maintaining air movement of 100 linear feet per minute throughout the area is also necessary. A filtered air intake is another requirement. To prevent contamination of the newly painted vehicle, the air spray may be used as a drying area. Or, another clean, dry, enclosed area should be provided.

### TABLE OF AIR PRESSURE DROP

#### AIR PRESSURE DROP AT SPRAY GUN

| SIZE OF AIR HOSE INSIDE DIAMETER | 5-FOOT LENGTH | 10-FOOT LENGTH | 15-FOOT LENGTH | 20-FOOT LENGTH | 25-FOOT LENGTH | 50-FOOT LENGTH |
|---|---|---|---|---|---|---|
| 1/4-inch | Lbs. | Lbs. | Lbs. | Lbs. | Lbs. | Lbs. |
| At 40 lbs. pressure | 6 | 8 | 9-1/2 | 11 | 12-3/4 | 24 |
| At 50 lbs. pressure | 7-1/2 | 10 | 12 | 14 | 16 | 28 |
| At 60 lbs. pressure | 9 | 12-1/2 | 14-1/2 | 16-3/4 | 19 | 31 |
| At 70 lbs. pressure | 10-3/4 | 14-1/2 | 17 | 19-1/2 | 22-1/2 | 34 |
| At 80 lbs. pressure | 12-1/4 | 16-1/2 | 19-1/2 | 22-1/2 | 25-1/2 | 37 |
| At 90 lbs. pressure | 14 | 18-3/4 | 22 | 25-1/4 | 29 | 39-1/2 |
| 5/16-inch | | | | | | |
| At 40 lbs. pressure | 2-1/4 | 2-3/4 | 3-1/4 | 3-1/2 | 4 | 8-1/2 |
| At 50 lbs. pressure | 3 | 3-1/2 | 4 | 4-1/2 | 5 | 10 |
| At 60 lbs. pressure | 3-3/4 | 4-1/2 | 5 | 5-1/2 | 6 | 11-1/2 |
| At 70 lbs. pressure | 4-1/2 | 5-1/4 | 6 | 6-3/4 | 7-1/4 | 13 |
| At 80 lbs. pressure | 5-1/2 | 6-1/4 | 7 | 8 | 8-3/4 | 14-1/2 |
| At 90 lbs. pressure | 6-1/2 | 7-1/2 | 8-1/2 | 9-1/2 | 10-1/2 | 16 |

## SPRAY BOOTHS

A spray booth is a compartment, room or enclosure, generally of fireproof construc-

In many cities fire underwriters require that automotive vehicles be painted in spray booths designed for the purpose. But even if such requirements are not in force, it always

Fig. 28-20. Type of drive-through spray booth.

pays to use a spray booth. The initial cost is soon offset by better paint jobs and improved health of workers.

There are two basic types of spray booths: 1. Dry type. 2. Air washer type.

Some variations of the dry type booth are used almost exclusively by auto body re-finishers while the air washer type is used in production work.

In the dry type spray booth, Fig. 28-20, contaminated air is drawn through baffles or removable filters and is expelled directly outside. In the watertight spray booth, air is drawn through a series of water curtains and baffles to remove solids from the overspray, before it is exhausted. Commercially con-structed booths are desirable, but some auto refinishers construct their own booths by partitioning off a corner of the shop. A large exhaust fan is installed and air is drawn into the booth through filters such as are com-monly used in hot air heating systems. The spray booth must be so designed that all joints are sealed and the filtered air intake must be of adequate area to filter all air being moved through the booth by means of the ex-haust fan. The fan should be capable of maintaining air movement of 100 linear feet per minute throughout the booth.

## PAINT DRYING EQUIPMENT

In order to hasten the drying of the finishes used in refinishing the automobile, various types of drying equipment are used. Such equipment ranges from a single bulb type

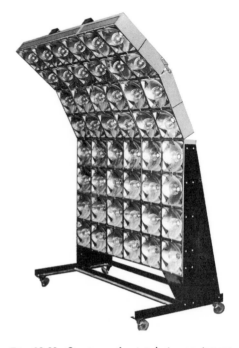

Fig. 28-21. One type of paint drying equipment.

190

Fig. 28-22. Paint drying equipment.

Lacquers dry primarily by evaporation of their solvents. Enamels dry because of two chemical changes, oxidation and polymerization. In the oxidizing process of drying, the enamel absorbs oxygen which causes the enamel to dry. In the case of polymerization, the synthetic resin in the enamel acts somewhat like an egg when heat is applied. It solidifies, becomes hard, and will not return to a liquid state, no matter how much heat is applied.

Polymerization speeds up drying beyond that which would take place with oxidation alone. It also makes the paint harder, improves water and chemical resistance, and enhances its durability and gloss.

Force drying temperatures of below 165 deg. F. dries the finish only by increasing oxidation, and does not start polymerization. The higher the temperature of the baking system, the greater the oxidation, and polymerization. With true baking temperatures around 300 deg. F., finishes can be dried in a few minutes.

unit, Fig. 13-11, to huge batteries of infrared lamps, as shown in Figs. 28-21, 28-22, and 28-23. In some operations, the drying

Fig. 28-23. Drive-through type of drying equipment.

equipment is installed in a spray booth. In large establishments, a baking tunnel type oven is placed at the end of the spray booth. As soon as the spraying is completed the vehicle is rolled forward into the drying room.

Paint baking equipment is used particularly when the vehicle is refinished with enamel.

There are two basic types of baking equipment: Radiant and convection. The latter bakes with hot air, circulated in well-insulated ovens into which the vehicle is pushed. The heat in such cases is usually produced by natural gas or oil.

Radiant units bake with electrically powered infrared lamps or ceramic heating units. The lamps use 125, 250 or 500 watt bulbs, Fig. 28-23. A shop turning out more than 10 cars per day, will usually find the tunnel type equipment economical. Smaller shops will use equipment shown in Figs. 28-21 and 28-22.

When an infrared baking unit is used, consideration must be given to the fact that darker colors absorb more heat than the lighter colors. Excessive heat may cause loss of gloss and discoloration, blistering and wrinkling. Baking time of different colors must therefore be kept in mind.

Before putting the car in the baking oven, 10 to 15 minutes should elapse to provide time for the solvents to "flash off." Heavy fills of putty and 10 or 12 coats of old surfacer have a tendency to cause blistering when placed in the bake oven.

Loss of gloss can be caused by applying

Fig. 28-24. Type of respirator.

insufficient enamel, porous old finish or undercoat, too much heat or too long a bake, too much reducer, insufficient ventilation. Windows of the vehicle should be left partly open during the baking process. This will provide better distribution of heat and reduce any tendency for the glass to break.

## RESPIRATORS

Paint fumes are toxic, particularly if inhaled constantly. When spraying paint, or when working in an area where paint is being sprayed, a respirator should be worn. See Fig. 28-24. A respirator is a mask worn over the nose and mouth to prevent the inhalation of toxic pigment particles, harmful dust and vapors from various types of paints and lacquer. The hood type respirator which protects the eyes of the wearer is a popular type. The organic type respirator is equipped with replaceable cartridges that remove organic vapors by chemical absorption and also any dust particles that may be present.

Some respirators are designed to remove dust only, and are satisfactory only if the material being sprayed contains no toxic fumes.

## QUIZ - Chapter 28

1. A spray gun uses air to atomize the material being sprayed.
   True.
   False.
2. The spray gun with an air valve is known as a bleeder gun.
   True.
   False.
3. An external mix gun is usually used when refinishing an automobile.
   True.
   False.
4. The air cap is located at the front of the spray gun and directs the material stream into the compressed air to atomize it and form it into a spray.
   True.
   False.
5. What size fluid tip is usually used when refinishing an automobile? (Suction feed gun.)
   .041 in.
   .025 in.
   .100 in.
   .014 in.
6. A major advantage of a spray gun is that it is not necessary to clean it after each use.
   True.
   False.
7. If small holes in air cap become clogged, what should be used to clean them?
   Wooden match stick.
   Wire nail.
   Fine wire as used for attaching tags.
8. What type of lubricant should be used on fluid needle packing, air valve packing and trigger bearing screw?
   Light oil.

Transmission lubricant.
Lubriplate.
Wheel bearing grease.

9. In a pressure feed system, the spray gun can be held at any angle.
   True.
   False.

10. In a two-stage compressor, air is first compressed in which cylinder?
    Larger cylinder.
    Smaller cylinder.

11. Cooling fins of compressors should be kept clean.
    True.
    False.

12. A high quality air transformer will keep air pressure within what limits?
    3/4 lb. variation.
    2 lb. variation.
    5 lb. variation.

13. Air hose used in painting is usually what color?
    Red.
    Green.
    Black.

14. What is the inside diameter of fluid hose used when refinishing automobiles? (Large gun.)
    1/2 in.
    3/8 in.
    1/4 in.

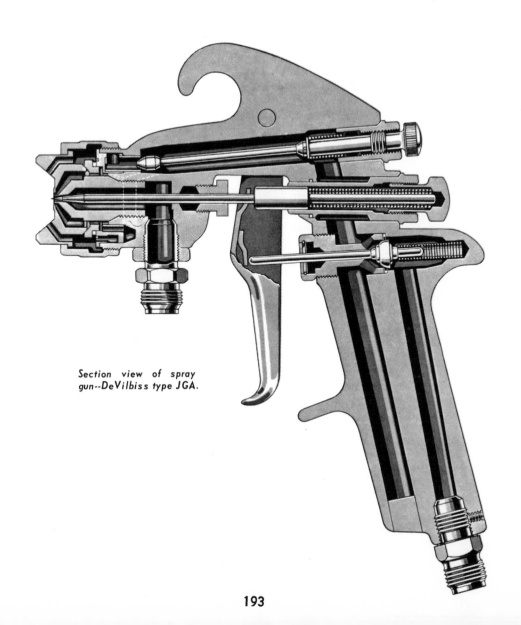

*Section view of spray gun--DeVilbiss type JGA.*

# Chapter 29

# HOW TO
# SPRAY PAINT

## USING A SPRAY GUN

A production type spray gun, clean and in good condition is required to obtain proper atomization and application of paint in a minimum amount of time. Either a suction feed gun, or a pressure feed type may be used, Fig. 29-1.

For suction feed work a suitable air cap and fluid tip are needed. A one quart capacity suction feed cup attached directly to the spray gun is generally used.

*Fig. 29-1. Using a suction feed gun to spray a car.*

The fluid tip or nozzle normally used for suction feed guns will be .070 in. For faster application a .086 in. tip is used. The air cap for the .070 in. tip will require 11.5 cubic feet of air per minute at a spraying pressure of 60 lb. For the .086 in. tip, an air cap consuming 13 cu. ft. of air at 60 lb. pressure is needed.

For pressure feed work, a fluid tip in the range from .0425 in. to .046 in. should be used. A pressure feed cap consuming 14 cu. ft. of air will be needed.

Spray guns as used in auto body refinishing, Fig. 28-10, have two manual adjustments that must be properly set to achieve good operating results. This is true for both suction and pressure feed guns. The two adjustments found on both types of gun are the spreader adjusting valve for side port control, and fluid adjustment. The spreader adjusting valve when fully closed shuts off the air to the horns on the air cap and a round spray pattern results, Fig. 29-2. As this valve is gradu-

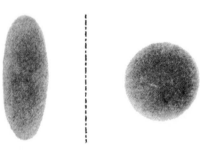

*Fig. 29-2. When spreader adjusting valve is fully closed, a round pattern results as shown at the right. When valve is opened the pattern becomes oval as shown at the left.*

ally opened, air is emitted from the horns on the air cap and the spray pattern is changed to an oval, Fig. 29-2. This adjustment allows the operator to select a spray pattern width to suit the job. For touch-up-work or spotting in a round pattern a small fan is used. For panel and large areas the gun is adjusted to a wide or oval pattern.

The fluid adjustment, Fig. 28-10, controls the amount of paint coming from the gun. When fully closed, no paint leaves the gun. When fully open, maximum paint flow is provided. This adjustment permits the operator to select a setting that will give the proper paint flow for the job. On spot work a minimum flow is used, and on panels or other large areas, maximum flow is used.

## AIR PRESSURE

The air pressure used at the gun to atomize the paint will vary with the viscosity of the paint and to some extent the type, that is lacquer, enamel or acrylic. Gun air pressure

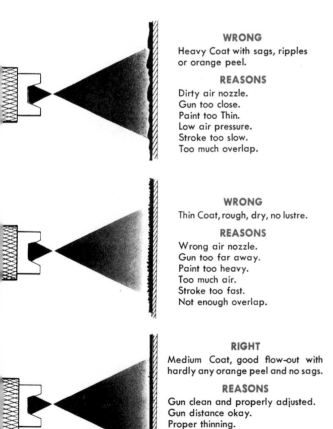

**WRONG**

Heavy Coat with sags, ripples or orange peel.

**REASONS**

Dirty air nozzle.
Gun too close.
Paint too Thin.
Low air pressure.
Stroke too slow.
Too much overlap.

**WRONG**

Thin Coat, rough, dry, no lustre.

**REASONS**

Wrong air nozzle.
Gun too far away.
Paint too heavy.
Too much air.
Stroke too fast.
Not enough overlap.

**RIGHT**

Medium Coat, good flow-out with hardly any orange peel and no sags.

**REASONS**

Gun clean and properly adjusted.
Gun distance okay.
Proper thinning.
Right amount of air.
Stroke okay.
Overlap 50%.

*Fig. 29-3. Right and wrong ways of operating a spray gun.*

is adjusted and controlled with the air regulator which is part of the air transformer, Fig. 28-18. The correct pressure to use is a matter of experience and is arrived at by a series of test patterns, Fig. 29-2. Not only is the shape of the pattern altered, but also its size. Varying the pattern is accomplished by the selection of the setting of the spreader adjustment valve. The spreader adjustment valve is a key to lower cost painting. Select the setting most suitable to the size and contour of the area being finished. Never have a pattern wider than the surface being refinished.

Too low an air pressure will result in under-atomized paint, Fig. 29-3, which will be rough or show a heavy orange peel. Atomizing pressure too high will result in a dry spray and may also cause an orange peel due to lack of proper flow-out in the material. As a matter of general practice the atomizing pressure at the gun will range from 30 lb. to 60 lb. A pressure feed gun will require less atomizing air pressure than a suction gun.

The first step in operating a spray gun is therefore to adjust the gun and air pressure until the desired pattern and atomization are obtained. Test the spray pattern on paper, or on a scrap panel. If the air cap or tip is not clean, or is worn, a defective pattern will result. Fig. 29-4. In general the height of the oval should be 5 to 6 in., and the width 2 in.

To correct the pattern distortions, clean the air cap and fluid tip thoroughly inside and out, using solvent, and a soft bristle brush.

"Spitting" is caused by dried-out packing around the material needle valve permitting air to get into fluid passageways. Loosen knurled nut on air valve and lubricate with machine oil. Spitting is also caused by dirt between fluid nozzle seat and body, loosely installed fluid nozzle, or by a defective swivel nut on syphon cup or material hose.

It is important, when spraying paint, that the gun be held at the correct distance from the surface of the work. For synthetic enamels, the correct distance is 8 to 10 in. or about the hand span of a normal size hand. For lacquers the correct distance is 6 to 8 in. If the gun is too close to the work, paint goes on too heavy and tends to sag. If the gun is too far from the work, there is ex-

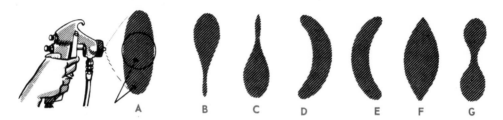

Fig. 29-4. Detail A—Spray guns can be adjusted to either round or oval patterns. B—Top heavy patterns caused by horn holes partly clogged, obstruction on top of fluid tip, dirt on air cap seat or fluid tip seat. C—Heavy bottom pattern caused by horn holes partly clogged, obstruction on bottom side of fluid tip, dirt on air cap seat or fluid tip seat. D—Heavy right side pattern caused by right side horn holes partly clogged, dirt on right side of fluid tip, or twin jet air cap right jet clogged. E—Heavy left side pattern caused by left side horn holes partly clogged, dirt on left side of fluid tip, or on twin cap left jet clogged. F—Heavy center pattern due to too low setting of the spreader adjustment valve, with twin jet cap too low, an atomizing pressure or paint too thick, with pressure feed too high a paint pressure for the atomization air being used or the material flow is in excess of the normal capacity of the cap, too large a nozzle for the material being used, too small a nozzle. G—Split pattern due to air and paint not being properly balanced. Reduce width of spray pattern by means of spreader adjustment valve or increase fluid pressure.

cessive dusting and a sandy finish, Fig. 29-3.

It is important to remember that the gun should be held at the correct distance the entire length of the stroke and always perpendicular to the surface of the work, Fig. 29-5. When the gun is held at an angle to the

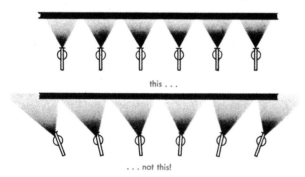

Fig. 29-5. To get even paint distribution and film thickness always hold gun perpendicular to the surface of the panel.

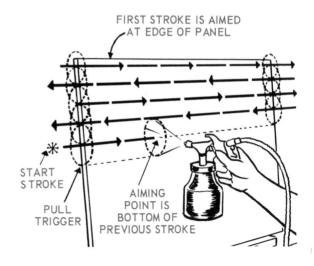

Fig. 29-6. In this method of spraying, the gun is triggered at edge of panel.

painted surface, more material is applied at one part of the spray pattern, less at the other. This results in streaks, sags, runs and wasted paint.

Always work for a wet coat. Use slow steady strokes across the surface from one side to the other. Never use a fanning motion. To insure smoother coverage, each stroke should overlap 50 percent.

When spraying a panel, the stroke may be started off to one side the surface of the work. The trigger is pulled when the gun is opposite the edge of the panel, Fig. 29-6. The

spray gun is then moved to the other side of the panel and the trigger is released at the edge of the panel, but the stroke is continued for a few inches before reversing direction for the next stroke. The triggering is part of the spraying technique. It maintains full coverage, without overspray. The quality of the paint job is improved and little paint is wasted.

Another method of painting a panel is to first "band-in" the ends of the panel, moving the gun vertically, Fig. 29-7. Then spray the face of the panel horizontally triggering the gun at the beginning and end of each stroke. After the edges have been "banded-in" the operator can begin each stroke and then pull the trigger. He can release the trigger before completing the stroke. Smooth, complete coating will result with a minimum waste from overspray. Incidentally, corners should be sprayed so that both edges of the corner are covered at the same time.

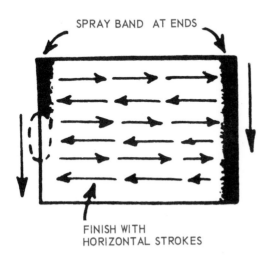

Fig. 29-7. In this method of spraying, the sides of the panel are first banded-in.

Some authorities estimate that 30 percent of the material atomized by the spray gun does not fall on the vehicle but on the inside of the spray booth. When the edges have been "banded-in" the habit of whipping the gun is more easily controlled. The banded surfaces act as a signal to "trigger" at exactly the correct moment of the stroke.

The stroke must be smooth and easy, allowing enough time for sufficient material to be applied, but fast enough so too much material is not applied and causes sags. "Whipping" the gun wastes energy and material. Strokes should overlap each other approximately 50 percent, Fig. 29-8.

When spraying a hood, top or other wide horizontal surface, always start at the near side and work to the far side. This is particularly important when lacquer is being sprayed. The reason is that any overspray will land on a dry surface. Overspray landing on a wet surface will result in a sandy surface. If a pressure gun is not available, the suction gun can be tilted slightly to be as near a right angle to a painted surface as possible.

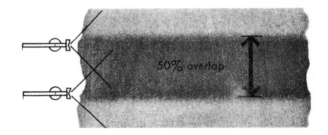

Fig. 29-8. Allowing a 50 percent overlap with each pass of the gun.

## SPRAYING THE ENTIRE CAR

Two suggested area painting sequences are shown in Fig. 29-9. First paint the hidden edges, door jambs, inside the trunk lid, hood edges, etc., leaving the door slightly ajar to avoid sticking, and to permit proper drying. Then proceed with the exterior of the car, following the numbered sequence shown in either of the drawings in Fig. 29-9. Most painters prefer to do one-half of the top and complete it as they work around the car. When spraying the door jambs use air pressure of about 20 lbs. Then increase pressure as indicated by paint manufacturer's instructions--usually about 40 lbs. for lacquers and acrylics and 60 lbs. for synthetic enamel. Spray inside the trunk lid, in back of bumper and bumper guards, and under the hood.

At no time should it be necessary to spray or lap into a semidry area, as that would cause air streaks to show up on the finished job.

## SPRAYING TEMPERATURES

There is an ideal temperature for spraying paint at which it will behave most satisfactorily through the gun and produce a paint job of high quality. If the material is too cold, it becomes thick and heavy bodied. When overheated, the viscosity drops and the material becomes more liquid. The correct temperature of the paint should be close to

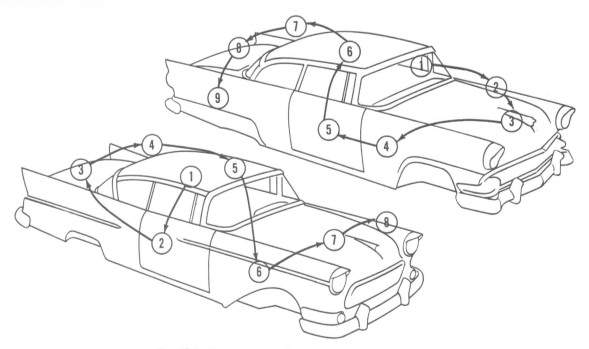

*Fig. 29-9. Two procedures for spraying a complete vehicle.*

70 deg. F. The temperature should be checked as it is put into the pressure pot or suction cup.

Painting materials and equipment should be stored at temperatures ranging between 70 and 85 deg. F. When stored and applied at higher or lower temperatures, poor quality paint will usually result. Remember that to put paint of the correct temperature into hot or cold container, will affect the temperature of the material to be sprayed.

The vehicle to be sprayed should also be at from 70 to 85 deg. F. Never attempt to paint a car that has just been standing in the sun or in extreme cold.

On lacquer color only, to remove overspray or dry spray resulting from overlapping, spray over the entire car with lacquer thinner to which a little color has been added. Use care to avoid excessive wetting as this will cause runs. The thinner coat is applied to pick up overspray and put it back into the finish. It also helps to level any "orange peel" that may be on the surface. Less rubbing and polishing will be required.

## SPECIAL NOTES ON REFINISHING

It is hardly possible to give detailed instructions for car refinishing that would be applicable to all jobs because the exact procedure will vary with the make of car and type of refinishing material used. So when refinishing an automotive vehicle, it is well to keep in mind at all times that the instructions provided by the individual paint manufacturer should be carefully followed.

There are however, a few basic procedures that are applicable to all jobs.

First of all, the surface must be smooth and free from minor imperfections of scratches and dents. The surface must then be treated to remove all traces of oil, dust and rust. Modern primer surfacers, while capable of filling in some fine scratches, are designed primarily to provide adhesion.

The next step after cleaning the surface is to spray the primer surfacer. The type of primer surfacer depends on the original finish and the type of material to be used for the color coat, that is, nitrocellulose lacquer, synthetic enamel, acrylic lacquer or acrylic enamel. Applying heavy coats of primer surfacer in one pass of the gun is definitely not recommended. Primer surfacers applied in that manner will usually have a surface hardness, but will not be dry close to the metal. Excessively heavy coats can lead to hard sanding, poor holding, pin holes and other film defects. It is better to apply thin wet coats of surfacer and allow a short solvent flash-off time between coats.

In spot spraying bare metal spots with primer surfacer, using a narrow fan-shaped spray from the gun, and building up the bare spot gradually, will usually produce good results.

After the primer surfacer has dried, putty can be applied to any rough areas. The time required for primer surfacer to dry will depend on the thickness of the coat, the type of thinner and atmospheric conditions.

The next step is to water sand the surface using No. 320 grit paper, Fig. 29-10. If, as

Fig. 29-11. Polishing to improve lustre.

Fig. 29-10. Wet sanding a primer surfacer.

a result of sanding, the primer surfacer should be cut down to the metal, it will be necessary to respray the surface with another coat of primer surfacer. When sanding, do not bear down too hard but let the abrasive paper do the work. To eliminate sand scratches at any featheredge, use fine grit paper such as No. 400 to obtain a smooth surface. Some painters will use rubbing compound on the featheredge rather than fine sandpaper.

After sanding is completed, wash the sanded area with water to remove all traces of the primer surfacer which have been sanded from the surface. Then allow the surface to dry thoroughly. Blow out crevices and moldings with compressed air.

## SPRAYING COLOR COAT

Just before spraying the color coat, all crevices should be blown and cleaned with compressed air and then carefully wiped with a tack rag to remove all traces of dust.

If the finish coat is nitrocellulose lacquer, the usual procedure is to spray three or four double coats, thinned in accordance with the

manufacturer's instructions. Allow each coat to flash (thinner evaporate) before applying succeeding coats. Pressure at the gun is usually 40 to 45 lbs.

Allow to dry at least four hours, preferably overnight, then hand rub with rubbing compound or machine polishing compound. Polish or dry buff with polishing disk or lamb's wool bonnet, Fig. 29-11. Allow 30 days for lacquer to harden before waxing.

If the finish is acrylic lacquer or acrylic enamel, many paint manufacturers recommend that after wiping with a tack rag, one or two coats of special sealer be applied. When that is dried, three or four wet double coats of acrylic, (thinned in accordance with manufacturer's instructions) are sprayed on. In hot weather a "retarder" may be added to the thinner to aid leveling and to prevent blushing (taking on white or grayish cast while drying). Allow each double coat to "flash" before applying succeeding coats. In spot repair of acrylic lacquer finishes, extend each color coat a little beyond previous coat to blend into surrounding finish. Next, spray a mist coat of retarder and thinner to increase loss and reduce compounding and level overspray roughness.

For most brands of acrylic allow at least four hours for air drying, or preferably overnight. If force dried with infrared or oven, heat the finished area at least thirty minutes to 165 deg. F. Then process the repaired area with rubbing compound. Acrylic retains most of its original gloss and appearance for at least 18 months, so polishing is not normally needed. Wax may be applied after allowing 60 days for acrylic to harden. Acrylic may lose some of its original luster, if not thoroughly dry prior to compounding and polishing. If such after shrinkage occurs, the original luster can be restored by lightly buffing after two weeks or longer aging.

When the color coat is enamel, the usual

Fig. 29-12. Lifting. A puckering and wrinkled effect usually resulting from the application of material carrying strong solvents over a partially oxidized surface. May also be caused by lack of cleanliness, wax, etc. Remedy: Sand and refinish.

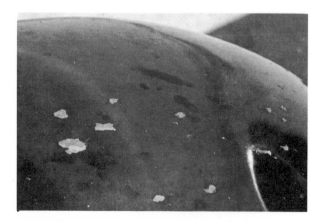

Fig. 29-13. Bruises and chipping. Caused by stones, etc., striking the surface, NOT due to finish. Remedy: Sand out and refinish.

Fig. 29-14. Peeling over solder spot. Usually noticeable a few weeks after refinishing. Typified by loss of lustre. Gets progressively worse until paint peels from surface. Remedy: After soldering, surface should be washed with a solution of equal parts of ammonia, alcohol and water. Be sure surface is thoroughly dry before refinishing.

Fig. 29-15. Orange Peel. This condition results from a number of causes: Improper air pressure at the gun, insufficient reduction and selection of solvent. A thinner that dries too fast will produce orange peel, as well as lacquer sprayed on a hot surface. Remedy: Check thinner, air pressure, and make sure surface temperature is 70 deg. F.

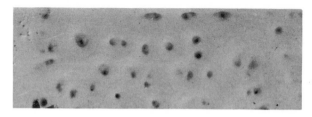

Fig. 29-16. Fish-eyes. Usually caused by failure to remove silicone polish. Remedy: Sand thoroughly, clean surface, refinish.

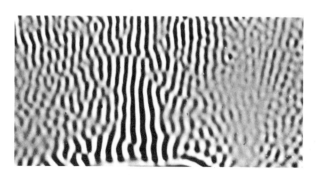

Fig. 29-17. Wrinkling. Usually found only in a synthetic enamel finish. Results from the application of a heavy coat. Aggravated by high temperatures. Remedy: Apply thinner coats.

procedure after the primer surfacer has been applied, is to spray the area with one medium coat of primer sealer. After drying, the crevices are blown out with compressed air and the entire surface wiped clean with a tack rag. The finish enamel is then sprayed, making sure the enamel is thoroughly stirred and mixed with the correct amount of reducer. Spray a medium first coat and after drying spray a full second coat. The drying time of enamels vary greatly with different brands, and also with weather and atmospheric conditions. Special reducers are available to aid in drying with different shop temperatures.

Some manufacturers recommend spraying one panel at a time, applying two full wet coats to each panel, one immediately following the other. Then move to the next panel. Metallic colors may require an additional coat, a mist coat.

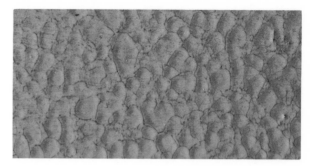

Fig. 29-20. Pitting. Usually caused by oil or moisture escaping through the air line. Remedy: Sand down to smooth surface and refinish. Overhaul compressor and separator to correct trouble.

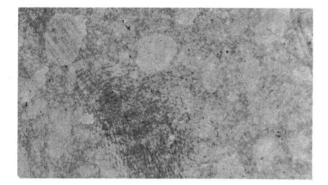

Fig. 29-18. Water Spotting. Usually caused by washing car in bright sunlight. Remedy: Use paste cleaner and polish or wax.

Pressure for spraying enamel is usually at or near 65 lbs., when a regular syphon gun is used. The greatest error in spraying enamel is putting on too much. A thick film

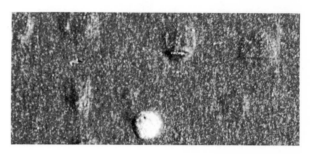

Fig. 29-21. Blistering is caused bu rust, moisture, oil, grease or other foreign materials working in between coats and causing them to separate. Oil or water in air lines will cause blistering as will high temperatures and high humidity. Remedy: Remove finish to metal and refinish.

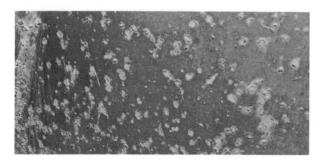

Fig. 29-19. Rust under finish usually appears as a raised section of the finish, or blistering. Usually caused by poor penetration and cleaning of surface. Remedy: Sand surface, treat surface with rust remover and refinish.

of enamel is no more durable than a film of normal thickness. In some cases a thick film is even less durable. Two coats of a quality enamel will usually hide any color. Solid colors spray easiest by applying a good medium coat first. Allow this first coat to get tacky and then spray a full coat. Polychromatic colors will give best metallic effect by spraying on the full coat first, then applying a light coat.

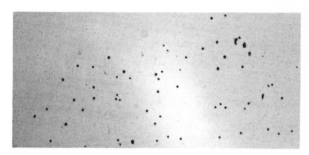

Fig. 29-22. Pin Point Blistering. This type of blistering is often confused with pitting because small broken blisters have the appearance of pits. These pin point blisters range in size from a pin point to a pin head. Remedy: Sand down to metal and refinish.

Be sure to keep the gun at right angles to the panel and at the proper distance--about 10 in. If the gun is held too close, it will cause poor distribution of the enamel, and if too far away dry spray will result.

Examples of paint that have been applied to various types of poorly prepared surfaces are shown in Figs. 29-12 to 29-25.

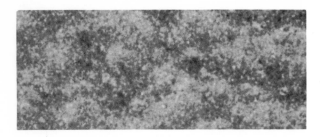

Fig. 29-23. Paint will have a mottled appearance if applied on surface which had been polished with silicone type polish. It is therefore imperative that all traces of such polish be removed from the surface before refinishing.

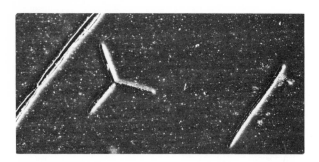

Fig. 29-24. Cracking and checking may extend to the metal. Or, it may go only as far as the undercoating. Depressions in the film caused by cracks in the undercoat also are typical. Simple line cracks are caused by temperature stresses, flexing of body panels, second coat application before first is dry, and poor paint mixing. Remedy: Remove finish to bare metal and refinish.

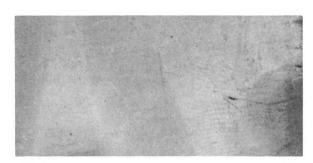

Fig. 29-25. Chalking is surface disintegration. Primarily due to weathering and sunlight and is characterized by dulling and powdering of the surface. Remedy: Apply paste cleaner, followed by polish. In extreme cases complete refinishing is necessary.

## QUIZ - Chapter 29

1. Spray pattern should always be larger than surface being refinished.
   True.
   False.
2. When atomizing pressure is too high a dry spray results.
   True.
   False.
3. As a matter of general practice what will be the range of the atomizing pressure?
   30 to 60 lbs.
   75 to 90 lbs.
   15 to 25 lbs.
4. When spraying synthetic enamels, what is the correct distance between the gun and the work?
   8 to 10 in.
   6 to 8 in.
   10 to 12 in.
5. If a panel is not banded-in, where should the trigger be pulled when painting the panel?
   At the edge of the panel.
   Just before the edge of the panel.
   Just after the gun passes the edge of the panel.
6. When spraying a hood, where should the spraying be started?
   At the near side.
   At the far side.
   At the center.
7. What is considered the best temperature for spraying a car?
   70 deg. F.
   65 deg. F.
   80 deg. F.
   60 deg. F.
8. When refinishing with acrylic lacquer, how many coats should be applied?
   Single heavy coat.
   Three or four wet double coats.
   One heavy and one mist coat.

# Chapter 30

# CUSTOMIZING
# AUTO BODIES

Customizing or altering the lines of automobile bodies can be easily accomplished by using epoxy resins and fiber glass. Such work can range from a simple job of filling in joints between two metal panels, to providing new fender lines, and even a complete new body.

A simple job is to remove chrome trim and use epoxy resin to fill the holes used for the clips that held the chrome trim in place. The procedure for such work is similar to that explained in Chapter 13 for filling in dents. Filling in seams between panels is done in the same manner.

When altering the lines of an auto body, the basic procedure is to first build up a frame work of wire mesh. The epoxy resin and fiber glass are then applied over this form. When dry, the surface is sanded smooth, and painted.

The purpose of the wire mesh is to provide a form for the resin. Instead of wire mesh, some body men use stiff cardboard, which is taped in position on the auto body. However, wire mesh is generally preferred as it is more easily formed to the desired shape, and will retain that shape more easily than cardboard. The wire mesh is formed to the desired shape, and is welded or soldered in position on the automobile. If desired, self-tapping screws can be used to hold the wire form in place, instead of welding.

When "hooding" headlights or wherever a form is required in duplicate for the other side of the vehicle, it is essential that the two forms be identical. An excellent method is to first make a master (male) form. This must be the exact shape desired. Its outer surface must be smoothed, sealed and covered with a parting agent.

To seal the surface it is simply sprayed with a clear lacquer. When that is dry, it is coated with a parting agent, or mold release, which is usually a wax emulsion. The next step is to lay on a couple of laminations or layers of fiber glass material. When this has hardened, the mold which has been formed (female mold) is completed and is lifted off the male mold. This may be used to make as many identical lamp hoods, tail fins, wind scoops, etc. as desired.

Making female mold models, which are then used as master molds, is the preferred method. However, many body men when customizing, will simply build a wire form of the shape desired, and fasten the form in position. The wire form is then covered with fiber glass material. Sufficient fiber glass is used to permit considerable sanding so that the two forms on each side of the body can be duplicated.

The fiber glass is cut to the desired shape, and is dipped in the solution of resin and hardener, as described in the chapter on filling dents. The glass is then positioned on the form. When dry it is sanded smooth. Heat lamps can be used to speed the drying.

As previously mentioned, lamps may be hooded, air scoops formed, and tail fins altered by this method. In addition, complete auto bodies can be built.

## BUILDING COMPLETE BODY

Briefly the method of building a complete auto body is to first build a form of wood, wire and plaster of paris. The plaster of paris is sanded to produce the exact form desired. This is known as the male form, from which a female form is made which in turn is used to produce the final body.

Fig. 30-1, shows the first step of making

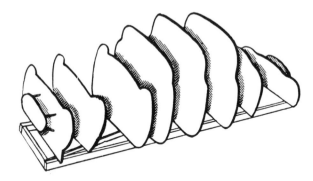

Fig. 30-1. Skeleton frame built up of plywood used as basis for building body of fiber glass.

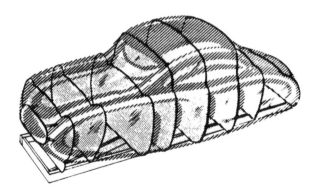

Fig. 30-2. Here the skeleton frame is covered with chicken wire prior to the application of fiber glass.

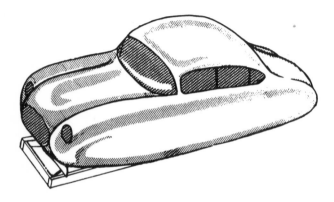

Fig. 30-3. The completed body after application of fiber glass and preliminary sanding.

a form. This consists of a series of plywood panels, the edge shapes of which conform to the shape of the desired auto body. This must be well made and strongly braced so that it will support the weight of plaster of paris and the stresses when the form is sanded.

This wooden form is in turn covered with wire netting, Fig. 30-2. This is covered with plaster of paris, Fig. 30-3. After the plaster of paris has dried, it is carefully sanded to produce the exact form, curves and contour desired. When sanding the plaster of paris be sure to wear a respirator as the air will be filled with powdered plaster of paris.

Fig. 30-4. Special body on Plymouth.

Fig. 30-5. Special body designed for land speedster.

The next step is to seal the plaster of paris by spraying it with clear lacquer. Two coats should be used to be sure that the pores of the plaster of paris are sealed.

When the lacquer sealer has dried, it is covered with the mold release, or parting agent. This is necessary so the fiber glass body (when completed) can be lifted from the form. The parting agent is usually in the form of a wax emulsion. After the mold release has been applied, the form is ready for the fiber glass, or if preferred a female form can be made. The female form is another form made from the male form. The easiest

Fig. 30-6. Special roadster type body.

material to use is fiber glass. Simply lay on a couple of laminations of fiber glass after it has been dipped in the epoxy resin mixture. When it has hardened, the female form is completed. The inside of this form is coated with a mold release and then fiber glass sheets are pressed into position in the female form. After it has hardened, the fiber glass body is lifted out and fitted to the vehicle chassis.

The amount of materials needed will depend, of course, on the size of the body being made. One manufacturer estimates it takes from 12 to 15 gallons of resin and 20 to 30 sq. yds. of fiber glass cloth, and about 10 yds. of matte. Two laminations (with the long weave at right angles) are generally sufficient for the female mold. One gallon of resin will saturate 30 to 40 sq. ft. of cloth, and 15 to 20 sq. ft. of matte. Matte is about twice the thickness of cloth. Use a layer of cloth and then a layer of matte and then a final layer of cloth for the auto body.

After the body is completed, add more glass underneath in the form of ribs or strips to reenforce corners and other areas which are subject to greater stress.

Doors can be fabricated by making wooden frames and covering them with wire mesh,

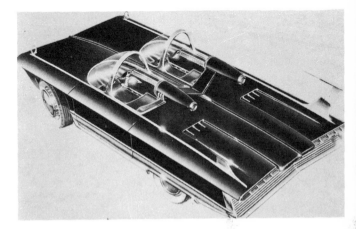

Fig. 30-7. Highly modernized body.

then fiber glass. Hinges can be attached by laminating them in position with several strips of fiber glass cloth. Accessories also can be mounted in a similar manner.

Brackets for mounting the body onto the chassis can be attached to the body by means of several layers of fiber glass cloth. The body can be supported along its sides and at the front and rear to chassis cross members. Such points should be considered when making the original plans. The location of the fire wall behind the engine is particularly important.

Fig. 30-8. Special body on Cadillac.

To stimulate the design of fiber glass bodies, Figs. 30-4, 30-5, 30-6, 30-7 and Fig. 30-8, are presented.

The fiber glass cloth method of making repairs can be used extensively when repairing auto bodies, particularly when it is impossible to obtain replacement panels for repairing antique cars and foreign cars where replacement parts are not available in the U. S.

For additional details on the fixing of the epoxy resin and the application of fiber glass cloth the reader is referred to Chapter 13.

## QUIZ - Chapter 30

1. When altering the lines of an auto body, the basic procedure is to first build up a frame work of wire mesh.
    True.
    False.
2. A parting agent is used so that the female mold can be easily lifted from the male mold.
    True.
    False.
3. Describe briefly how a form for a complete fiber glass auto body is made.

# Chapter 31

# WHEEL ALIGNMENT

As the result of collisions, the alignment of the front wheels is often changed and it is, therefore, important that auto body repairmen understand the fundamentals of front wheel alignment.

No attempt will be made in these pages to describe the use of the various types of equipment used in measuring the alignment of automobile front wheels because there is great variation in the design of such equipment. The reader is, therefore, referred to the instruction book which accompanies such equipment.

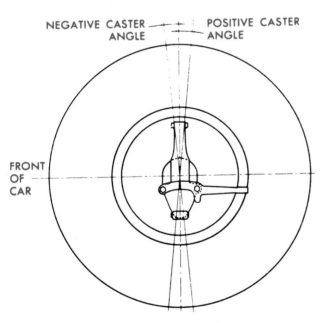

NEGATIVE CASTER ———— POSITIVE CASTER
ANGLE                ANGLE

FRONT
OF
CAR

*Fig. 31-1. Illustrating positive and negative caster.*

Front wheel alignment and front end service are the keys to good steering control, safe handling and maximum tire life. Correct alignment calls for the use of reliable accurate equipment to aid in making critical checks and precise adjustments of caster, camber and toe-in.

However, correct alignment of the steering angles is so interrelated with good working condition of steering and suspension parts that many preliminary checks and adjustments are required along with any needed repairs and/or parts replacement. Among the more common causes of steering and suspension troubles are: Worn ball joints or tie rod ends; unbalanced wheels; bent wheels; weak or inoperative shock absorbers; unlike tread patterns or different degrees of tread wear on the front tires; improperly adjusted steering gear. Trouble shooting details are given in the accompanying list at the end of this chapter.

## CASTER

Caster is the steering angle that utilizes the weight and momentum of the vehicle to lead the front wheels in a straight path, and is illustrated in Fig. 31-1. It is measured in degrees, and is the backward or forward tilt of the ball joint (or king pin) axis from the vertical axis of the front wheels. It tends to stabilize steering in a straight direction by placing the weight of the vehicle either ahead or behind the area of the tire-to-road contact. POSITIVE caster is the angular amount the steering axis is tilted at the top toward the rear of the car. NEGATIVE caster is the amount the steering axis is tilted toward the front of the car. Caster can be adjusted to the manufacturer's specifications by means of shims, strut rods, or eccentric bolts, bushings, pins or oversize bolt holes.

## CAMBER

Camber, as shown in Fig. 31-2, is the outward tilt of the wheels at the top. It is also measured in degrees, and is closely associated with steering axis inclination,

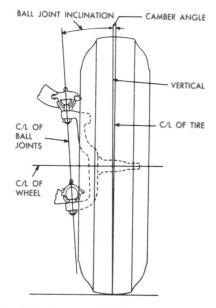

*Fig. 31-2. Camber and ball joint inclination.*

which is the inward tilt of the steering knuckle. These two steering angles share a common side (the vertical axis of the wheel) and form what is known as the included angle. Its purpose is to place the turning point of the wheel at the center of the tire-to-road contact area. Camber can be adjusted by means of shims, eccentric bolts, bushings, pins or oversize bolt holes. A typical adjustment is shown in Fig. 31-3.

## TOE-IN

Toe-in, as shown in Fig. 31-4, is the amount in inches that the front wheels are "pigeon-toed," or closer together in front than at the rear, as measured at hub height (with one or two exceptions). Its purpose is to prevent slipping and scuffing of the tires on the road. The small amount of toe-in serves to keep the front wheels running parallel by offsetting the forces that tend to spread them apart. Toe-in is adjusted by turning the tie-rod ends which are also known as the steering connecting rod ends, to

shorten or lengthen the tie rod. On some cars, as shown in Fig. 31-5, the adjustments are made by means of sleeves on the connecting rods.

Toe-out on turns, as shown in Fig. 31-6, refers to the correct relative position of the front wheels on turns. Since the outside wheel on turns is approximately five feet further away from the point about which the car is turning, it must swing through a greater arc than the inside wheel. To accomplish this, the steering arms are designed to angle several degrees inside of the parallel position. This serves to speed the action of the arm on the inside of the turn as it moves toward the center line of the wheel spindle. The effect on the outside wheel is to slow it down to obtain true rolling contact of the tires rather than slipping and scuffing. The amount of toe-out on turns is not adjustable

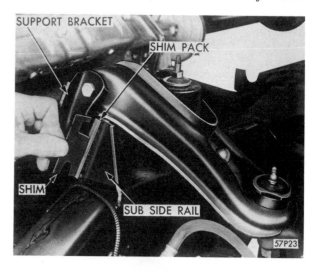

*Fig. 31-3. A popular method of adjusting camber is by means of shims.*

*Fig. 31-4. Front wheels are toed-in when dimension B is less than dimension A.*

**FRONT OF CAR**

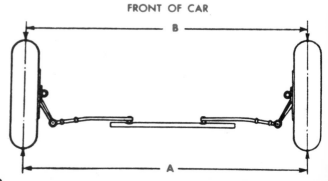

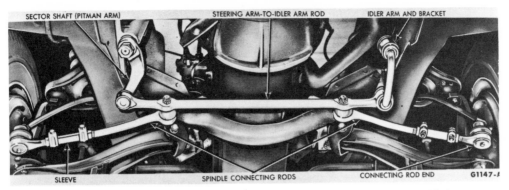

Fig. 31-5. Layout of *steering* linkage on Ford cars. Note *sleeves which are adjustable for toe-in.*

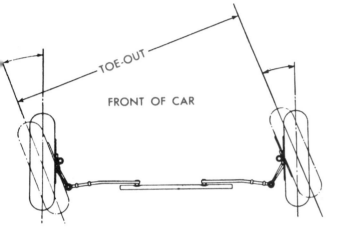

Fig. 31-6. Note the wheels toe-out on turns.

but is controlled by the angle of the steering arm. Should these become bent, they should be replaced. In no case should heat be used to straighten steering arms or any other steering parts which are heat treated.

Causes of steering difficulties include:

HARD STEERING
Lack of lubrication.
Under-inflated tires.
Maladjustment of steering gear.
Incorrect front wheel alignment.
Bent frame.
Sagged front spring.

LOOSE STEERING
Maladjustment of steering gear.
Defective front wheel bearings.
Worn steering knuckle ball joints.
Worn pitman shaft bushings.
Worn steering linkage.
Loose gear assembly at frame.
Worn control arm bushings.

SHIMMY
Unbalanced front wheels.
Faulty front wheel bearings.
Loose wheel nuts.
Defective front brakes.
Worn steering linkage.
Defective shock absorbers.
Bent wheels.
Low tire pressure.
Incorrect caster.
Incorrect toe-in.
Worn steering knuckle bushings.
Defective ball joints.
Worn control arm bushings.
Inoperative stabilizer.

WHEEL TRAMP
Unbalanced wheel assemblies.
Defective shock absorbers.
Inoperative stabilizer.

ROAD WANDER
Under-inflated tires.
Maladjustment of steering gear.
Defective front wheel bearings.
Worn steering linkage.
Worn steering knuckle bushings.
Worn ball joints.
Incorrect wheel alignment.
Shifted rear axle.
Worn steering gear.
Binding upper or lower control arm shaft.

CAR PULLS TO ONE SIDE
Low or uneven tire pressure.
Incorrect caster or camber.
Uneven car height at front.
Bent frame.
Shifted rear axle.

Incorrect toe-in.
Broken or weak rear springs.
Bent steering knuckle or knuckle support.
Inoperative shock absorber.
One brake dragging.

SIDE WEAR ON TIRES
Outside wear.
Excessive positive camber.
Inside: Excessive negative camber.
Outside and Inside: Under-inflated tires or
vehicle overloaded.

CENTER RIB WEAR OF TIRES
Over-inflation.

SHARP RIB EDGES ON TIRES
Inside: Excessive toe-in.
Outside: Excessive toe-out.
Inside on one tire, outside on opposite tire:
Bent arm or steering knuckle.

TIRE THUMP, TRAMP, SQUEAL
Damaged fabric.
Unbalanced condition.
Incorrect air pressure.
Incorrect wheel alignment.

ABRASIVE ROUGHNESS

HEEL AND TOE WEAR
High speed driving.
Excessive use of brakes.

UNIFORM SPOTTY WEAR
Lack of tire rotation.

UNEVEN SPOTTY WEAR
Unusual driving habits.
Worn or loose parts.
Incorrect wheel alignment.

## QUIZ - Chapter 31

1. Caster is the amount the wheels are tilted to the side.
    True.
    False.
2. Camber is the outward tilt of the wheels at the top.
    True.
    False.
3. What method is usually used to adjust toe-in?
    Shims.
    Threaded tie-rod ends.
4. List four causes of hard steering.
5. List five causes of why a car will pull to one side.

# Chapter 32
# AUTO BODY MAINTENANCE

## FIXING DUST AND WATER LEAKS

Car owners frequently complain of dust and water leaks occurring in their automobiles. Such leakage is often difficult to locate, as it frequently occurs at joints between panels which are normally sealed with special sealers, when the vehicle is being manufactured. It is important when repairing an auto body that all such sealing material be replaced whenever it has been removed or disturbed.

Dust and water leaks also occur at doors, windows, deck lids, ventilators and windshields whenever windlace, weather stripping and similar material has become damaged, is loose, or otherwise defective.

## LOCATING LEAKS

The three principal methods used to locate water and dust leaks are:
1. Spraying car with water.
2. Driving car on dusty road.
3. Directing beam of light on car.

Before making the actual test, it is generally advisable to remove interior trim from the general area of the leak. In that connection it is important to emphasize that the actual source or entrance of the dust or water is often quite remote from its appearance in the interior of the vehicle. It is, therefore, suggested that the following should be removed:
1. Cowl trim panel.
2. Quarter trim panel.
3. Rear seat back and seat cushion.
4. Luggage compartment floor mats, spare wheel and side trim panels.

Fig. 32-1. Using water from a hose to locate body leaks.

5. Center trim panel on four door sedans.
6. Scuff plates.
7. All floor mats.

After removing such trim the location of most leaks will be readily evident.

Entrance dust is usually indicated by a pointed shaft of dust or silt at the point of entrance. Seal all such points with an appropriate type of sealer. Then recheck to make sure that the difficulty has been corrected.

## CHECKING LEAKS WITH WATER

After removing the interior trim in the general area of the leak, spray the vehicle with a stream of water, Fig. 32-1. While that is being done, one man should be inside the vehicle with the windows shut, to act as an observer and carefully note just where the water is entering.

Testing for water and dust leaks by using water is to be preferred, as water under pressure is always available.

Fig. 32-2. *Applying sealer to windshield to stop water leaks.*

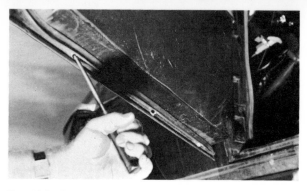

Fig. 32-3. *Opening drain holes on lower edge of door. (Ford)*

## DRIVING CAR TO LOCATE LEAKS

Another method of locating dust leaks is to drive the car over a dusty road. Keep the windows closed so that the observer will not be confused by any dirt which may enter through the windows. Dusty roads are not always available.

## USING LIGHT TO LOCATE LEAKS

Simple leaks can often be located by moving a light around the car, while an observer remains inside the vehicle. This method is satisfactory only when the course of the leakage is straight. If the path is devious, as is usually the case, a light beam will not be able to pass through the "turns."

Some body men light a candle in the car. As the candle is held in different areas of the car, the reaction of the flame to drafts is noted. Sometimes it is possible to find a leak by this means.

## PLUGS AND GROMMETS

There are many plugs and grommets used in the floor pan and dash panels of automotive vehicles to keep out dust and water from the interior of the vehicle. These areas should be carefully inspected to make sure that all the plugs and grommets are in place and in good condition.

## WEATHER STRIP LEAKAGE

When the weather stripping on doors and deck lids becomes loose or damaged, dust and rain leakage results.

On most vehicles the weather stripping used on doors and deck lids is cemented in place. Should it become loose, or when replacement is required, all that is necessary is to recement it in place. Fig. 32-2, shows special weather strip cement being used around the edges of a windshield.

To check for correct positioning of the weather strip around door and deck lid weather stripping, place a feeler gauge or card about .020 in. thick between the weather strip and the door frame. Then with the door closed, withdraw the feeler gauge. The weather strip should be checked all around the door or deck lid, as the case may be, and if there is little or no resistance when withdrawing the feeler gauge, the weather strip should be moved closer to the edge of the door, or replaced completely. For details on the procedure for removal and installation of various types of weather stripping, the reader is referred to Chapter 18.

## PREVENTING RUST

One of the major causes of rusted auto body panels is parking the car out of doors where rain, snow, fog and sun deteriorate the finish and rusting of the panels takes place.

Contributing largely to the rusting of the panels is the failure to keep drain holes open. Drain holes are located on the lower edge of the doors, rocker panels and quarter panels. The construction of the drain holes varies with different manufacturers. The type used on Ford cars, recent models, is shown in Fig. 32-3, on late model General Motors vehicles in Fig. 32-4. It is important that these holes be kept open so that any water that seeps down past the windows will not collect in the panels.

In the case of the construction shown in Fig. 32-3, the valves are located in the lowest points in the panel. The weight of the water will open the valve and allow the water to escape the panel. After the water has drained, the valve will close automatically and prevent entry of dust. If for any reason the door trim panel, rocker panel, scuff plate or luggage compartment trim panel has been removed, the metal should be inspected to make sure the drain holes are not obstructed.

On late model General Motor cars the door bottom drain hole sealing strips, Fig. 32-4, are attached to door inner panels over door bottom drain holes. These are designed to prevent entry of dust at these areas, and also permit water to drain.

The sealing strips are retained by two retaining plugs, which are in integral part of the sealing strip. These new sealing strips are of vinyl construction, and should not require lubrication. The sealing strip is easily pried out for inspection.

On older type bodies of all makes, drain holes are usually not provided with automatic seals, and it is particularly important to check the drain holes regularly to be sure they are opened and not plugged with dirt.

## BODY MAINTENANCE

Regular body maintenance preserves the appearance of the car and reduces the cost of maintenance during the life of the car. The following steps are suggested as a guide for regular body maintenance.

1. Vacuum the interior and wash the car regularly.

2. Check all openings for water leaks; seal where necessary.

3. Cement all loose weather strips which are still usable.

4. Replace weather strips which are unfit for service. Apply silicone lubricant to the weather stripping.

5. Replace all cracked, fogged, or chipped glass.

6. Align hood, doors and deck lid, if necessary.

7. Inspect windshield wiper blades and replace if necessary.

8. Tighten sill plate and garnish molding screws.

9. Clean the seats, door trim panels and head lining.

10. Touch up or paint chipped or scratched areas.

11. Drain holes located on the underside of doors, rocker panel and quarter panel should be cleared periodically.

## RATTLE ELIMINATION

Most rattles are caused by loose bolts or screws. Foreign objects, such as nuts, bolts, or small pieces of body deadener in the door wells, pillars and quarter panels are often the source of rattles. Door wells can be checked by carefully striking the underside of the door with a rubber mallet. The impact made by the mallet will indicate if loose objects are in the door well. All bolts and screws securing the body to the frame should

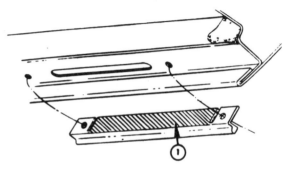

*Fig. 32-4. Drain hole sealing strips on Fisher bodies should be lubricated. (Chevrolet)*

be tightened periodically. In the event tightening bolts and screws, located on such assemblies as doors, hood and deck lid does not eliminate the rattles, the trouble may be caused by misalignment. If this is the case, follow the adjustment and alignment procedures for those assemblies.

Rattles and squeaks are sometimes caused by weather stripping and antisqueak material that has slipped out of position. Apply additional cement or other adhesive and install the material in the proper location to eliminate this difficulty.

## REAR COMPARTMENT LID DRAIN HOLES

Deck lids on Fisher body styles B-C-D-E are louvered to accommodate the flo-thru ventilation system. Water entering these louvers is channeled rearward between the deck lid inner and outer panels outside of the body through holes provided at the lower edge of the lid assembly. These holes are equipped with drain valves, Fig. 32-5. These drain valves must form a complete and flat peripheral seal around the drain holes. If for any reason a drain valve is removed or missing, it must be reinstalled properly or replaced. Torn, mutilated or deformed valves must be replaced.

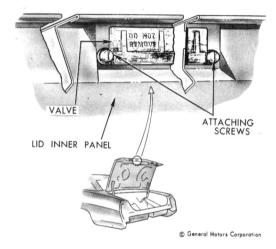

VALVE

ATTACHING SCREWS

LID INNER PANEL

© General Motors Corporation

*Fig. 32-5. Details of rear compartment lid drain holes.*

## HOOD NOISES OR PANEL FLUTTER

Squeaks or grunting noises in the hood when driving over rough roads, do not necessarily indicate misalignment of hood and fenders. These noises may be caused by metal contacts at some point where clearance should exist, or by worn or dry hood bumpers.

If hood squeaks, check with 1/16 in. thick feeler gauge all around hood for clearance at fenders and cowl. If an edge of metal is making contact at any point where clearance should exist, a bright metal spot will usually be found. Such spots can be depressed by spring hammering to provide clearance.

A grunting noise in hood is usually caused by dry rubber bumpers or cowl ledge lacing. Lubricate all rubber bumpers on rails and cowl with silicone rubber lubricant. To correct case of squeaking or grunting, where hood top panel contacts ledge lacing, even when lubricated, cement 1/16 in. thick strip of felt to panel where lacing makes contact.

To prevent hood panel flutter, the rear end of the hood panel must have firm contact with the lacing attached to cowl ledge. It may be raised or lowered by adjustment.

## EXTERIOR CLEANING

The outside finish should be washed frequently. Never wipe the painted surfaces with a dry cloth. Dusting the finish when it is dry tends to rub the dust and dirt into the finish and leaves a sandpaper effect on the surface. To keep finish bright and attractive and eliminate necessity of using polish, it is advisable to wash the car whenever it has accumulated a moderate amount of dirt and road salt.

## CLEANING BRIGHT PARTS

The bright metal parts of the car if made of stainless steel require no special care. Periodic cleaning will preserve the beauty and the life of such material. Wash with clear water or if any parts are very dirty use a special cleaner for stainless steel.

Chrome plated parts rust or corrode because chemical agents present in road silt and traffic film seep through pores in plating and attack underlying base metal. A plating of nickel is applied underneath chrome to seal plating and protect base metal.

Deterioration of chrome plated parts can be avoided by keeping parts clean and by periodic application of a preservative which will aid in retarding seepage of destructive agents through plating. Plated parts should be washed with clear water only, using mild detergent when necessary. Avoid using scouring powders, cleaning compounds or stiff brushes.

## INTERIOR CLEANING

Use a vacuum cleaner to remove dust and dirt from the upholstery or floor covering. Vinyl and woven plastic trim that is dusty can usually be cleaned with a damp cloth. Do not use cleaning materials containing kerosene, naphtha, toluol, xylol, lacquer thinners, cellulose acetate, butyl cellulose, carbon tetrachloride, body polish, battery acid, antifreeze, gasoline, motor oils, or other type lubricants.

# HOW TO REMOVE SPOTS

In automobiles the seats are covered with what is called trim material. There are four general types of this material being used in current model vehicles. In order to remove spots most easily, it is important to know what is the best cleaner to be used for each type of material.

The four general types of material used to upholster the seats in automobile bodies are:

1. Fabrics - - either plain fabrics (broadcloth, gabardine, etc.), or pattern fabrics which are made with either natural or synthetic (nylon, orlon, rayon, viscose, etc.) fibers.

2. Genuine leather.

3. Coated fabrics (vinyl or nylon).

4. Polyurethane foam.

Dust or dirt particles that accumulate on the upholstery of a car should not be allowed to accumulate, but should be removed regularly.

Do not use a whisk broom on fabrics having a raised tapestry pattern since damage to fine threads may result. On polyurethane foam materials use only a soft bristle brush. Do not use a vacuum cleaner or a whisk broom.

# REMOVING SPOTS

For best results stains should be removed as soon as possible after they are made, as the longer they remain in the fabric, the more difficult they are to remove.

Cleaning precaution: Do not use any of the following to clean upholstery fabrics: Colored gasoline or gasoline which may contain tetraethyl lead, acetone, lacquer thinners, enamel reducers, bleaches, hydrogen peroxide, chlorine.

# TYPES OF CLEANERS

There are four basic types of cleaners commonly used for removing spots and stains from automotive upholstery materials.

1. Volatile cleaners, which are usually colorless and include such liquids as benzine, carbon tetrachloride.

2. Synthetic detergents.

3. Neutral soap.

4. Ammonia.

# USING VOLATILE CLEANERS ON FABRICS

When using volatile cleaners, it is generally advisable to do the work out-of-doors and care must be exercised that there is no flame in the vicinity. Avoid inhaling the fumes of cleaners, as many are toxic. Also avoid prolonged contact with the skin and take special care to keep the cleaner away from the eyes and mouth.

Do not use too much cleaner. Apply the cleaner with a clean cloth. Remember the solvent is designed to dissolve the material forming the spot or stain, which is then absorbed by the cloth. Use only a minimum of pressure.

First brush away all loose particles of dirt or soil. Then dampen a clean cloth with the volatile cleaner. Open the cloth and allow a portion of the solvent to evaporate so that the cloth is just slightly damp.

Using a very light pressure and circular lifting motion, rub the stained area, starting at the outer edge and working toward the center until the entire area has been covered. When the cleaning cloth becomes dirty it should be discarded and a new one used.

Before proceeding, wait several minutes to allow most of the cleaner that is in the upholstery to evaporate. This will avoid the danger of a cleaner penetrating into the padding under the upholstery. Repeat the foregoing procedure until the spot has been removed.

If a ring should be formed when removing a stain, repeat the cleaning operation but start well beyond the area of the ring and again work toward the center. Old upholstery is often so full of dust it is almost impossible to treat a single spot without leaving a telltale ring. In such cases it is advisable to go over the entire seat area with a cloth dampened with cleaner.

# USING SYNTHETIC DETERGENTS ON FABRICS

In addition to special synthetic detergents designed specifically for cleaning upholstery fabrics, many body shops use such materials as Tide, Lux, etc.

Make a solution of the synthetic detergent in lukewarm water. With a clean cloth or sponge dampened with the solution, apply to the surface of the upholstery using light pressure. Repeat several times, taking care that clean areas of the sponge or cloth are used each time. With a second clean cloth dampened with lukewarm water (no detergent) rub over the area to remove excess detergent. Follow with a clean dry cloth and wipe off the excess moisture.

Allow fabric to dry and if necessary repeat cleaning operation.

## CLEANING LEATHER AND COATED FABRICS

Care of genuine leather and coated fabrics, including vinyl coated formed head lining is relatively easy. The surface should be wiped occasionally with a clean dry cloth. Whenever dirt accumulates the following cleaning procedure should be followed: Use lukewarm water and a neutral soap. Apply a thick suds to the surface worked up on a piece of clean cheesecloth. Use a damp cloth but no soap to remove all traces of soap. Then dry with a clean cloth.

Polishes and cleaners used for auto body finishes, volatile cleaners, furniture polishes, oils, varnishes or household cleaning and bleaching materials should never be used on leather and coated fabrics.

## CLEANING POLYURETHANE FOAM MATERIAL

Normal soilage, such as dirt and fingerprints can be removed with a cleaning solution of approximately 2 oz. of white detergent powder mixed in a gallon of water. Immerse a clean cellulose sponge in cleaning solution. Wring the sponge out thoroughly leaving suds only; then clean soiled area carefully. Rinse off the clean area with a sponge and clean water. Do not soak the clean area. Soilage such as cements, sealers and grease can be removed by first cleaning the soiled area with a detergent solution as described previously. Do not rinse. Leaving suds on the soiled area, clean area with a

clean cloth that has been dipped in a good volatile upholstery cleaner and thoroughly rung out. Then clean soiled area with detergent suds and rinse as described before.

## CLEANING FLOOR CARPETS

Thoroughly brush or vacuum the floor carpet. In many instances the floor carpet may require no further cleaning. If carpet is extremely soiled remove carpet from car and thoroughly vacuum to remove loose dirt; then with a foaming type upholstery cleaner, clean approximately one square foot of carpet at a time. After each area is cleaned, remove as much of the cleaner as possible using a vacuum cleaner. After cleaning the carpet use an air hose to fluff the carpet pile, then dry the carpet. After the carpet is completely dry, use an air hose again to fluff the carpet pile.

## REMOVING SPECIFIC STAINS

Some types of stains and soilage, including blood, ink, chewing gum, etc., require special consideration for most satisfactory results. For these and other stains specific instructions are outlined in the following paragraphs. It must be expected, particularly where water treatment is specified, that some discoloration and finish disturbance may occur. By following the procedures outlined with normal care and caution, reasonably satisfactory results can be expected.

## BATTERY ACIDS

Apply ordinary household ammonia water with a brush or cloth to the affected area, saturating it thoroughly. Permit the ammonia water to remain on the spot about a minute, so that it will have ample time to neutralize the acid. Then rinse the spot by rubbing with a clean cloth saturated with cold water.

## BLOOD

Do not use hot water or soap and water on blood stains since this will set the stain and make its removal very difficult.

Rub the stain with a clean cloth saturated with water until no more of the stain will come out. If this treatment does not remove all the stain, apply a small amount of household ammonia water to the stain with a cloth or brush. Let stand a moment, then continue to rub the stain with a clean cloth dipped in clear water. If the stain remains after the use of ammonia and water, a thick paste of corn starch and cold water may be applied to the stained area. Allow the paste to remain until it has dried. Then carefully brush off the dried corn starch. Several applications may be necessary.

## CANDY

Candy stains, other than candy containing chocolate, can usually be removed by rubbing the affected area with a cloth soaked with hot water. If the stain is not completely removed, rub area lightly (after drying) using a cloth wet with a volatile cleaner. This will usually remove the stain.

Candy stains resulting from cream and fruit filled chocolates can be removed more easily by rubbing with a cloth soaked with lukewarm soapsuds (mild neutral soap) and scraping while wet with a dull knife. This treatment is followed by rubbing the spot with a cloth dipped in cold water.

Stains resulting from chocolate or milk chocolate can be removed by rubbing the stain with a cloth wet with lukewarm water. After the spot is dry, rub it lightly with a cloth dipped in volatile cleaner.

## CHEWING GUM

Harden the gum with an ice cube and scrape off particles with a dull knife. If gum cannot be removed completely by this method, moisten it with a volatile cleaner and work it from the fabric with a dull knife, while the gum is still moist.

## FRUIT, LIQUOR AND WINE

Practically all fruit stains can be removed by treatment with hot water. Wet the stain well by applying hot water to the spot with a clean cloth. Scrape all excess pulp, if present, off the fabric with a dull knife; then rub vigorously with a cloth wet with very hot water. If the stain is very old or deep, it may

be necessary to pour very hot water directly on the spot, following this treatment with the scraping and rubbing. Direct application of hot water to fabrics is not recommended for general use since discoloration usually results.

If the above treatments do not remove stain, allow fabric to dry thoroughly; then rub lightly with a clean cloth dipped in a volatile cleaner. This is the only further treatment that is recommended.

Soap and water are not recommended since they will probably set the stain and cause a permanent discoloration. Drying the fabric by means of heat (such as the use of an iron) is not recommended.

## GREASE AND OIL

If grease has been spilled on the material, as much as possible should be removed by scraping with a dull knife or spatula before further treatment is attempted. Grease and oil stains may be removed by rubbing lightly with a clean cloth saturated with a volatile cleaner. Be sure all motions are toward the center of the stained area to decrease the possibility of spreading the stain.

## ICE CREAM

The same procedure is recommended for the removal of ice cream stains as described for removing fruit stains.

If the stain is persistent, rubbing the spot with a cloth wet with warm soapsuds (mild neutral soap) may be used to some advantage after the initial treatment with hot water. This soap treatment should be followed with a rinsing, by rubbing with a clean cloth wet with cold water. After this dries, rubbing lightly with a cloth wet with a volatile cleaner will help to clear up the last of the stain, by removing fatty or oily matter.

## NAUSEA

Sponge with a clean cloth dipped in clear water. After most of the stain has been removed in this way, wash lightly with a soap (mild neutral) using a clean cloth and lukewarm water. Then rub with another clean cloth dipped in cold water. If any of the stain remains after this treatment, gently rub clean with a cloth moistened with a volatile cleaner. Another method is to use a cloth dampened with ammonia and rub until the spot has been cleaned.

## SHOE POLISH AND DRESSINGS

On types of shoe dressing which contain starch or dextrine or some water soluble vehicle, allow the polish to dry; then brush the spot vigorously with a brush. This will probably be all the treatment that is necessary. If further treatment is required, moisten the spot with cold water and after it has dried repeat the brushing operation.

Paste or wax type shoe polishes may require using a volatile cleaner. Rub the stain gently with a cloth wet with a volatile cleaner until the polish is removed. Use a clean portion of the cloth for each rubbing operation, and rub the stained area from outside to center.

## TAR

Moisten the spot lightly with a volatile cleaner and then remove as much of the tar as possible with a dull knife. Follow this operation by rubbing the spot lightly with a cloth wet with the cleaner until the stain is removed.

## URINE

Sponge the stain with a clean cloth saturated with lukewarm soapsuds (mild neutral soap) and rinse well by rubbing the stain with a clean cloth dipped in cold water. Then saturate a clean cloth with a solution of one part household ammonia and five parts water. Apply the cloth to the stain and allow solution to remain on affected area for about a minute; then rinse by rubbing with a clean wet cloth.

## LIPSTICK

The composition of different types of lipstick vary greatly, making the stains very difficult to remove. In some instances a volatile cleaner may remove the stain. If some stain remains after repeated applications of the volatile cleaner, it is usually best to leave it rather than try other measures.

## QUIZ - Chapter 32

1. Spraying a car with water is one method of locating water leaks.
   True.
   False.
2. On most vehicles the weather stripping is cemented in place.
   True.
   False.
3. Indicate the location of water drain holes.
   Lower edge of doors.
   Wheel housing.
   Rocker panels.
   Quarter panels.
   Deck lids.
4. Rattles and squeaks may be caused by weather stripping which has slipped from position.
   True.
   False.
5. Scouring powders should be used to clean chrome plate.
   True.
   False.
6. Gasoline is recommended for cleaning spots from upholstery.
   True.
   False.
7. Which of the following should be used to clean genuine leather upholstery.
   Gasoline.
   Neutral soap and water.
   Carbon tetrachloride.
8. Is household ammonia satisfactory for use when battery acid gets on upholstery?
   Yes.
   No.
9. What should be used to remove fruit stains?
   Hot water.
   Carbon tetrachloride.

# Chapter 33
# SAFETY IN THE
# AUTO BODY SHOP

Safety is everyone's responsibility. This is particularly true in the auto body shop where there are greater possibilities of accidents than in most any other department. This results from the use of combustibles, such as the highly flammable lacquers, enamels, thinners and other highly volatile chemicals, coupled with the use of welding equipment. Because of the nature of the work, the body shop floor is usually more cluttered than shops doing other types of repair work. Also, there is a greater possibility of cuts and bruises when handling dented and torn sheet metal.

One of the basic rules of safety in any shop is the proper and correct conduct of every individual. There can be no running, no practical jokes, no horseplay. Such conduct invariably results in accidents as well as distracting others in the shop from the work they are supposed to do.

As previously pointed out, there is great danger from fire because of the great use of combustibles. Paints and thinners should always be kept in closed containers. This will not only prevent fires but also will reduce loss due to evaporation.

Smoking and unprotected flames should never be permitted. No Smoking signs should be prominently displayed.

Painting should always be done in a spray booth provided with exhaust fans and conforming to underwriters' requirements. In addition painters should always wear respirators, as the inhalation of the fumes from lacquer and enamel will result in respiratory ailments.

All auto body shops should be provided with an ample number of fire extinguishers. Everyone should be familiar with their location, and the owner or manager of the shop should make it his personal responsibility to check the fire extinguishers regularly to be sure they are in operating condition. Remember that water cannot be used to extinguish a fire from lacquer, thinner, gasoline or grease. For such fires a carbon tetrachloride or foam type extinguisher is specified. If nothing else is available, sand can be used.

As a further protection against fire, oil and paint rags, together with used abrasive paper, should be kept in suitable containers. Care must be taken so that spontaneous combustion does not occur.

Depending on the nature of the collision to a vehicle, the electrical wiring may be damaged so that there is a strong possibility of electrical shorts occurring. It is, therefore, always good policy to disconnect the starting battery as soon as any car is brought into a shop. In that way the possibility of fire is greatly reduced.

When using sanders or grinders, auto body mechanics should always wear goggles as protection for the eyes, Fig. 33-1.

It is particularly important that the shop be well lighted, not only to avoid eye strain, but also to reduce the possibility of accidents resulting from tripping over parts on the floor which cannot be seen because of lack of proper illumination. Special attention should be paid to keeping the aisles clear and free from parts removed from vehicles undergoing repair. This is a difficult problem in auto body shops, as panels and other parts are often removed so that other parts can be more easily reached. In such cases,

Fig. 33-1. Note safety mask being worn by mechanic, and that oxyacetylene tanks are chained to prevent tipping.

care must be taken to place such parts as are removed, against the wall of the shop or in some other areas where they will not be in the way.

Floors must always be kept clean, and particularly, free from grease and oil. Such spots are a fire hazard and also very slippery and consequently are the cause of accidents to mechanics and other persons walking through the shop. Whenever any oil or grease is spilled on the floor or drips from a vehicle, it should be immediately wiped up. Special preparations are available for absorbing oil and cleaning such spots.

Much repair work done on auto bodies is performed with the car raised on jacks or horses. It is, therefore, important to make sure that all such equipment is in safe operating condition and is capable of supporting the various vehicles. If garage type jacks are being used, care must be taken so that the jack handle does not protrude in such a way that it will cause someone to trip and fall.

## USING TOOLS SAFELY

Files should never be used without protective handles, as there is always the danger of injury from the pointed tang. Neither should files be used as pry bars, or hammered. Files are made with hard temper and consequently are quite brittle and when hammered, small pieces may fly off and

cause severe wounds or loss of eyesight. Hardened surfaces, such as the face of an anvil, should not be struck with a hammer as bits of steel may fly off and cause damage. Further in connection with hammers and sledges, care must always be exercised that the head is always securely attached to the handle. Loose hammer and sledge heads may fly off when the tool is used and anyone standing in the way will be struck and severly injured.

When the head of a chisel becomes swagged over, it should be discarded or reground to remove the swagged edges. This will prevent bits of steel from flying off and causing damage.

Whenever grinding is done, the mechanic should wear goggles to protect his eyes. The grinding wheel should always be provided with a protective guard. The reason for the guard is that in the event of the grinding wheel flying apart due to centrifugal force, the danger to the operator will be minimized. Unless the grinding wheel is designed to take such strains, its side surfaces should not be used for grinding.

As there is always a possibility of a driving belt breaking or a rotating wheel bursting, it is always advisable to stand away from the plane of rotating parts. In the event of any such breakage, parts will be hurled with terrific force and anyone standing in line with the rotating part may be severely injured.

When using a wrench, there is always danger to the mechanic if he pulls on the handle, rather than pushes on it. Should the wrench slip when pushing on it there would be less danger of skinning the knuckles. Further in that connection, when the jaws of a wrench become worn or are sprung, the wrench should be discarded, as it will no longer fit the nut securely and will tend to slip.

Compressed air is an important "tool" in every shop. The air gun should never be pointed at anyone. The high pressure of the air can blow dust and dirt particles at such high speed that they will puncture the skin and get into the eyes.

Care must always be exercised, when working around any machinery, engine or motor that there is no chance of loose clothing being caught and entangled in rotating parts. Neckties should always be tucked within the shirt. If long sleeves are being worn, these should always be buttoned at the cuff. Caps without brims are considered safer than those with brims, because of the possibility of the protruding brim being caught in some rotating part.

In regard to safety precautions when using oxygen and acetylene for welding, there are many points to observe. Never allow oil or grease to contact oxygen under pressure. Do not lubricate welding and cutting apparatus. Never use oxygen as a substitute for compressed air, as a source of pressure, or for ventilation. Before starting to weld or cut, make sure that the flame, sparks, hot slag, or hot metal will not be likely to start a fire. Always wear goggles when working with a lighted torch.

Be sure to keep a clear space between the cylinders and the work as you may find it necessary to reach and adjust the regulators quickly. Do not risk hand burns by lighting the torch with a match. Use a friction type lighter as it is safer and also easier. Never use acetylene pressure higher than 15 psi.

Never release acetylene where it might cause a fire or an explosion. Always check equipment before starting to work. Never braze, weld, or use acetylene flame on gasoline or other fuel tanks. Acetylene and oxygen tanks should always be in a special carrier, or chained to a post to prevent falling.

## QUIZ - Chapter 33

1. Paint and thinners should always be kept in closed containers.
   True.
   False.
2. What material can be used to extinguish lacquer, gasoline, grease and thinner fires?
   Water.
   Carbon tetrachloride.
3. Why should the starting battery be disconnected on vehicles after they have been in a collision?
4. Files may be used as pry bars.
   True.
   False.
5. It is always advisable to stand in the plane of rotating parts.
   True.
   False.

# Chapter 34
# GLOSSARY OF TERMS

ABRASIVE: A substance used for wearing away a surface by rubbing. Examples of abrasives as used in the automotive painting field are, aluminum oxide paper, silicon carbide paper.

ABRASIVE COATINGS: In closed coating paper no adhesive is exposed as the complete surface of the paper is covered with abrasive. In opening coating, adhesive is exposed between the grains of abrasive.

ACID CORE: Solder supplied in tubular wire form with the interior filled with acid flux in paste form.

ACRYLIC RESINS: Synthetic resins of excellent color and clarity used in both emulsion and solvent based paints. Available as a lacquer and also as an enamel.

ADHESION: How well a paint sticks to a surface to which it is applied. Surface preparation has considerable effect on adhesion.

AIR DRY: To dry paint at ordinary room temperatures.

ALUMINUM OXIDE: Hard and sharp abrasive made by fusing mineral bauxite at high temperatures.

ATOMIZE: The extent to which the air at the nozzle of the paint spray gun breaks up the paint and solvent into fine particles.

BAKELITE: A registered trademark identifying phenolic products used in varnish manufacture.

BINDER: The nonvolatile portion of a paint which serves to bind or cement the pigment particles together.

BLEEDING: Stain which works up or "bleeds" through succeeding coats of finish materials. Also when applied to hydraulic systems - the removal of air from the hydraulic fluid.

BLENDING: Mixing one color with another so colors mix or blend gradually.

BLISTERING: Formation of bubbles on surface of paint, usually caused by moisture behind film of paint.

BLOOM: Clouded appearance on finish coat.

BLUSHING: A finish coat is said to "blush" when it takes on a white or grayish cast during drying period. It is usually caused by the precipitation or separating of a portion of the solid content of the material, causing an opaque appearance.

BODY: Thickness of a fluid; that is, its viscosity.

BRONZING: The information of a metallic appearing haze on a paint film.

BUFFING COMPOUND: Soft abrasive in stick form bonded with wax.

BUTYL ACETATE: A lacquer solvent made from butyl alcohol by reaction with acetic acid.

CARBON TETRACHLORIDE: A nonflammable liquid with good solvent properties.

CARNAUBA WAX: A hard wax obtained from species of palm grown mostly in Brazil and used in some body polishing materials.

CAST: Inclination of one color to look like another. For example, sulphur is yellow with a greenish cast.

CAULKING COMPOUND: A semidrying or slow drying plastic material used to seal joints or fill crevices.

CELLULOSE: An inert substance, the chief component of the cell walls of plants. Nitrocellulose, used extensively in making lacquer, is prepared from cotton linters by treatment with chemicals.

CELLULOSE ACETATE: A binder made by chemical reaction of acetic acid on cellulose.

CELLULOSE NITRATE: A binder made by chemical reaction of nitric acid on cellulose (cotton linters). Also known as nitrocellulose and pyroxylin.

CHALKING: The decomposition of paint film into a powder on the surface.

CHECKING: The formation of short narrow cracks in the surface of a paint film. These cracks may assume many patterns, but the usual ones resemble the print of a bird's foot or small squares.

CHIPPING: Where small segments of top coat break away from the finish. Loss of adhesion.

CLEAR: A finish having no pigments or transparent pigments only.

COLOR RETENTION: When a paint product exposed to the elements shows no signs of changing color, it is said to have good color retention.

COMPATIBILITY: The ability of two or more materials to work together.

COMPRESSOR: A device used to compress air which in turn is used to spray paint.

COOL COLORS: Hues or colors in which blue predominates. The term "cool" is used because of association with ice, sky and water.

CORROSION: Break down of a metal caused by chemical action. Rusting for example.

COVERAGE: The area a given quantity of paint will cover; also how well paint conceals the surface being painted.

CRATERING: Formation of holes in the film. Usually caused by surface contamination.

CRAZING: Minute interlacing cracks on the surface of a finish.

CURING: The complete or final drying stage where a paint reaches complete strength and dryness as the result of chemical change.

DECALCOMANIA: Paint films in the form of pictures or letters which can be transferred from a temporary paper mounting to other surfaces.

DIE BACK: The loss of gloss in a finish coat usually caused in an acrylic or lacquer by continued thinner evaporation after the color has been polished.

DINGING HAMMER: A special hammer used for dinging or removal of dents from an auto panel.

DOLLY: A hand held metal tool or anvil designed to be held on one side of the dented panel while the other is struck with the dinging hammer.

DOUBLE COAT: A term used in acrylic and lacquer application. A single coat immediately followed by a second coat. (Often the second coat is sprayed in the opposite direction to the first - one horizontal and the other vertical.)

DRIER: A material added to paint to reduce drying time.

DRY SPRAY: The atomized paint that does not dissolve into the material being sprayed. Presents a rough dull appearance. Usually caused by too fast a reducer or thinner for the temperature, holding the gun too far from the surface so that too much of the solvent evaporates in the air, or too high an air pressure.

ENAMEL: Type of paint made by grinding or mixing pigments with varnishes or lacquers or acrylics.

EPOXY RESINS: Resins obtained by condensation reaction between phenols and epichlorohydrin.

ETHYL LACTATE: A solvent made by a reaction between ethyl alcohol and lactic acid.

FEATHEREDGE: When a paint surface is broken by stone bruises, grinding, etc., it usually leaves a sharp edge. This edge must be slanted or tapered with sandpaper or featheredging solvent. This taper edge of the paint is called the featheredge.

FIBERGLASS: Fine spun filaments of glass used as insulation and also in the repair of auto bodies.

FINISH COAT: Last coat applied of finish material.

FISH-EYES: Blemishes in the finish coat usually of a circular and opalescent character. Generally caused by failure to remove all traces of silicone polish prior to painting.

FLAKING: Detachment of small pieces of paint film.

FLASH OFF: Flash off is the rapid evaporation of thinner.

FLINT PAPER: Abrasive paper which is grayish white in color. Inexpensive but has short working life. Seldom used in auto body refinishing.

FLOW: The ability of particles of paint spray to merge together to form a smooth surface.

FOG COAT: A thin, highly atomized coat to obtain a fast flash off of the thinner and therefore, minimum penetration of the thinner into the old finish. Usually achieved by reducing the fluid speed while leaving air pressure at 45 lb. at the gun.

GARNET PAPER: Abrasive which is reddish in color, hard and sharp; comes from same source as semi-precious jewel by that name. It is more expensive than flint paper, but it lasts longer.

GLOSS: A term used to indicate the shine, luster or sheen of a dried paint film.

HEADLINING: The cloth or other material used to cover the inner surface of the car roof.

HUMIDITY: Amount of water vapor in the air.

INDUCTION BAKING: Using heat induced by electrostatic and electromagnetic means for baking finishes.

JIGSAW: A saw with a narrow blade, mechanically driven and used for cutting body panels.

LACQUER: Finishing material that dries by the evaporation of the thinner or solvent. There are many different types of lacquers, a popular type being that based on cellulose nitrate. Besides the cellulosic compound, lacquers contain resins, plasticizers, solvents and diluents.

MASKING PAPER: A special paper used to cover areas of body panels to protect them from paint spray.

MASKING TAPE: Adhesive coated paper tape used to mask or protect parts of surface from spray paint. Also used to attach masking paper to body panels.

METAL CONDITIONER: Special preparation to be applied to unfinished metal and designed to prevent the formation of rust and also slightly etch the surface.

METALLICS: A class of finishes or paints which include flakes of metal in addition to the pigment.

MINERAL SPIRITS: Petroleum product which has about the same evaporation rate as gum turpentine. Frequently used for cleaning spray guns.

MISCIBLE: Capable of being mixed.

MIST COAT: Over thinning the color and spraying very wet. Usually the final coat for flow with lacquer or acrylic polychromatic colors.

NEUTRAL FLAME: The flame of an oxyacetylene torch so adjusted to eliminate all of the acetylene feather at the inner cone of the flame.

NITROCELLULOSE: See cellulose nitrate.

ORANGE PEEL: A nubby surface looking like the skin of an orange. It may or may not have a good gloss. Caused by poor flow because of too fast a reducer or lack of atomization.

ORIGINAL FINISH: The paint applied at the factory by the vehicle manufacturer.

OVERLAP: That part of the spray band that goes on top of the previous swath of paint. Also that part of the spray that overlaps a previously painted area.

OVERSPRAY: An overlap of dry spray gun particles on areas where they are not wanted.

OXIDATION: Combination of oxygen from the air with the paint film. This process dries and continues to harden enamel for several weeks. The chalking (surface powder) of a paint film, that takes place in the aging of the film, is also a form of oxidation.

PAINT FILM: The thickness of the paint on the surface.

PAINT REMOVER: A mixture of active solvents used to remove paint and varnish coatings.

PEELING: Detachment of a paint film in relatively large pieces. Paint applied to a damp, or greasy surface usually peels. Sometimes it is due to moisture back of painted surface.

PHENOLIC RESIN: Resin based essentially on reaction between phenol and formaldehyde.

PIGMENT: Material in the form of fine powders. Used to impart color, opacity and other effects to paint.

PINHOLING: Holes that form in the top coat or undercoat.

PLASTIC FILLER: Special compounds used to fill dents and cracks in automotile panels.

POLYCHROMATIC: This term is used by some paint manufacturers for the metallic effect imparted to color coats. It is produced by adding aluminum powder in flake form to the paint.

PRIME COAT: Primer or primer surfacer applied to bare metal to obtain adhesion.

PUTTY: A heavy-body material used to fill flaws that are too large to be filled by primer surfacer.

REDUCER: The solvent combination used to thin enamel is usually referred to as reducer.

RESPIRATOR: A device designed to filter particles out of the air so that they do not reach the lungs.

RETARDER: A very rich, slow drying solvent that slows down the rate of evaporation.

RUBBING COMPOUND: An abrasive used to smooth and polish the paint film.

SAGS: A paint film that drips or runs.

SAND SCRATCHES: The marks made in metal or old finish by abrasives. Also those showing in the finish coat due to lack of fill or sealing.

SANDERS: Power driven tool used to sand auto bodies. Some sanders give a rotary motion to the abrasive, while others give a reciprocating motion.

SEALER: A liquid coating composition, usually transparent, for sealing porous surfaces to prevent previous coatings from bleeding through.

SHROUD: Sheet metal used to contain or direct air blast from cooling fan.

SILICON CARBIDE: Abrasive crystals are shiny black and iridescent; very hard. Made by fusing silica and coke in an electric furnace.

SILICONE: An ingredient in waxes and polishes which makes them sleek to the touch and improving the appearance of the finish coat. Must be removed before new paint is applied.

SINGLE COAT: Usually just referred to as a coat of paint. Once over the surface to be painted with each stroke overlapping the previous coat 50 percent.

SKIRT: That portion of the fender that extends down along the side of the wheel.

SLIDE HAMMER: Special tool on which the hammerhead is slid along a rod and against a stop, so that it will pull against the object to which the rod has been hooked or otherwise fastened.

SOLDER: A mixture of tin and lead, having low melting point and used to fill dents and cracks in auto body panels.

SOLIDS: That part of the paint that does not evaporate, but stays on the surface.

SOLVENT: A liquid capable of dissolving a material.

SPECIFIC GRAVITY: The weight of a given volume of a liquid compared to the same volume of water at the same temperature.

SPOON: A tool used in much the same manner as a dolly (i.e. an anvil) but so designed it can be used in areas where there is little clearance and there would be no room for a dolly. Also used to pry panels back into position.

SPRAY GUN: A device to mix paint and compressed air so that the mixture is ejected in a controlled pattern and highly atomized.

STRIKER PLATE: That portion of a door lock which is mounted on the body pillar and which is struck or engaged by the latch or lock extension when the door is closed.

SURFACE DRYING: Drying of a finishing material on top while the lower portion remains more or less soft.

SYNTHETIC RESIN: An artificial resin or plastic produced by systematic exploitation of chemical reaction of organic substances.

TACK COAT: The first coat with enamel. This is a full coat and is allowed to dry until it is quite sticky. From 10 to 30 minutes, depending on drying conditions and reducer used.

TACK RAG: A cloth impregnated with varnish and used to remove abrasive dust from surface just before applying finishing material.

TEMPLATE: A form or pattern made especially so that other parts can be formed exactly to the same shape.

THINNER: The solvent combination used to thin lacquers and acrylics to spraying viscosity is usually called thinner.

TOLUOL (TOLUENE): Lacquer diluent made normally by coal tar distillation.

TONE: A graduation of color, either in hue, a tint, or a shade; as a gray tone.

TOOTH: Roughened or absorbent quality of a surface which affects adhesion and application of coating.

UNDERCOAT: Second coat in three coat work, or first coat in repainting.

WARM COLORS: Colors in which red-orange predominate.

WATER SPOTTING: Water droplets mar the finish before the finish has become completely dry.

WEATHERING: The change or failure in paint caused by exposure to weather.

WINDSHIELD HEADER BAR: That area immediately above the windshield to which the windshield header molding is attached.

WINDLACE: Special trim of a rope-like nature placed around the edge of the door frame as a decoration and also to reduce drafts.

WRINKLING: Skinning of a heavy coat of paint before the underpart of the film has properly dried.

# Chapter 35
# USEFUL TABLES
# AND CHARTS

## DECIMAL EQUIVALENT OF THE NUMBERS OF TWIST DRILL AND STEEL WIRE GAUGE

| No. | Size of No. in Decimals | No. | Size of No. in Decimals | No. | Size of No. in Decimals | No. | Size of No. in Decimals | No. | Size of No. in Decimals | No. | Size of No. in Decimals |
|---|---|---|---|---|---|---|---|---|---|---|---|
| 1 | .2280 | 17 | .1730 | 33 | .1130 | 49 | .0730 | 65 | .0350 | | |
| 2 | .2210 | 18 | .1695 | 34 | .1110 | 50 | .0700 | 66 | .0330 | | |
| 3 | .2130 | 19 | .1660 | 35 | .1100 | 51 | .0670 | 67 | .0320 | | |
| 4 | .2090 | 20 | .1610 | 36 | .1065 | 52 | .0635 | 68 | .0310 | | |
| 5 | .2055 | 21 | .1590 | 37 | .1040 | 53 | .0595 | 69 | .0292 | | |
| 6 | .2040 | 22 | .1570 | 38 | .1015 | 54 | .0550 | 70 | .0280 | | |
| 7 | .2010 | 23 | .1540 | 39 | .0995 | 55 | .0520 | 71 | .0260 | | |
| 8 | .1990 | 24 | .1520 | 40 | .0980 | 56 | .0465 | 72 | .0250 | | |
| 9 | .1960 | 25 | .1495 | 41 | .0960 | 57 | .0430 | 73 | .0240 | | |
| 10 | .1935 | 26 | .1470 | 42 | .0935 | 58 | .0420 | 74 | .0225 | | |
| 11 | .1910 | 27 | .1440 | 43 | .0890 | 59 | .0410 | 75 | .0210 | | |
| 12 | .1890 | 28 | .1405 | 44 | .0860 | 60 | .0400 | 76 | .0200 | | |
| 13 | .1850 | 29 | .1360 | 45 | .0820 | 61 | .0390 | 77 | .0180 | | |
| 14 | .1820 | 30 | .1285 | 46 | .0810 | 62 | .0380 | 78 | .0160 | | |
| 15 | .1800 | 31 | .1200 | 47 | .0785 | 63 | .0370 | 79 | .0145 | | |
| 16 | .1770 | 32 | .1160 | 48 | .0760 | 64 | .0360 | 80 | .0135 | | |

## LUBRICANTS FOR CUTTING TOOLS

| Material | Turning | Chucking | Drilling Milling | Reaming | Tapping |
|---|---|---|---|---|---|
| Tool Steel | Dry or Oil | Oil or Soda Water | Oil | Lard Oil | Oil |
| Soft Steel | Dry or Soda Water | Soda Water | Oil or Soda Water | Lard Oil | Oil |
| Wrought Iron | Dry or Soda Water | Soda Water | Oil or Soda Water | Lard Oil | Oil |
| Cast Iron | Dry | Dry | Dry | Dry | Oil |
| Brass | Dry | Dry | Dry | Dry | Oil |
| Copper | Dry | Oil | Oil | Mixture | Oil |
| Babbitt | Dry | Dry | Dry | Dry | Oil |
| Glass | | | Turpentine or Kerosene | | |

Mixture is 1/3 Crude Petroleum, 2/3 Lard Oil; when two lubricants are mentioned, the first is preferable.

# Tables and Charts

## HIGH TEMPERATURES JUDGED BY COLOR AND COLORS FOR TEMPERING

| Degrees Centigrade | Degrees Fahrenheit | High Temperatures Judged by color | Degrees Centigrade | Degrees Fahrenheit | Colors for Tempering |
|---|---|---|---|---|---|
| 400 | 752 | Red heat, visible in the dark | 221.1 | 430 | Very pale yellow |
| 474 | 885 | Red heat, visible in the twilight | 226.7 | 440 | Light yellow |
| 525 | 975 | Red heat, visible in the daylight | 232.2 | 450 | Pale straw-yellow |
| 581 | 1077 | Red heat, visible in the sunlight | 237.8 | 460 | Straw-yellow |
| 700 | 1292 | Dark red | 243.3 | 470 | Deep straw-yellow |
| 800 | 1472 | Dull cherry-red | 248.9 | 480 | Dark yellow |
| 900 | 1652 | Cherry-red | 254.4 | 490 | Yellow-brown |
| 1000 | 1832 | Bright cherry-red | 260.0 | 500 | Brown-yellow |
| 1100 | 2012 | Orange-red | 265.6 | 510 | Spotted red-brown |
| 1200 | 2192 | Orange-yellow | 271.1 | 520 | Brown-purple |
| 1300 | 2372 | Yellow-white | 276.7 | 530 | Light purple |
| 1400 | 2552 | White welding heat | 282.2 | 540 | Full purple |
| 1500 | 2732 | Brilliant white | 287.8 | 550 | Dark purple |
| 1600 | 2912 | Dazzling white (bluish-white) | 293.3 | 560 | Full blue |
|  |  |  | 298.9 | 570 | Dark blue |

## FIGURING PULLEY SIZES AND RPM

To Find:

| | |
|---|---|
| RPM of Driven Pulley | Multiply diameter of driving pulley by its rpm and divide by diameter of driven pulley. |
| Diameter of Driven Pulley | Multiply diameter of driving pulley by its rpm and divide by rpm of driven pulley. |
| RPM of Driving Pulley | Multiply diameter of driven pulley by its rpm and divide by diameter of driving pulley. |
| Diameter of Driving Pulley | Multiply diameter of driven pulley by its rpm and divide by rpm of driving pulley. |

## MELTING POINT OF METALS

| Metal | Degrees Fahrenheit |
|---|---|
| Aluminum | 1220.4 |
| Copper | 1981.4 |
| Iron | 2795.0 |
| Lead | 621.2 |
| Platinum | 3224.0 |
| Silver | 1761.0 |
| Solder (50-50) | *415.0 |
| Solder (63% tin--37% lead) | 360.0 |
| Solder (40% tin--60% lead) | *459.0 |
| Tin | 449.4 |
| Tungsten | 6120.0 |
| Zinc | 787.2 |

*First melting point 360°.

## METRIC CONVERSION FACTORS

| TO CONVERT | INTO | MULTIPLY BY |
|---|---|---|
| Centimeters | Inches | 0.3937 |
| Feet | Meters | 0.3048 |
| Inches | Centimeters | 2.540 |
| Meters | Feet | 3.281 |
| Sq. Centimeters | Sq. Inches | 0.1550 |
| Sq. Feet | Sq. Meters | 0.093 |
| Sq. Inches | Sq. Centimeter | 6.452 |
| Cu. Centimeters | Cu. Inches | 0.06102 |
| Cu. Inches | Liters | 0.0164 |
| Cu. Feet | Cu. Meters | 0.0283 |
| Gallons U. S. | Liters | 3.785 |
| Ounces | Grams | 28.35 |
| Pounds | Kilograms | 0.4536 |
| Kilograms | Pounds | 2.205 |

## THE METRIC SYSTEM OF MEASUREMENT
### MEASURES OF LENGTH

1 Millimeter (mm.) = ....................................0.03937079 inch, or about 1/25 inch
10 Millimeters = 1 Centimeter (cm.) = ........................................0.3937079   inch
10 Centimeters = 1 Decimeter (dm.) =........................................3.937079    inch
10 Decimeters = 1 Meter (m.) =...39.37079 inches, 3.2808992 feet, or 1.09361     yards
10 Meters = 1 Decameter (Dm.) = ................................................32.808992 feet
10 Decameters = 1 Hectometer (Hm.) = ..........................................19.927817 rods
10 Hectometers = 1 Kilometer (Km.) = ...................1093.61 yards, or 0.6213824 mile
10 Kilometers = 1 Myriameter (Mm.) = ........................................6.213824 miles

1 inch = 2.54 cm., 1 foot = 0.3048 m., 1 yard = 0.9144 m., 1 rod = 0.5029 Dm.,
1 mile = 1.6093 Km.

# ACKNOWLEDGMENTS

This book contains material obtained from many different sources. The publishers wish to record here, their deep appreciation of the splendid co-operation of the individuals and organizations which has made this book possible. Special credit is due:

Acme Quality Paints, Inc., Detroit, Mich.
Air Reduction Sales Co., New York, N. Y.
American Lacquer Solvent Co., Phoenixville, Penn.
American Motors Corp., Detroit, Mich.
Ammco Tools, Inc., North Chicago, Ill.
Arco Div., Mobile Finishes Co., Inc., Cleveland, Ohio
Automotive Finishes, Inc., Dearborn, Mich.
John Bean Division, F.M.C. Corp., Lansing, Mich.
Bear Manufacturing Co., Rock Island, Ill.
Bee Line Co., Davenport, Iowa
Behr Manning Div., Norton Co., Troy, N. Y.
Binks Manufacturing Co., Chicago, Ill.
Black and Decker Mfg. Co., Towson, Md.
Blackhawk Mfg. Co., Milwaukee, Wis.
Bonney Forge & Tool Works, Alliance, Ohio
Buick Motor Div., General Motors Corp., Flint, Mich.
Cadillac Motor Car Div., General Motors Corp., Detroit, Mich.
Carborundum Co., Niagara Falls, N. Y.
Car Fastener Company, Cambridge, Mass.
Chevrolet Motor Div., General Motors Corp., Detroit, Mich.
Chicago Pneumatic Tool Co., New York, N. Y.
Chrysler Corp., Detroit, Mich.
Chrysler Plymouth Div., Detroit, Mich.
Clayton Mfg. Co., Elmonte, Calif.
DeVilbiss Co., Toledo, Ohio
Ditzler Color Div., Pittsburgh Plate Glass Co., Detroit, Mich.
Dodge Div. Chrysler Corp., Detroit, Mich.
E. I. DuPont deNemours & Co., Wilmington, Del.
Fairmount Tool & Forging Div., Houdi Industries, Inc., Cleveland, Ohio
Fisher Body Div., General Motors Corp., Warren, Mich.
Ford Motor Co., Dearborn, Mich.
Hein-Werner Corp., Waukesha, Wis.

Herbrand Div., Bingham-Herbrand Corp., Fremont, Ohio
Ingersoll Rand Co., New York, N. Y.
K-D Mfg. Co., Lancaster, Pa.
Kelite Corp., Los Angeles, Calif.
Kester Solder Co., Chicago, Ill.
Lincoln Electric Co., Cleveland, Ohio
Lincoln Mercury Div., Ford Motor Co., Dearborn, Mich.
Lubriplate Div., Fisk Brothers Refinishing Co., Newark, N.J.
Magnus Chemical Co., Garwood, N. J.
Marquet Mfg. Co., Div., Marquet Corp., Minneapolis, Minn.
Martin Senour Co., Chicago, Ill.
Minnesota Mining & Manufacturing Co., St. Paul, Minn.
Mystik Tape, Inc., Northfield, Ill.
Nason Products, South San Francisco, Calif.
Norton Co., Worcester, Mass.
Oakite Products, Inc., New York, N. Y.
Oldsmobile Div., General Motors Corp., Lansing, Mich.
Owatonna Tool Co., Owatonna, Minn.
Paasche Air Brush Co., Chicago, Ill.
Permacel, New Brunswick, N. J.
Pontiac Motor Div., General Motors Corp., Pontiac, Mich.
H. K. Porter, Inc., Sommerville, Mass.
Rinshed-Mason Co., Detroit, Mich.
Sherwin-Williams Co., Cleveland, Ohio
Skil Corp., Chicago, Ill.
Snap-On Tools Corp., Kenosha, Wis.
Sommer and Maca Glass Machinery Co., Chicago, Ill.
Steck Mfg. Co., Dayton, Ohio
Studebaker Corp., South Bend, Ind.
Taylor & Art, Inc., Oakland, Calif.
Technical Tape Corp., New Rochelle, N. Y.
Union Carbide Corp., New York, N. Y.
Weaver Mfg. Co., Div. of Dura Corp., Springfield, Ill.

# INDEX